Publisher—Jack Stevenson
Editors—Pat Hollis, Jack Stevenson
Typographer—Cindy Gold
Special Typesetting Assistance—Phil Milstein
Special Graphics Assistance—Ken Feinstein
Illustrator—Jeff Gaither
Photographer—Harry Bartlett
Projectionist—Phil Kelly
Layout—Jack Stevenson
Contributors—Mark Feldman, Tom Fielding,
Dale Ashmun, Gary Miller

● ● ● ● ● ● ● ● ● ● ● ●

Ordering, distribution and wholesale information can
be obtained from Jack Stevenson, 171 Auburn Street,
Apt. #11, Cambridge, MA 02139
●

Library of Congress Catalog Number: 89-80312

ISBN Number: 0-9622239-0-5

● ● ● ● ● ● ● ● ● ● ● ●

We would like to thank the following individuals and
organizations for their generous support and invaluable
contributions:

Kris Gilpin   Carl Abrahamsson
Doug Pelton   David Kleiler
Marc Adams   Udo Breger
Candy Kohls   Dennis Dermody
Graf Haufen   Chris Von Camp
Eric Wagner   Jerri Rossi
Jim Condon   · · · · · ·
Beth Cataldo   The Primal Plunge
Kim Anderson   Etant Donnes
Geir Skaugen   Typo-Tech
Gary Gold   Color-Tek
John AES-NIHIL   CHET'S LAST CALL
Mike McInnis   SCREW Magazine
R.K. Sloane   THE QUEERS: Bobby, Joe, Kevin & J.J.

● ●

PHOTO CREDITS BY CHAPTER: PEARCE: Dreamland Productions; Bruce Moore (F.T. prints); Steve Yeager (D.L. prints);
New Line Cinema; M. Pearce. HILL: Joe Casarona—p. 17, 28, 29, 34, 36; *Comstock Cards*—p. 32, 33, 35; Judith Pringle—
p. 36 (bottom); New Line Cinema; Steve Yeager—p. 25. STOVER: Dave Klein—p. 40 (top right); Steve Yeager—p. 37 (top
right); Bruce Moore—p. 37 (bottom photos). WATERS: Bruce Moore; Roger Yeaton; Joe Casarona—p. 46, 48 & 54 (photos
left); Steve Yeager; Dreamland Productions; Karl Esch—p. 47 (top left); Allen Brand—p. 53; Dale Ashmun—p. 56 (top left);
R.V. Gerenser—p. 56 (left photos); New Line Cinema. G. KUCHAR: The British Film Institute; Anthology Film Archives;
Harry Bartlett; David Hallinger; Curt McDowell (T.C. prints, also p100); Pieter Vandermeer—p. 79; *Arcade Comics*—
p. 83-84; Linda Martinez—p. 93; Ivar Brynnjolfsson—p. 94, 95 (bottom). M. KUCHAR: Anthology Film Archives; Camille
Cook; G. Kuchar. ONDINE: P. Hollis. ANGER: *Photo-Fest (NYC)*; Moderna Museet (Sweden); Anthology Film Archives;
Smithsonian Institution; K. Anger; K. Feinstein. SELBY: *Variety;* H. Selby; John Sotomayor. WISEMAN: film stills courtesy
of Zipporah Films. ECK: Anaconda press; Howie Kusten; MGM; Museum of Modern Art stills archive; *Photo-Fest (NYC)*;
Paper Cinema (Dracut, MA); *Saturday Matinee* (N. Hollywood); *Hollywood Book and Poster; Cinema Collectors* (Hollywood); *Baltimore Sun Papers;* J. Eck.(Many photos were uncredited or credits impossible to ascertain. We apologize for
possible omissions.)

Johnny Eck
PAGE **153**

Mary Vivian Pearce
PAGE **1**

Jean Hill PAGE **17**

Kenneth Anger
PAGE **119**

Out of Print

12—
61

George Kuchar
PAGE 59

John Waters
PAGE 41

HUBERT SELBY JR. • PAGE 131
ONDINE • PAGE 113
FREDERICK WISEMAN • PAGE 143

Mike Kuchar PAGE 101

INTRODUCTION

by Stevenson

● ● ● ● ● ●

The cast of characters in this issue comprises a diverse bunch, connected only, perhaps, by their various experiences with the medium of film.

They have used film and been used by film. They have utilized the medium to give context and force to their obsessions, their investigations, their fantasies — while on the other hand the camera has captured, exposed and, at times, exploited them as only film can. They have employed the medium as a stage from which to let their personalities and visions shine, and, in turn, film has opened the trap doors to the backsides of their brains.

And like some underpaid teenage usher swinging his flashlight toward suspect activity in a cave-dark theater, they've cast light into the murky crevices of society itself, whether it be the exaggerated and symbolic (and deadly accurate) "Cavalcade of Perversions" in John Waters' *Multiple Maniacs*, or the gut-wrenching filmic diary of life in the mental wards of Wiseman's *Titicut Follies*.

...

Rather than a standard "film book," I consider this a roundabout testimonial to the transcendental power of a device known as the movie camera, a mechanical contraption that equals far more than the sum of its parts. This movie camera that transforms "everyday people" into movie stars (the Kuchar brothers) by utilizing — some would call it kidnap and rape — color and music without guilt ... the same movie camera that peels back normal exteriors to reveal the psycho-subconscious (Pearce) and that unleashes upon the masses a full-blown personality who was living life in cinemascope and technicolor long before she ever met a movie camera (Jean Hill). The movie camera that attempts the invocation of magic and dreams (Anger) as well as the invocation of vomit-splattered Brooklyn gutters and back alleys (Selby – *Last Exit to Brooklyn*) ... the movie camera that inspired the erection of flimsy plywood-and-cardboard cities teeming with garish grotesques (Waters/*Mortville*) ... and that silently records the even more shocking daily activities of our "real world" — be they the mental wards of *Titicut Follies* or the blood-drenched slaughterhouses of *Meat* (Wiseman). The movie camera that six decades ago brought famous half-man and King of the Freaks, Johnny Eck, across the continent by majestic rail caravan to Hollywood to star in a movie that proved so shocking it ultimately destroyed the career of its director, Tod Browning and was banned for decades in many countries.

...

To be sure, the movie camera has a strange effect on people when it's pointed in their direction — sometimes even loaded.

It can exert the same power over us that ancient idols and icons exerted over our pagan stone-age ancestors, sparking wild irrational behavior, indecent, almost epileptic, insane, stricken, possessed behavior — as if these puny humans contorting recklessly before the cameras were in the grip of some animal god or magic force. Some people will do anything if you point a movie camera at them; the examples are as numerous as they are unprintable.

Sometimes even great acting takes place before the cameras, acting comparable to the magnificent performances rendered by virgin stone age goddesses, possessed battlefield heroes and even the young village girls who masterminded the bloody pageantry of the Salem witch hysteria in a stellar example of late 17th century improv street theater ... these episodes of great cinematic potential that illuminate the moldy pages of history in a lurid and gushing technicolor glow. Too bad nobody was hanging around with a movie camera to record it all.

It's as if film possesses some (un)holy or supernatural power. And of course, it does. It grants eternal youth for one. The nursing homes of Hollywood are full of fragile withered old women who, at the flick of a projector switch, can once again be beautiful, voluptuous young bleached blondes.

But sometimes nothing happens — sometimes you can even capture real life.

The camera can be catalyst, instigator, provocateur ... or it can be just a movie camera, a disembodied battery-driven eyeball seeing the world with more clarity, dimension and courage than our own human eyes can match, clouded as they often are with emotion and prejudice.

Much of the essence of film is inferred, indirect, peripheral. Maybe you can't explain it but you can sense it, feel it ... get <u>flattened</u> by it. Flattened is precisely what happened at a recent movie show I attended where the power of film was vividly demonstrated before my bulging bloodshot eyes.

That memorable night the projector beam actually chased half the audience from the building and left two viewers slumped unconscious (fainted) in their chairs. The second fellow made ominous death-like rattling sounds deep in his throat, sparking panic in the darkened room as people scrambled to clear chairs and lay him out while the shadows of heads bobbled on the screen.

Such was the symbolic standing ovation the young man had given to Stan Brakhage's unflinching autopsy film, *The Act of Seeing With One's Own Eyes*. That film had been preceded by Anne Severson's *Nearing the Big Chakra*, while the final film of the night, viewed by a mere handful of stalwarts and masochists, was Otto Muehl's *Materialacktionfilm*. God, what a night!!! It was ...

But I'm getting carried away. This volume is not strictly about film and to set it in that context is a bit misleading as well as constraining. Johnny Eck, for example, had a fabulous and varied career (and life) and his role in the movie *Freaks* is only one piece of the much larger picture. And Hubert Selby is inarguably a man of the written language, not the language of cinema (even though, as we speak, a movie of *Last Exit to Brooklyn* is in post-production).

Generally speaking, the conversations, photos and writings here often wander far afield from the subject of film and I'm glad they do. The boundaries between film and life are and can only remain indistinct, each ever invading and plundering the other's realm.

I feel, nonetheless, that film does provide whatever backbone this reptilian book has. For me personally, film is the motivating obsession in life. Nothing looks real until I see it up on the movie screen.

Jimmy Swaggart and other hardcore gut-busting Christian preachers have warned that film is intrinsically unnatural, an evil occurrence, and that nobody should go to see any film. I can think of no higher praise. To them the movie projector is that evil idol, that releaser of pagan spirits.

Would it be that film could always scale such heights.

Jack Stevenson

THE FUTURE

Originally the line-up for this issue was to include Gilles de Rais, a wealthy 15th century French battlefield hero and personal saviour of Joan of Arc, later turned heretic, devil worshipper and mass killer of hundreds of kidnapped peasant children — he was brought to trial by the Catholic church, garroted and burned in 1440.

As work on this issue progressed, we collected more material for each chapter than was initially expected, since almost all the living contributors were most generous with their cooperation. Facing financial and time constraints, we decided to publish the Gilles de Rais material in a separate magazine at a later date. I would like to take this opportunity to thank Carl Alessi and Mike Matthews for the great amounts of time and talent they have already invested in this now delayed project.

Plans for future publications also include a comprehensive, photo-intensive volume of the history of freaks in America and a fully-illustrated retrospective compilation of Rick Sullivan's pioneering trash-gore-exploitation film fanzine, *Gore Gazette*.

"Unlike the low-pressure television experience (during which the viewer remains aware of room environment and other people), the film experience is total, isolating, hallucinatory." — Amos Vogel, 1974: *Film as a Subversive Art*

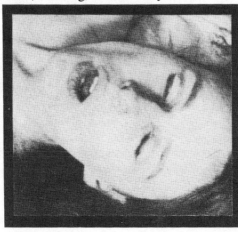

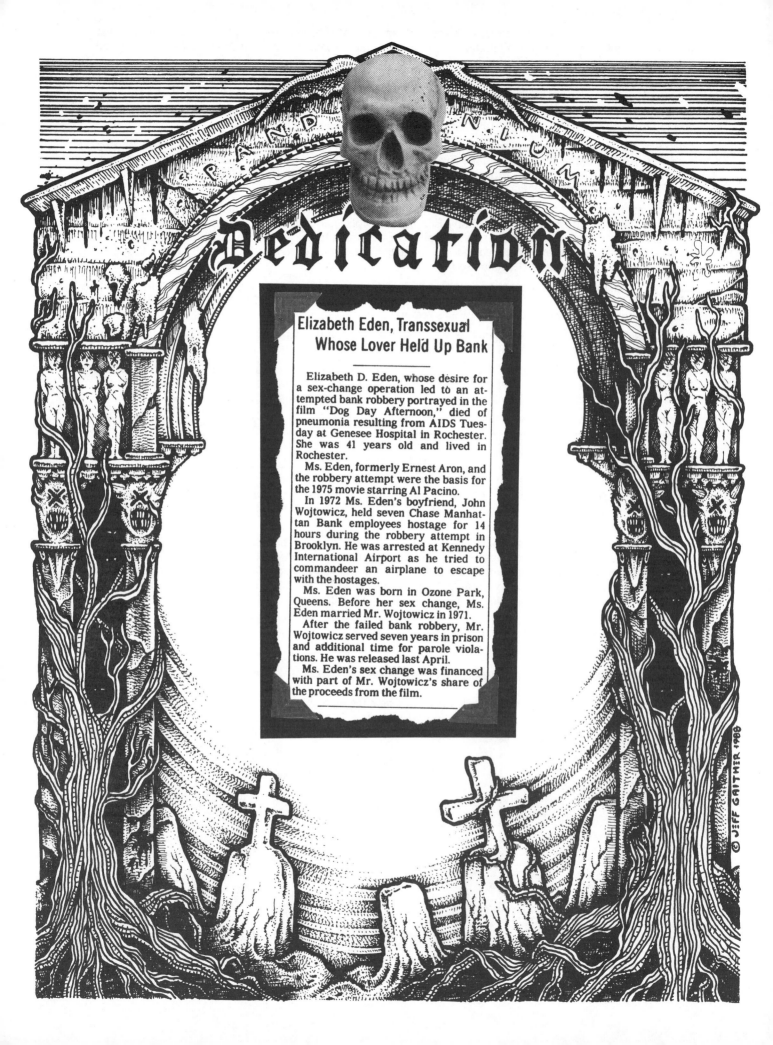

Dedication

Elizabeth Eden, Transsexual Whose Lover Held Up Bank

Elizabeth D. Eden, whose desire for a sex-change operation led to an attempted bank robbery portrayed in the film "Dog Day Afternoon," died of pneumonia resulting from AIDS Tuesday at Genesee Hospital in Rochester. She was 41 years old and lived in Rochester.

Ms. Eden, formerly Ernest Aron, and the robbery attempt were the basis for the 1975 movie starring Al Pacino.

In 1972 Ms. Eden's boyfriend, John Wojtowicz, held seven Chase Manhattan Bank employees hostage for 14 hours during the robbery attempt in Brooklyn. He was arrested at Kennedy International Airport as he tried to commandeer an airplane to escape with the hostages.

Ms. Eden was born in Ozone Park, Queens. Before her sex change, Ms. Eden married Mr. Wojtowicz in 1971.

After the failed bank robbery, Mr. Wojtowicz served seven years in prison and additional time for parole violations. He was released last April.

Ms. Eden's sex change was financed with part of Mr. Wojtowicz's share of the proceeds from the film.

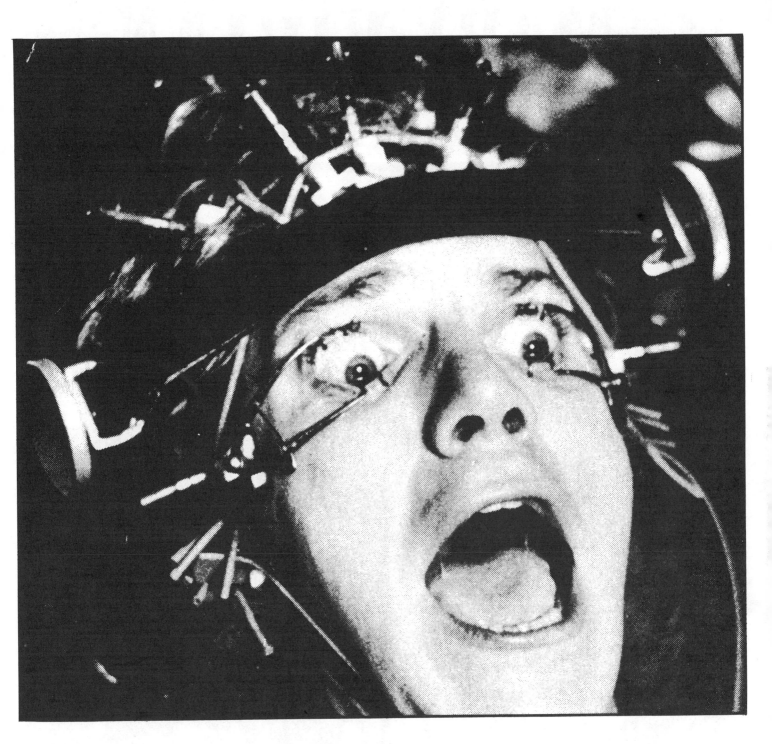

"Stop the film!
Please, please stop it!!!
I can't stand any more."
—Alex, A CLOCKWORK ORANGE

MARY VIVIAN PEARCE

Love will conquer all: Cotton and Crackers, Forever and Always

AS DONNA DASHER
MRS. LINKLETTER
MISS COTTON
PRINCESS COO-COO

Introduction

by J. Stevenson

Mary Vivian Pearce, known to friends as Bonnie, is a long-time "travelling companion" of John Waters and a star actress in his early films. As maladjusted teenagers, they scandalized local C.Y.O. dances, hooked school, crashed parties and just generally indulged in juvenile delinquent behavior that would go on to provide inspiration and subject matter for some of the most hilarious scenes in John's films.

While only appearing in brief cameo roles in John's last two big-budget mainstream films, *Polyester* (1980) and *Hairspray* (1988), Bonnie was one of John's first stars and an important weird character in his earliest (and greatest in my opinion) films where she always appeared as a platinum blonde.

Hag in a Black Leather Jacket (1964), a 15-minute, 8mm, black and white film, was Bonnie's stunning world debut — even if no one's ever seen it and John keeps it locked in his closet today. John uses terms like "terrible" and "mercifully short" to describe it, yet credits Bonnie with salvaging it from complete shitheapism as in one scene she launches into a wild rendition of an obscene dance known as the "Bodie Green," garbed in a cocktail dress young John purloined from his mother's closet.

Bonnie went on to co-star in John's next film, *Roman Candles* (1966), a twisted take-off of Andy Warhol's *Chelsea Girls*, complete with three-screen projection and tape sound of obnoxious radio ads, rock and roll, and press conferences with Lee Harvey Oswald's mother.

Bonnie played a kidnapped fashion model who is forced to "model herself to death" in front of a pack of screaming maniacs in John's next film, *Eat Your Makeup*. This endeavor, his first in 16mm, was shot mostly on his parents front lawn and in John's newly rented slum apartment in the Baltimore ghetto.

On the set of *Eat Your Make-Up*, L to R: David Lochary, Mary Vivian Pearce and Marina Melin

These first three films are today unobtainable in any form and comprise the "holy trinity" that hardcore Waters fanatics would kill to see.

●●●●●●●●●

John made his first feature film in 1969, *Mondo Trasho*. Bonnie, dolled up in hot pants and stockings as a jailbait Hollywood slut, co-stars with Divine and is the subject of much aimless camera time and ends up being carried around "unconscious" for much of the film. (She claims she boycotted the Oscars that year — and all years.) Waters proudly calls this a "gutter film" and promoted it as a "combination of cheap theatrics, obsessional fantasies, and a true love of all that is trashy in film today." The sound track is a run-on mash of every conceivable type of music, spliced in with radio snatches. The plot is either the most complicated since *War and Peace* or there is no plot at all, I can't figure out which.

Snapshot taken during the making of Mondo Trasho

Bonnie's career didn't go down the tubes like Clara Bow's when John started shooting "talkies" in 1970 with *The Diane Linkletter Story*. Shot as a 10-minute sound check the day after Diane "tripped" out her window in the throes of a bad LSD trip, this quickie stars an overweight, five o'clock shadowed Divine dressed in ridiculous hippie glad-rags as the little lady. Bonnie and David Lochary play the concerned parents, mouthing ridiculous "parent talk."

Later that same year, John made his first talkie feature, *Multiple Maniacs*, heavily influenced by the Manson killings hysteria then sweeping the nation. Bonnie plays David Lochary's "brainless chatterbox" girlfriend who steals him away from a vengeful Divine. This movie is as rampant, gritty and manicly paced as *Mondo Trasho*, yet, now able to employ dialogue, John's obsessions are more belligerently manifest. And after this, dialogue would never be the same. The film had showings in 16 cities, including London, but its longest run as a midnight film was at the Palace Theater in North Beach, San Francisco in 1971.

Mary Vivian Pearce armed and dangerous in *Multiple Maniacs* (1970)

Finally, in 1972 Bonnie and her co-stars exploded on an unsuspecting world with vomitous force in the now legendary *Pink Flamingos*. Bonnie plays Divine's "travelling companion," Miss Cotton, the voyeuristic sexual deviant accomplice of Divine's hippie white-trash son, Crackers (Danny Mills). With her blonde looks, expressive eyes, and soft voice, Bonnie was able to evoke a twisted weirdness that the movie-going public had never seen the likes of before.

Playing the elegant and arrogant Donna Dasher in John's next movie, *Female Trouble* (1974), Bonnie was again cast as the wife of David Lochary. Bonnie had a god-given talent for portraying frail, effette, psychotic society wrecks ... wealthy, genetically exhausted, hemophiliac blue-bloods, and Lochary was an excellent complement to such a role. True chemistry. Donna Dasher, just like Miss Cotton, is a frigid, sex-hating, sex-fearing gal who compensates with an out-of-control and perverted-to-the-core

imagination. And she was born to wear a fur coat. Wrapped in furs and silks and shawls and big hats, sneering at a world full of morons and inferiors, she was the essence of arrogant corrupted perversion. Her costumes took on this "society bitch" look from the end of *Pink Flamingos* through *Female Trouble* (until the money ran out).

Bonnie's last and perhaps most incredible starring role was in John's insane fairy tale, *Desperate Living* (1977), a genetic celluloid mutation of the French Revolution, Disneyland, Jean Genet and the Baltimore skid row. Here Bonnie is cast as Princess Coocoo, the rebellious daughter of evil Queen Carlotta (Edith Massey) who rules over Mortville, a shabby make-believe trash town crawling with winos, criminals, psychotics and lesbians. This is my personal favorite of Bonnie's roles. She is perfect as the unhappy, cloistered, medieval princess, resplendent in doily-laced gowns and looking like something that fell off an over-embalmed wedding cake, buried under tons of eye make-up. There are threads of the Miss Cotton and Donna Dasher characters in Princess Coo-coo taken to the extreme. This was John's best looking movie yet, quality-wise, and the color photography is lush to the point of gushing.

While never targeted for the attention and fame of other John Waters stars such as Divine, Edith Massey, Jean Hill and Mink Stole, Bonnie was perfect for certain types of roles and often came off as the strangest character of the bunch.

She was a perfect counterpoint to the massive jabbering grotesques who hogged all the notoriety in John's films, yet her characters were equally striking in the perverted and sickening scheme of things. Bonnie projected a more introverted personality, and John was always keenly aware of exactly the type of character she should play and he wrote these custom-tailored roles into his movies. Bonnie's characters remain a basic part of John's early film successes and she commands the fanatical devotion of a hardcore underground sub-cult of Waters' junkies who would gladly bring her the severed head of anyone she named.

Desperate Living was John's swan song in a sense. It was his most excessive movie and the only money loser, and was followed by a conscious attempt to assault the mainstream, to expand his audience. Since Bonnie is not a trained actress and never especially wanted to be one, her starring days appear to be over as John adopts more conventional approaches on all fronts. I personally liked *Polyester* and *Hairspray* very much, but the five bastard children he raised from *Mondo Trasho* to *Desperate Living* are some **real** sonofabitches.

I have come to know Bonnie at some of John's parties over the years. She's a friendly, soft-spoken person, yet extremely quick on the up-take, with a slightly (?) twisted sense of humor. I talked to her by phone at her apartment in Baltimore near Pimlico race track on March 13, 1988 ironically, only a week after Divine's death.

3

Well, I guess it's hard to start with anything else considering this tragedy that happened a week ago — Divine's death. I just wondered where you were when you heard about it and what your gut reaction was.

It was really AWFUL the way I heard about it. It was Tuesday morning and I didn't get a newspaper, it didn't arrive as usual, so I went over to the track and got one out of the machine. I put a quarter in — I had all my stuff with me — and the door slammed shut! So I had to go back to my car, get another quarter (laughs) and I — just read the race results. And I got really busy at work, and I never looked at the front page. And then this trainer comes up and starts saying — tells me that he had died and saying all these TERRIBLE things about him! About him being gay, being overweight and stuff, and I turned over the paper and I thought OH MY GOD and I just started screamin' at him. I thought that was just — SO rude! (laugh of disbelief) You just don't DO ... I mean you know somebody that had a friend that DIED, it was — was really horrible.

Yeah, I GUESS ...

So I went stormin' in the track kitchen after work, I was hoping he would be there so I could YELL at him some more 'cause I was really upset ... and I really thought I had things under control, and he wasn't there, but these two Washington Post writers were ... "What's the matter with YOU!!!," so I told them that Divine had died and ... one of them knew who Divine was and stuff, and that we had grown up together — and they were really sympathetic so that was nice to run into ... I was sort of glad that I didn't run into the other guy ... but I was really upset all day on Tuesday ... and Wednesday was pretty rough.

Did you talk to John?

I talked to John on Wednesday.

I'm sure he must have been taking it bad, of course.

He took it pretty bad. But he's ... in pretty good spirits. First ... few days were pretty rough for him. But he's, ah ... he had a BEAUTIFUL speech written yesterday, at the funeral.

Yesterday (3/12/88) was the funeral, so ... probably you saw a lot of people you don't normally see.

Oh yeah. Yeah, there were about 300 people there.

Oh yeah?

Yeah. A lot of people I didn't know. And a lot of people I hadn't seen for a long time ... and he was buried up in the, ah — Towson Cemetery, near where we all grew up, where we used to play hooky and ... get into the graveyard and drink beer, and (laughs) Divine used to steal flowers from the graveyard there, because he used to decorate his apartment for parties — always Easter Sunday was the best day (to get flowers).

Rather appropriate ... and John had a speech that he wrote?

Yeah, it was REALLY nice.

It was so ironic that it happened just now, and I'm sure that struck everybody ...

Yeah.

So you knew Divine way back when, I guess ... you knew John, like ...

Yeah. I've known Divine for about 25 years. And I've known John all my life. Our fathers went to school together.

Right, that's what he says (in *Shock Value*).

Yeah, but he didn't, uh — you know we just saw each other at family gatherings until I was about 13 or 14, and then we started hanging around together ... gettin' in trouble.

Right and then your parents started not speaking to each other.

Right. (laughs) We were juvenile delinquents. And, ah — we were forbidden to see each other, so naturally we ... kept seeing each other. We didn't have "dates," we went out like, as kind of a group? So to sneak out we'd arrange a fake date. We'd get somebody real straight lookin' to come to the door and pose as my date? And the guy would be really embarrassed ... and a little bit nervous, which my parents thought that — was NICE, you know? They thought that nice boys were nervous when they met the date's parents. So it really fooled them, and the next day they'd say, "Oh, that was a really nice boy you went out with!" (laughs) And so one night I couldn't set up a fake, and I wanted to go to this big dance called "Night Train" after the James Brown song, it was popular at the time, so this guy that I didn't like at all, but he had been NAGGIN' me to go out with him for a long time, and so I said, okay ... when I got to the end of the driveway I bailed out! (laughs) ... just to get out of the house. (very brief attempt at seriousness) That was really mean. ... (laughs)

Yeah, that was the inspiration for that scene in *Polyester*.

Yeah.

So did you know David Lochary, or did you meet Divine —

Oh yeah, I met David Lochary about the same time I met Divine ... twenty, twenty-five years ago.

When you were in your early teenage years?

Uh-huh. Yeah, I was 14 ... when I went to David Lochary's.

And then those — John started to shoot those early films, right? Like *Hag In a Black Leather Jacket*?

L to R: Bonnie, John Leisensing and David Lochary brainstorming during shooting of *Mondo Trasho*

Mary Vivian Pearce in *Mondo Trasho*

NOV   68

The making of *Mondo Trasho*: Bonnie relaxes with a copy of *Hollywood Babylon* while pervert approaches

Hag ... yeah, about three years later.

Right, in his book (*Shock Value*) he describes — says he has that one (*Hag in a Black Leather Jacket*) locked in his closet and he doesn't want to show it, he refuses to show it, but he says it's pretty dull actually except the best part is when you do a dance in it.

(laughs) Yeah, I do the "Bodie Green" in it ... always getting in trouble for doing the Bodie Green.

Oh yeah?

Well, the Immaculate Conception, of course that was a C.Y.O. dance, you know you weren't ... we'd always do it and Father Morrison would (laughs) we'd get caught, and ... at Beaver Springs, when we had

dances there in the summer time — it was a swimming club, out in Cockeysville — and Josh Cockey would catch us doing the Bodie Green and he really would get furious. (shouts in imitation) "YOU CAN GO FROM SIDE TO SIDE YOUNG LADY BUT NO BUMPS AND GRINDS!!!"

So there was no chance the dance would go unnoticed by ... people of decent morals?

NO.

Do you have any memories of those early films, like *Roman Candles*?

Roman Candles, yeah, I remember that. That was the triple projection. It happened on Flower Mart day.

EAT YOUR MAKEUP

L to R: Mona Montgomery, Mary Vivian Pearce and Marina Melin in *Eat Your Make-up.*

Right, that's —

Well, it was a "one day only" (laughs). Lou Cedrone reviewed it — he gave it a nice review. Said it went off with, not a whimper but with a bang, or something. It was pretty nice ... it was the only nice review he gave any of John's movies — except for *Hairspray*. And he really wasn't nice about that.

He gave a mixed review to *Hairspray*?

Well, he said he liked the first forty minutes but that was all.

Huh ... yeah that's weird. Yeah, it's been getting unbelievable reviews — it's really been, ah ... did he say how — when you saw him (at the funeral) — how it's been doing or give any news on that, on *Hairspray*, or ...

No. (dead silence)

I guess the earliest film that's being rented out now is *The Diane Linkletter Story* — do you remember shooting that one?

(fondly) Oh yes. Yeah, that was our first "talkie."

All the others were silents?

Uh-huh. The sound wasn't on the thing, there was a TAPE that went with it. So that was just a rehearsal to practice ... TALKING and we'd just read a thing in the newspaper and it was improvised.

Divine as Diane Linkletter

So that happened the day after she jumped out the window, right?

Uh-huh.

So it was ALL improvised?

Well, we just read the story we ... had a basic idea of what we were gonna do, you know ... yeah, it was a lot of fun! (laughs)

There are some great lines in that one. You (as the mother) trying to talk Divine into going to "the club" ... (in a shabby Divine imitation): "I don't WANNA go to the club!"

Yeah, I thought David Lochary was really good.

Yeah, he was great in all those ... I think ... which was your favorite of those films? You mentioned *Mondo Trasho* as ...

(thoughtfully) *Mondo Trasho* ...

Mary Vivian Pearce on the road to stardom in snapshots of 11/68 [during shooting of *Mondo Trasho*]

A lot of people who've worked with John say they liked *Female Trouble*. Is the —

Female Trouble, yeah, I like that one a lot too. I like 'em ALL. (laughs)

Me too! I think your greatest roles were as "Cotton" (*Pink Flamingos*) and "Princess Coo-coo" (*Desperate Living*).

Princess Coo-coo?!!

Yeah — that was UNBELIEVABLE, that was — you're not like that in real life, are you?

What?!!

Like Princess Coo-coo?

(helpless laughter) ... No.

I just HAD to ask that. Do you remember what that green bile was made out of that you dribbled out of your mouth at the end of that movie? (*Desperate Living*)

Yeah — it's Alka Seltzer and green food dye, and you just mix 'em together and put it on your tongue and it — you foam, because when Alka Seltzer mixes with saliva it just ... foams out, like when you drop it in water.

Well that's a great recipe, and I hope maybe some people will take a hint from that ...

(laughs)

... because it looked almost phosphorescent, that was really a wonderful last scene.

Yeah, it does look ... (laughs)

Of course Donna Dasher in Female Trouble was a great role, and you wore some stunning fashions in

"Sneering at a world full of morons ..." Donna Dasher reclines in what appears to be a silk straight jacket in *Female Trouble* □ □ □ □ □ □ □ □ □ □ □ □ □ □ □

that. Now, you said before, the costumes got less fancy as the money ran out during the shooting?

Yeah, the first costume I wear — that white silk suit? That was made for me. And the others were just my clothes, and ah, the one in the (later) hospital scene is just some scarves thrown together.

You were recognized in New Orleans once on the street for being in Pink Flamingos. Could you describe that encounter briefly?

Yeah, I was there on vacation.

That was a few years ago?

Yeah, and I had gone to the racetrack — The Fairgrounds — lost all my money, I was walking home (chuckles) and I was just looking at the marquee for the show *One Mo' Time,* and the guy came out and he just started looking at me really weird. (laughs) I thought, "God, what's the matter?!" — he says "Can I help you?" and well, I'll ask how much it is — don't have any MONEY to go to it, but ... and he told me it was 19 or 20 dollars. And then he says (shouting) YOU WERE IN *PINK FLAMINGOS,* WEREN'T YOU???!!! (laughs) I said, oh, that's why he was looking at me like that. I was kind of relieved. I said yes and he let me go to the show for free, and that night three of us went to Tipitinas to see some live music. He told me that he had seen *Pink Flamingos* 17 times ... when the Toulouse was a movie theater.

Are you recognized often on the street, or ...

(emphatically) No.

That's surprising.

Well, I don't have platinum blonde hair anymore.

Right, that's true. So your natural haircolor was always brunette? But you used to dye your hair a lot, or ...

Oh yeah. Uh-huh. I really wanted to be a platinum blonde (chuckles), but when I was a little kid I didn't know how to do it. So — I didn't know how hair

Bonnie in street clothes on the set of *Female Trouble*

Lochary and Pearce as Donald and Donna Dasher in *Female Trouble,* outraged and repulsed ━━━

Van Smith applies the finishing touches on the set of *Desperate Living*

Desperate Living

dyes worked or anything, I just knew Clorox had bleach in it? So I went in my mother's laundry room and I dumped Clorox all over my hair, and then BOOSTED it with Ajax! And so presto! I was PLATINUM BLONDE!!! Well, my parents weren't too PLEASED with the look, (laughs) you know, I thought I looked like Kim Novak. And it was, oh — it was really — the ends were all broken up — SMELLED horrible! (laughs)

Yeah, that's amazing — that was straight Clorox? Or ...

Yeah, STRAIGHT Clorox!

Wow, if you soak clothes in that they come apart, disintegrate!

I know!

(laughs) ... and then your natural color would grow back after a while?

Yeah ... and then I'd do a touch-up with Clorox. But that was when I was 13 or 14 ... then I learned how to use dye properly.

Yeah, you were a blonde in most all of those (films), as "Cotton" and ah ...

Uh-huh.

I guess you knew Danny Mills, "Crackers," back then pretty well.

Uh-huh.

I guess he's in jail today or something?

Well, he's in a half-way house, he's out of jail. He's doin' really well.

Yeah, John said in his lecture in Los Angeles about half a year ago, said he was ... the prosecutor was trying to get him for LSD distribution or something.

Uh-huh.

Were any of those people at all like the characters — especially *Pink Flamingos* I'm talking about — were any of those people at all like the characters they played in that movie?

(quiet disbelief) ... Are you kidding? (laughs)

Or should I say were any of them NOT like the ... (attempts to repair this line of questioning are unsuccessful as Bonnie drowns them out with incredulous laughter)

(laughs die down) Ah ... no.

I mean some of them couldn't possibly be —

No. (flat, serious tone)

Because the production values obviously weren't slick or anything, and there wasn't a lot of ... you know, make-up and stuff ... a lot of the people seemed to be acting naturally ... (loss for words) ...

(laughter of toleration) No, (deadpan response) no one's like that.

Didn't Danny run a health food restaurant for a while?

No. His — it's just a restaurant. It wasn't "healthy." (laughs) The food was pretty good.

Was that a while ago?

Just before he went to prison. Supposedly they used the restaurant as a front.

So back in 1973 before *Pink Flamingos* came out, the three of you, you, John and Danny, moved to New Orleans and moved into, John describes it in his book *Shock Value*, as "the worst dump" he's ever seen.

The worst dump?!! (laughs) Well, it, uh ... yeah, it was a dump, it was a little shotgun style house right outside the French quarter ... and we didn't have much money. We didn't have any FURNITURE (laughs) ... and we just had a mattress on the floor, and ah ... had a little backyard and the hot water heater was OUTSIDE, so the pilot light was constantly going out, and so we never had hot water. And then across the street was this food store that — was always making these announcements about what was on sale, and (laughs) I could hear it from our house.

And you worked in a bar?

Uh-huh.

Do you remember the name of that bar?

The Gunga Din.

Wonder if it's still open? Do you, when you go back to New Orleans on a vacation or something, do you still know the neighborhood you used to live in then?

Uh-huh.

Everything is still there, the house and everything?

Yeah.

Do you have fond memories of those months in New Orleans? You were there for about half a year? I guess John went back to New York.

Oh yeah, we had a wonderful time.

So otherwise outside of that time you lived in the Detroit area, you've lived mostly in Baltimore?

Yeah.

You worked on a horse farm? Does your family own that?

No, a guy I knew from a long time ago was the trainer there. And I got the job from him. It was breaking yearlings and schooling two-year-olds.

When you grew up did you have horses at your house? Did you live on a large estate or something like that?

No. I had a horse but I kept it at a friend's house, about three miles away from where I lived. They had a barn and a ... it was near Windy Valley — that's where I got involved with the race horses, they corrupted me. It was the strangest place. It was about a half mile from where I stabled my horse, and that's where I learned how to ride. The trainer there, he owned it ... it was a frozen custard store and then up the driveway he had a barn with — his racetrack was

really a PLOUGHED PATH (laughs) and ah, he asked me to exercise one of his horses and taught me to ride, put me on a real quiet horse named SAM FIREBALL. And I galloped him every day, and then this other guy that worked at the racetrack showed me how to tie the reins and do all this stuff that you do when you gallop racehorses. It was really fun.

You were really young then?

— and they had this frozen custard store that he owned, the trainer of the horses, that was just a really strange place. It was a kind of restaurant and they had this man that worked there that made the donuts, his name was "Sarge" and he lived in a shack behind the barn, and he was an alcoholic, and some say he was shell-shocked from the war — something had happened to him and it might have happened on Joe's place because for some reason they adopted him — and then he worked in the store and then he'd go on a drunk. But he made the donuts and the ice cream and he'd usually go down to the store in these blood spattered pants, (chuckles) right out in the open making these donuts in the most awful looking grease .. and wipe his nose. (chuckles) And the donuts were delicious! (seriously meant) He also made ice cream, the health department would close him down once in a while. They had RATS roaming freely in the back of the store, a SKUNK picking through ... Sundays they sold pony rides ... small ponies Joe had up there. And they had these race-horses.

Bonnie's Dad and Bonnie on her horse, Shamrock

This was near your house?

Uh-huh, 'bout three miles. And then everyday at noontime there'd be a big card game ... trainers, exercise riders ... and, my favorite was Marie Fox? An ex-stripper from The Block. (chuckles) She played cards every day. I learned how to play "Pitch." And then every NIGHT they had a card game. It was wonderful.

Yeah, it sounds like a lot of people hung out there and stuff, it wasn't just a ... So that was where you were first corrupted, and then ...

(laughs)

You were quite young when you hung out there?

Uh-huh. About 16, 17.

And then, would you say, well you knew John during this period.

Uh-huh. I was still hanging around with John then. He would call me at Windy Valley.

Did, ah — did you ever go ... go straight after that or has it been a LIFE of corruption?

(laughs hard) No, I've gone straight! I'm still a race-track degenerate. An' I played poker last night. Yeah, I realized how well I've learned to play Pitch 'cause — which is kind of unfortunate because now no one will play with me. And all the characters are gone that played — it's a REGIONAL game, you know, it's very popular in Baltimore. You probably never heard of it.

Well, I'm not — I don't know much about cards anyway.

Well, no one's ever heard of it outside Baltimore, especially SOUTH Baltimore. It's very popular there. And um ... it's really a complicated game, it's ... much more complicated than poker. It's a TRUMP game? And there's different points and you bid.

So, you go out today —

Yeah, we go out to — if I go out to play cards everybody will play poker because I play Pitch too well.

And that's Pimlico Racetrack that you live next to now, right?

Uh-huh.

And you work there, too, right?

Right.

So you know a lot of people that — racetrack people?

Uh-huh.

John said in his early — those early films when they had openings, and there was publicity and festivities and ... a lot of show business stuff, that you didn't care too much for all the spotlight type of things. Would you say that's true? Would you say you love the life of show business, or you like to live more quietly?

Yeah, I like — more quietly. I always helped adver-tise. At *Eat Your Make-up* in Provincetown I gave out candied lipstick ... and *Eat Your Make-up* flyers. I always helped out with the publicity, to push the movies, we'd go out in the streets and just hand out flyers and stuff.

Right, that was back when it was more of a basic type of publicity.

Right.

Certainly it's come a long way, huh? With the Balti-more *Hairspray* premiere — that was incredible. Like John said, they don't even have openings like that in Hollywood anymore.

Bonnie in 1954 after receiving her first Holy Communion

"In my combination clothes" – March 1958

Bonnie barefoot in front of a Fells Point bar ["Mom says I look like a 'hooker' in this picture."]

Right, it was — yeah.

Did you hang out at Pete's Hotel back in Fells Point?

Uh-huh.

Do you ever go back to that neighborhood or have reason to go back to that neighborhood these days?

Oh yeah. I go back there occasionally on weekends.

Has it changed a lot over the years?

Uh-huh.

Yeah, I was talking with a black guy outside Edie's thrift shop — which I was surprised to learn was still open — and he was giving me the whole story about the neighborhood. I guess he's a character that's been hangin' out there for, he claims, 75 years. I don't know, you might recognize him.

For 75 years!? What's his name? "Hots?"

He's a black guy and he was sweeping up next to Edie's thrift shop.

Yeah, yeah — does he have a store right next ...

Yeah.

Yeah, that's Hots. He has a stable down the street too.

Oh really?

He has that store and he runs the stable around the corner ... they have the horses for the people who sell fruits and vegetables on the pony carts.

I'm not too familiar with ... I've been down there a few times but ... but he seemed to be a walking encyclopedia of the neighborhood.

Oh yeah.

And I was happy to see that the thrift shop was still open. I had thought it was closed, but it's still open.

Yeah, Bob Adams has it now.

And Pete's Hotel is STILL a bar. It's run by Greeks now.

Right, it's a Greek bar. He sold it.

Did they do a lot of renovation or is it still pretty much the same way —

No, they've changed it around. It's darker, and air conditioned and all closed up, and ... that's what I liked about it, because in the summertime you could, uh, it was the only bar that wasn't air conditioned some of 'em, ah — except on weekends when they're real crowded with body heat — were so air-conditioned that it was actually uncomfortable. So I'd always go over to Pete's to get warm. They had a nice big fan, you could look out onto the street ...

Of course that was quite a while ago — that was in the early '70s, right?

Uh-huh.

These days ... what sort of books do you like? The last

conversation you said you occasionally borrow books from John's collection. Do you have, ah ... gentle tastes in reading, or ...

(chuckles)

Or do you like sometimes the more crime type ...

Yeah ... I like — I love the crime type books.

WHO is the one you say you don't like at all?

Your fr — (she's about to say friend!) the one you like so much.

(laughs) I don't LIKE him!

Those letters! (referring to copies of John Gacy's love letters I'd sent her that had just appeared in the Chicago *Sun Times*) ... and that poor welfare woman! What'd she think!?

Yeah, what a tragic love affair. I mean, she's got ten kids.

(laughs) It won't work!!

Yeah, exactly, you feel like telling him — "Look!" You know? I mean, it's true that the Chicago *Sun Times* did BUY those letters off her, so she had a little spending money for a while. But I'm sure it got HIM plenty pissed. But ... no I don't ... you know (voice trails off) I don't LIKE him. He's ...

My favorite book I've read this year is *Detour*.

Is it fiction?

No, it's true. Cheryl Crane? Lana Turner's daughter? It's her autobiography and it's really good.

So, I guess ... you DID read some of those xeroxes I sent you?

(laughs) Yeah, THANKS a lot!

You know, a little "light reading" ...

I TOLD YOU I hated him so you send me these letters! I couldn't WAIT to finish *Buried Dreams*! I read *Detour* right after that (laughs) ... it was an "up" book by comparison. Even though her life was very tragic. Especially — if you got RAPED by Tarzan. And she became — she has a woman lover and she's been going with her for 18 years? So really it's the exact opposite of her mother, a STABLE gay relationship.

What sort of movies do you like? Are there any that stand out that you've seen recently?

Yeah — *Hairspray*.

Absolutely.

Before, I saw *Ironweed* and *Patty Rocks*. (dead silence)

Okay, I guess the last question is ... I just wondered if you ever got to Boise?

(laughs) No, I've never been to Boise.

No? Never got to Boise? Never got a crew cut?

No. Where is Boise?

Boise, IDAHO.

I know, where is that? (laughs)

(long pause then confused laughter, as Stevenson tries to figure out all possible metaphorical and Freudian meanings to this)

Is it in the midwest? Or the west?

Ah — (not sure if she's putting me on) actually I was near there once, hitch hiking a few years ago and I was going to stop in and just go through Boise, completely on the strength of *Pink Flamingos* ending. But instead I met somebody else who'd been there so I didn't have to make the pilgrimage.

(laughs)

Like John says today, he's shocked by it (Pink Flamingos) himself when he sees it again, how ugly some of the ... do you remember where it first opened by any chance?

Pink Flamingos? ... um ... Danny and I were still in New Orleans. John left because he was worried about what was happening to it. The distributor had it but it wasn't playing anywhere. It might've opened in ... New York?

I think it opened in a gay porno house in Boston.

Right!

In fact, the guy who ran the porno house (South Station Cinema, torn down in 1987), George Monsour, he's a big film booker in Boston now.

Right, he was there (at John's 1986 Boston show). But it didn't — he said it WAS the first place it was shown?

Well, I thought it was the first place in BOSTON it was shown, but that was the first place in the WORLD it was shown.

Oh really?

Yeah, 'cause John, in his book *Shock Value*, describes it in rather unflattering terms, he says it opened in a gay porno house in Boston — was ALL WRONG and the cast got pissed off when they heard about it.

That's right! And THEN it went to New York.

END

──── "I'm God — YOU'RE God!" ➹ Crackers and Cotton celebrate the execution of Connie and Raymond Marble

Divine takes aim at the Marbles while Cotton looks on

16

MISS

JEAN HILL

17

by J. Stevenson

After many unsuccessful auditions and at his wits end for a heavy black actress to star in his next film, *Desperate Living*, John Waters was introduced to Jean Hill. He extended his hand — instead she grabbed his crotch — and the rest is history. If the gods smiled when Bergman met Ullman then their lips twisted into a shit-eating grin when Waters met Hill.

John immediately gave her the role of Grizelda, Peggy Gravel's (Mink Stole) psychiatric nurse. Jean kills Mink's husband (George Stover) by sitting on him, and the two fugitives flee to Mortville to escape the flabby arm of the law. Now ensconced in Mortville as subjects of sadistic Queen Carlotta (Edith Massey), Grizelda and Peggy Gravel become lesbian lovers and ... well just go see the goddam movie for yourself!!! *Desperate Living* was Jean's first screen appearance — a star was born and a million minds were blown.

Jean followed this with a brief but hilarious role in John's next movie, *Polyester*, where she portrays a gospel lady who hijacks a crowded public bus in pursuit of a hot-rod full of juvenile delinquents. She immobilizes the car, blowing out a tire (by biting it), then proceeds to beat the shit out of Stiv Bators.

While not featured in John's most recent film, *Hairspray*, Jean has gone on to gain widespread infamy as a greeting card model for Rockshots and Comstock cards, actually sparking a bidding war between the two companies that's exploded in a flurry of lawsuits. At the time I talked to Jean she was featured in the current issue of *Jumbo* porno magazine. (Her layouts are wholly comprised of chaste if ever so bizarre greeting card stills.) Jean's received a multitude of other offers — not all of them printable — including a role as "Love Judge" in a People's Court style sex series, and in TWA commercials for wide body airliners.

While most people still identify her as a "John Waters discovery" on a par with Divine and Edith Massey, Jean is an amazing cut-the-bullshit type personality in and of herself, and it's an open question as to who discovered who. It's really a "Tale of Two Cities" to put in in a theatrical and overblown perspective: John circulated in white (and white trash) Baltimore for the most part and Jean in black Baltimore, otherwise it's inconceivable that they wouldn't have run into each other sooner. Yet, while Jean is linked to John in the public mind, she's fiercely outspoken and if she has a bitch with John she lets him know it full square. Future collaborations are probable but uncertain at this point, although the two remain good friends and mutual advisors and live in the same neighborhood near Druid Park. Jean's entrance at John's parties always causes a stir.

In fact I first met Jean at John's 1983 Christmas party and it's taken me this long to get the lead out of my ass and get an interview. I was staying in a cheap hotel that night and as Jean and I were given a ride home from the party she told me if I ever came down again to stay with her in the ghetto instead of some old sleazy-ass hotel room.

On the evening of Tuesday, March 22, 1988 I called Jean at her apartment in Baltimore. She had recently been released from Mercy Hospital after prolonged treatment for blood clots, obesity, high blood-pressure, diabetes and asthma. Now confined to the hospital style bed in her apartment, Jean was nonetheless within easy reach of her phone and what followed as the tape recorder spun and cassettes popped in and out was close to three hours of hilarity, equal parts history, philosophy, story-telling and sex advice, all of it delivered in Jean's animated, bellicose style, punctuated throughout by fits of laughter and demonstrating that her hard-ass spirit was unbowed and that she was still indeed the incomparable Miss Jean E. Hill. Words on paper can hardly do it justice.

Exhortation, Harangue, Manifesto ... all these terms apply. She answered all my questions and often went far beyond, leaving me gape-jawed in disbelief. Proper English takes a beating, but what the hell. ... And never did a hint of self pity creep through, which is amazing considering she's endured health problems that would have devastated the spirits of an ordinary mortal.

I have not censored any of her words and have tried to leave intact the spirit of her verbal barrage. What else can I say? ... Ladies and Gentlemen, Drag Queens and Winos, we now present Miss Jean E. Hill!

Hello?

Hi Jean, how you doin'?

Pretty good.

Well, I found the magazine (*Jumbo*) —

Am I on the front cover?

Yeah.

Am I?!!!!

Yeah, you are.

(laughs)

Yeah — it goes "Miss Jean Hill, Earth Shaking Sex Symbol."

(laughs) Aw — that's cute!

And the pictures are unbelievable, they're great.

Somebody else said it's not in poor taste even though it's a porno magazine. That the article is not in poor taste — 'cause I said, "Do you have it?" and he read it to me and I wasn't offended by any of it.

... I'm not gonna knock it. I'm not gonna knock it. It got me the exposure, and I got over 75 pieces of mail, and I'm pretty sure if I go back down there there'll be more mail down there.

Some unbelievable pictures, about six pages of pictures.

'Cause if they keep askin' for these videos — does it mention anything about that video? The "videos" were John Waters films?!! (laughs) They don't know that, they keep saying "Well, can you mail me one of your videos?"

It says you're in *Desperate Living* and it goes ... "Famous film producer, John Waters, who lives near Jean, thought she was good enough to put her in his film *Polyester* and star her in *Desperate Living* in which Jean portrayed a psychiatric nurse and appeared nude ..." So it says "appeared nude in *Desperate Living* — maybe they want videos of that!

I AM nude, though. But you gotta wait halfway through the film!!! (laughs) ... 45 minutes for a ... for two minutes of my ass rollin' on the bed!!! (hilarious laughter all around)

And by the time they get that far their minds will be so blown they won't — (ongoing laughter)

I LOVE the article, though! I mean it's not ob — sinful, it seems like it's in good taste in a bad magazine.

You got it. You got the whole thing right there. You're getting a lot of responses on the article, huh?

Yeah, because I got 75 pieces of mail between the — I noticed on each one it was between the 12th and the 15th.

You're gonna get BURIED in mail. Uh ... you say there were some crazy replies?

Oh, but all of 'em were so positive — I thought somebody would write "Why did you do this!" and ... I got NONE of that! All of 'em were cryin' for MORE! ... and some of 'em makin' — three marriage proposals, or be their mistress, and one guy said the thing with the two Cadillacs — I'm gonna DEFINITELY call him.

It says in the magazine —

It IS a lot of pictures in there, eh? Do they have any Rock-Shot pictures in there?

It's mostly like the greeting card type pictures, actually they don't have any pictures of your tits or, anything at all.

I GOTTA see this! I mean I'm wonderin' how this got OVER in a magazine like this. But it was like everybody sayin', "You gave us just enough, but give us MORE." You know it's like, "You're TEASING us, where can we get your video, where ..." I told somebody I'm beginning to ENJOY this part of it, because it's like "give us more, give us more!" 'Cause I love that one where the guy wrote on the computer paper, he said, "I don't even want to see the front, I want to see that big ASS, that big BEHIND." (laughs)

Yeah, and you know that was coming straight from the heart.

(laughs) That's all he wrote on there — "I want to see that ASS, that BIG ASS, that big behind." I said, now who is THIS?! He left his name and address.

Was he one of the — you said you got some letters from some crackers from Arkansas?

Oh! The one from Charlotte, North Carolina was cute, he said ... "I'm a white male and I'm from Charlotte, North Carolina and I weight 140 lbs. but I've always had this secret desire to have me a big black mama." ... I'm gonna pull some of 'em out and read 'em to ya. (laughs) Oh some of 'em were just wild! Then I had this staff sergeant who talked about lickin this pussy — all of 'em talked about eatin my pussy — I love it! (wild laughter)

Yeah! Talk about lively mail.

I had more offers to get this cunt ate than the law allows. (laughs) I told John, I said, "Come down here and read this shit!"

Right ... they've got one quote in here that says "Jean says that she's had sex with over 4,000 men in her life."

Not THOUSAND, four HUNDRED! (laughs all around) Four HUNDRED ...

Jean, they threw an extra zero on there!

She's got four THOUSAND in there! Oooooohh nnnnooooo honey!!! ... Yeah, 'cause one guy was sayin' to me, he said, "I know you got hundreds of boyfriends, but could you please clear it with one of

'em so that I could have you for a' evening" (laughs) ... he be in Baltimore, he says ... (looking through her mail) where IS he? ... and there's one seemed like Ku Klux Klan, lives in Arkansas. I told 'em I KNOW I have arrived now! (laughs wildly)

Definitely, this is some sort of peak of ... the industry, in a way.

He said, "I have a secret desire to ..." ... what did he say? He had a secret desire to screw a large black woman, he said, but — how did he put it? Wait a minute. And then he asked me was I "TV Mama" ... whoever she is, I don't know.

No, I've never heard of her either but this is hilarious: You said 400 and they just threw a little old zero on the end of it.

Jean Hill's motto is, "Live until you die." She's had sex with over 4000 men in her lifetime.

Oh my God! ... Four THOUSAND ... Oh my G O D !!! My friend said I was exaggeratin' with 400 — I said, "No girl, let's go back here and count." She been knowin' me a long time. So I start namin' 'em, I can name the first 65 of 'em. That was the second year I was havin' sex. And then the next year ... I started datin' — we used to go down to the Royal Thee-ater, and I used to mess around with those guys — I never went with the stars 'cause I knew they thought that they were lovers, and I've always been fearful of disease. So I would pick like, Tommy Hunt's drummer, or some man that looked like he just needed some self-esteem to stay in the band, or something like that. And THOSE are the ones that I would go to bed with. But I rarely went to bed with a star. "Cause if he didn't want you blowin' him or doin' somethin' crazy with him — the mothafucka thought he was better than you! And I ain't sleepin' with 'em like that.

Was this a club that used to be open?

No, it used to be a bar — I mean a, ah stage, like the Apollo? Well, this was the Royal Thee-atre and they used to let me backstage, and I used to get my pickin, 'cause I was about sixteen years old. And that was the very first time I ever encountered, ah ... gay women. I won't call her name, but she was the woman who used to sing (in a sing-song voice) "There she is, standin' in the rain," and I noticed that she wouldn't let any men in her dressing room, 'cause she said, "Baby, if YOU want to come in," so

I went in — first time I ever encountered dope, too, 'cause she and her friend were sittin' on the floor smokin' dope. Then when I seen these two women kiss I said, "Oh my Gawd!" (laughs) I was sixteen. Thought I knew it all but I didn't know a damn thing but what I read in books ... use to read Masters & Johnson's *Sexology* and all of that, but by the time I was eighteen honey, I think I had gone through everything there was to be gone through. I'd GO to orgies but I have never participated in 'em because I have this fearful thing of disease or somebody else, it just FRIGHTENS me.

And that theater was like ...

They used to have people like Dinah Washington, ah ... the first person I ever saw on stage down there was Dionne Warwick, "Walk On By," and then the Supremes used to come down there. And I used to tease people all the time and tell 'em Diana Ross was gonna be the star, because she had this thing where it looked like she would put her hands — I will NEVER forget it — up in front of those two girls and stand at least a foot in front of them, and (laughs) I said one of these days she's gonna walk away from 'em, and sure enough she did.

This was pretty much a black theater. Not many white people down there at this point?

Well, a few of 'em had started comin' down, but you know at the time it was still sort of racist here. But you had a lot of white promoters and white producers, and ... they had Fat Daddy Johnson, and then they had another white guy that used to like me. But I never would sleep with him, I'd tease him, always "gonna, gonna, gonna" but never got around to it.

Yeah, Baltimore is mostly blacks. What do you think — do a lot of blacks like John's films? Or ... do they "get the joke"?

No, you know when I first started, blacks sort of shunned me, in John's films. Because they said John Waters had never used any black people in his films before. I think he had one, Rod, which was a friend of mine. 'Cause Rod had told me that he was lookin' for somebody. I think Rod was the first one that ever told me that he was lookin' for a black woman to play this role. He said, "Jean, you'd be perfect," so I said, No, I'm not interested in bein' in the movies," 'cause you know at the time I thought about the consequences. One of the reasons I just stayed away and played "hobby" with it was because, before I went off and had my little emotional breakdown, I always worried about people findin' out my skeletons in the closet. I don't give a fuck no more. But I realized that my mother was right, and when people wanted to deal with who your father is — you know I never realized you didn't have to answer these questions. You can say "none of your business." And I never realized at that particular time that if they signified, you STILL could deny it, you understand what I'm sayin'?

Exactly.

But back then I'm one of these truth and honor people. Who can't tell a lie that much ... who if you ask me a question I will give you a legitimate answer honestly about, possibly can answer it or you either exaggerate the truth so that you won't know that it's, ah — but I can never really come out and tell a blanket lie. This is what SHOCKS me when I find people who can tell lies! I mean, it AMAZES me. And I say how can they actually say it and do it?! You know (laughs) ... I told a lie for the first time in my life yesterday, a blanket lie. And it's been eatin' at me ALL DAY. I was trying' to call this girl — because I know this girl is pregnant. And Malcolm is a good friend of mine, SHE'S a good friend of mine ... told me, "Don't tell anybody that she's pregnant, she will — they will know when she starts to show." So Malcolm came around and said, "Jean, if anybody would know that she's pregnant, YOU would know." He said, "Is she pregnant?" I said, "I really don't know." And honest to God, in a way I don't! (laughs)

Well, she's TOLD me this. And do you know that I want to call him up and tell him that as far as I know she told me she was pregnant. I — it's just been eatin' at he ALL DAY LONG. I said to myself — I told the lady that comes in downstairs to help me, I said you know the older I get the less loyal I am. 'Cause I'm one of them people, if I LOVE ya, I kiss ya ass. I go to the wall for ya. But I will never LIE for ya.

• • •

But I think sometimes it's all in that attitude that you carry, too. 'Cause I watched my doctor today, and he said, ah — he'll call on certain number of people, and he said, (politely) "Miss Jean —" (laughs) And the nurses are all askin' me how in hell did you win Doctors Franks and Lowe's respect?!!! because they don't even have respect for nurses. But when I first met them, they were rude to me. Franks, the first day I met him — Dr. Franks, the doctor that did my operation two years ago — I went to the clinic late, and he said, "I refuse to see you?" ... and looked at me and ROLLED HIS EYES! I didn't say ANYTHING, 'cause they said if you say anything to him he'll cut you out. So the second time I saw him I said, "WHAT THE FUCK!!! Do you mean —" (laughs) I call it old shock therapy, honey, and he took one look at me, an' I said, "What you gonna say?! 'What the fuck' back?" He said, "Miss, you somethin'!" I said, "I heard you're somethin' too."

And then George Lowe, when I met him just recently, he had said something' to me about fat people, and I said, "Let me tell you something right now!" I didn't say this the first day. He said, "As a matter of fact you got diabetes and your diabetes is 388, so I'm gonna suggest to Franks ... if you were my patient I'd send you him right now, but don't take your clothes off and get into bed ... I'm gonna call Dennis Franks right now and suggest to him that you go home until you get this diabetes taken care of, and THEN you'll come back here." He said, "Because your insurance will not cover all of this

and we don't have money or time to waste!" I said, "Oh my god — this is a tough cookie here." (chuckles) So I said, "It's past 9:30 at night, do you REALLY MEAN for me not to get into bed?" He said, (stern impatient tone) "You can go home any hour of the night at this hospital, up until 11:59 and won't be charged for it! (laughs) 'Cause I didn't come home until 6:30 — when I came home the other day! So I sat there ... 10 o'clock came. I said, "Nurse, should I go home or should I get in bed?" She says, "Miss, I don't know" ... (dramatically) Eleven o'clock came . . . 'cause the woman that was in the room, she said (pleading tone) "Miss Hill, get in the bed." I said I'm not takin' my clothes off 'cause that mothafucka was rude to me, and I ain't gonna have him wakin' me up outta the bed and sendin' me home! Eleven o'clock at night. (laughs) She said, "He's REALLY a nice doctor."

So he came around, he wouldn't even COME to my room the next day. He ordered a glucose kit ... I think he was upset, because from what I hear, Franks said, "Work her up the best you can 'cause I'm gonna do the operation Monday no matter what." So that evenin' he (Doctor Lowe) came around and he said to me, "I don't know what's between you and Franks but he told me to work you up." I said, "Look, by the time Monday comes my sugar will be right, my blood pressure will be down, and I'll be ready for surgery." He said, "I don't know how you're going to do that in four days. Miss Hill, you're morbidly obese and you're diabetic." I said to my self, you just keep havin' fun with me ... have fun now 'cause my day is comin' and I'm one of the one's responsible for you.

So the next day he comes to see me, he started lookin' through my lungs, then he got the pulmonary specialists in there. The nurse asked me, "How much money you payin'?" I said, "You can look on my card — I'm a welfare case." ... "Well, how do you get George Lowe to come and see you every day?!" I say, "He's a friend of Dr. Franks!" ... She says, "Well, he doesn't usually take charity patients." I said, "Well, there's exceptions to every rule." So then he came up to see me — I knew I had won him over when he came up to see Intensive Care to see me, he came with a smile. I said, "What you doin' up here?!! I don't need you — I got Dr. Jacobs up here." ... "I thought I'd come to just see whether you made it or not." (laughs) Then he was askin' me a lot of questions, and I know he started believin' me. 'Cause he started askin' me questions like, did I think that weight was a cultural thing, because he noticed that black women — and black males, but especially black women — have a tendency to be fatter, and more COMFORTABLE with their weight than white women did. And I was tellin' him that's how I got started in theater, because there was a play written for a white woman but they couldn't find white people that were more than 150 lbs. that wanted to go on stage and show their bodies. That's how I really got started in the theater . . . so then we started talkin' about somethin' else and he asked me how did I get my blood pressure and the sugar down, and I said, I don't know, I just ate the right things or somethin', I said but then again a lot of things are mind over matter. And another thing he respected me for was, I told him that the woman next to me was gonna die ... 'cause I get these little deja vu things — that's why I said I knew I wasn't gonna die, 'cause I'm gonna get four million dollars. That when I make four million dollars that's when I'm gonna start seein' death.

But I know I'm not goin' nowhere ... before I die I'm gonna be healthy. I'm off of pills I been takin' all my life. They took me off of all high blood pressure medicine. I said now can ya get rid of the ASTHMA? (laughs) Can ya'll get rid of the blood clots?

So the blood clots are the main problem now?

Well, that and — I'm gonna find some way to work THIS out in a year! But then after this he was askin' me different things, and then one day — I'm gonna tell you when I knew he loved me. He was off (work), and had his joggin' clothes on, musta been runnin down by the hospital. And he said, "I just dropped —" I said, "What you doin' here?! You don't work today!" ... "I know, but I just thought I'd drop in to see you." I said, "What, ya got LONELY for a conversation or somethin'?" (laughs all around) "Cause he used to spend sometimes 10 or 15 minutes with me. And a lot of patients he'd just go in — 'cause one morning at six o'clock I woke up, and he didn't even wake me up: he had the stethoscope up in my chest! ... "Sounds better today." (laughs)

So then he said to me, "Look, I'm goin' away for a week, if there's anything that you want me to do ... and when I come back I don't know whether you'll be here or not, but it was really nice knowin' you."

He came back, honey, the day after Divine died. And he seen me cryin' in the bed, and he said to me, he said, "How you feel about your friend dyin'? She was a good friend of yours, wasn't she?" So I said, "You know we were rivals at one time, at least I thought we were!" But two years ago when I saw him at 'Private Eyes' we got to be good friends, when he called me up on stage and called me his sister. 'Cause I was sorta gettin' close to Glen then. And then, eh — 'cause I said to Glen, "You know, people used to think that I hated you because I made that movie with John Waters and I thought you sorta hated me," and he said, "No no no! — wasn't nothin' like that, I was makin' another movie, and so-and-so and so-and-so." I said, "Well, a lot of people — I got nasty words and all of that." But I've gotten to the point now that I don't even worry (about) stuff like that, 'cause I have to be what I have to be. People still tease me that that's (*Desperate Living*) the only film John never made with him.

Right — with Divine. So you didn't know Divine until he, ah —

Nnnoooo! I knew Divine years ago, but Divine and I back THEN didn't even get along because Divine had lied and said she had had this operation. And we used to go down to Eddie's Bar, and I told the bitches

— this was when he was really tryin' to make a mark for himself. And — but I was just an ordinary girl, but ... gay guys and white guys — I'm serious — used to just LOVE me when I came to this club. And I said to Divine one night, I said (demanding tone) "Old bitch, you know you ain't had no damn operation!"

See, I knew the game already. Divine ain't had no sex change, honey. But that's the LIE he used to go around tellin' people ... and then he didn't like me for tellin' people he — because back then I pretty well knew, DOCTOR MONEY ... and a few other people who did that here, and then I was real tight with this white girl. One time you had to go to Tijuana, Mexico in order to get the operation, 'cause they weren't even doin' it here in Baltimore in '57, '60 and '61, and this was when Divine was tellin' people that he had gone over there and got this operation and shit like that. I said, "Bitch, you ain't got nothin' to show!"

So Divine was around back then raising hell?

Yeah, down to Eddie's Bar! And then I didn't see him no more and he went off to New York, and ... I STILL wasn't aware that he was with John Waters. But people used to TELL me about John Waters. I DID meet Marion Michaels a long time ago, who was really way out and ave-ant garde. Because at that time, '69, '70, I was goin' for white guys.

And who was this guy you met?

I was goin' with this white guy named "Skip." My mother, whenever the phone used to ring, she'd yell, "Are ya white or are ya black?!" and if they said they were white, she'd hang the phone up ... (begrudging laughter) ... But then when I got ahold of Skip she used to say, "That man don't want you!" and blah-blah-blah. My mama's a racist woman, 'cause John and all them tease me, said my mother is a BLACK Ku Klux Klan, she'd burn a cross on a white man's lawn.

So John has met her and stuff?

Ooohhhh yes!!! She cussed him out!!!! Talkin' about how he exploited me, and ooooo-weeeee! Oh baby — she can wear white people out! I don't even introduce her! She's nicer now than she's ever been in her LIFE. 'Cause she's learned to accept the fact that these are the people that I like, and this is the way I'm gonna be. But in the beginning, '68, '69, '70 — up till '75, oooh my god she was terrible! Ask John about it, (laughs) tell John... . "You USED my daughter!" — 'Cause I used to tell John, you gotta meet my mother, all she keeps tellin' me is I get used. And then a lot of people have put that in my head. But the, because she — John don't know this, I don't know whether he knew it — I wrote him an 18-page letter. After I found out he had offered one girl $450, another girl — I wound up meetin' these people later on in life . . . so with me, I think he offered me more money than any of 'em. But two people had also tried to convince me to do this film. I never read it in the papers, I never read it in anything.

23

Stover as husband Bosley Gravel confronts Hill in *Desperate Living*.

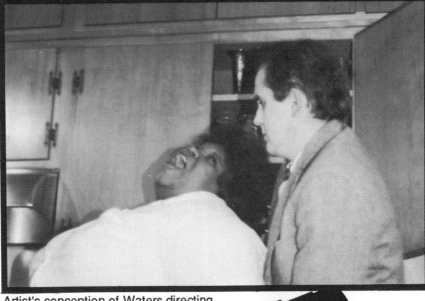

Artist's conception of Waters directing Jean Hill and George Stover on the set of *Desperate Living*.

•••••••••• Hill and Stover clash in *Desperate Living*. ••••••••••

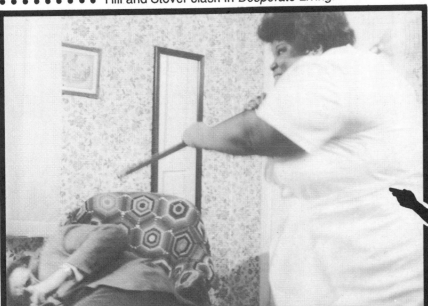

GRIZELDA BACK OFF, ASSHOLE! *(She hits him over the head with broom)* Are you all right, Mrs. Gravel? Did he hurt you?

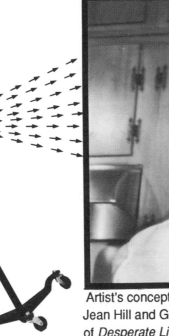

DESPERATE LIVING

Muffy St. Jacques ●●●●●●●●●●● LIZ RENAY	★	*Lt. Grogan* ●●●●●●●●●●●●●● STEVE BUTOW
Peggy Gravel ●●●●●●●●●●●● MINK STOLE	★	*Lt. Williams* ●●●●●●●●●● CHANNING WILROY
Mole McHenry ●●●●●●●●●● SUSAN LOWE	★	*Bosley Gravel* ●●●●●●●●● GEORGE STOVER
Queen Carlotta ●●●●●●●●● EDITH MASSEY	★	*Motorcycle Cop* ●●●●●●●●●●● TURKEY JOE
Princess Coo-Coo ●●●● MARY VIVIAN PEARCE	★	*Muffy's Husband* ●●●●●●●● ROLAND HERTZ
Grizelda Brown ●●●●●●●●●● JEAN HILL	★	*Baby-sitter* ●●●●●●●●●●●● PIRIE WOODS
Flipper ●●●●●●●●●● COOKIE MUELLER	★	*Big Jimmy Dong* ●●●●●●● H. C. KLIEMISCH
Shina ●●●●●●●●●●● MARINA MELIN	★	*Herbert* ●●●●●●●●●●●●● GEORGE FIGGS
Shotsie ●●●●●●●●●●●● SHARON NIESP	★	*Pervert* ●●●●●●●●●●●●● PAT MORAN
Lt. Wilson ●●●●●●●●●●● ED PERANIO	★	*Nurse* ●●●●●●●●●●● DELORES DELUXE

And that was *Desperate Living*?

Right. So I was stayin' upstairs with a friend of mine, which was Sonny Smith, on the 10th floor, and he asked Sonny, so Sonny said to me, "John is comin' upstairs," and wanted to know about a fat woman doin' a part. So when I came downstairs I immediately liked John, but I didn't know whether John liked me. So he made me so nervous I went to grab for his hand and I grabbed for his dick and shook it. (chuckles) He wrote that in the book *Shock Value*.

Yeah, he said you goosed him the first time.

Yes, honey, I grabbed the meat, and I said, (polite tone) "Hello Mister Waters, how are you?" — 'Cause that's where I always grab guys when I get nervous.

You just grabbed his crotch, eh?!

Ah-huh! (hilarious laughter all around) I'm famous for shakin' hands with the dick, honey.

Yeah, he said in Shock Value that he was totally unnerved by it — a famous first meeting if ever there was one!

'Cause when Pat (Moran) and them saw me they said, "Oh she don't even need to audition." So I told 'em I was doin' a play down at the Arena Playhouse, and I was really honored because about eight of 'em came down to see me in this play.

Eight of his people?

Ah-huh, it was him and Judith and John, and Pat, and the next — they took me out also for my birthday to dinner. We went to a bar. I'll never forget it. I said, "Oh, I like him." And then you know you got black people tellin' you, "Oh they used you, they used —" and then I said to myself, "Well I've never been paid anything for actin' anyway," so it didn't make no difference.

But see, I always took the stuff for a hobby. Then I

L to R: Liz Renay, Jean Hill and Mink Stole living it up in one of Mortville's finer lesbian S&M bars [*Desperate Living*].

Starring **LIZ RENAY · MINK STOLE · SUSAN LOWE · EDITH MASSEY · MARY VIVIAN PEARCE ·** and introducing **JEAN HILL**
Produced and Directed by **JOHN WATERS** ● From **NEW LINE CINEMA**

can show you some letters where my mother used to write me and tell me, (low, intimate tone) "Jean, you don't need to do things like that 'cause white people will EXPLOIT you, and they will do this and that. Just think of what John Waters did. He done made millions of dollars." ... But see, I UNDERSTOOD the business, 'cause I know he hadn't made no whole lot of millions of dollars, but it was just the idea that I was gettin' exposed to thousands and thousand of people at a time, and then ... I'm still teachin' school, not makin' no money, 'cause all my money I'm tryin' to take to pay to GO to school. That's why I told somebody, "I'm so proud of me I don't know what to think 'cause I never took a school loan out!" One time I borrowed $750, but I never, ever — since I went to college I paid my own way.

So, ah, what John paid me was extra money. Then I had my own apartment around the corner ... at the time I was stayin' with my mother but I had saved all the stuff up so that I would have a nice apartment, around the corner. So then I said to myself, "Oh my god, this is IT." So then I didn't know what to do because I — I didn't know I was gonna have this impact on people. I couldn't go nowhere.

Really?

NNNNOOOOWHERE! 'Cause John had said to me — this is his exact words — I said, "John, when I do somethin' people always remember me. He said, "Oh, child! Don't even worry about it because in a film like this ain't nobody gonna remember you." He said, "You're here today and a has-been tomorrow." He said, "Just think of . . ." and he would name different stars. So I took this for granted. GOD DAMN! The next semester? They didn't wanna give me any money! "Miss Hill, we need a W-2 form, you're in a movie." I mean it stopped me from getting EVERYWHERE. And I tried to explain to people, all I made was $750. "No, Miss Hill, where's the income tax?" So John never sent me income tax forms for it either. And I never argued with 'em about it 'cause I thought at that time that was his responsibility.

So in the meantime, my mother pumpin' my head up about that ... (slow, ominous tone) "There's no income tax form ... there's no John Waters . . ." And I was really likin' this guy, I thought he was one of the neatest people because . . . if he would admit to it, he can tell you he got that word "shock value" from me! And it came from a guy I used to know, he told me, "Jean, you know what? Underneath all that facade that you play, you are one of the nicest, kindest, quietest people, and you're shy." He sat there one day and really told me about me who I knew was me. He said, "But you know what you like to do? You like to SHOCK people." But anyway, to make a long story short, I was thinkin' to myself, I said, "You know what kind of humor it is? It's called "shock value" . . . and when I seen John had a book with *Shock Value*, I wanted to choke him! ASK him where he got *Polyester* from! I said, "You know what? People are gonna laugh at me but no matter how many millions I make I'll still wear polyester

clothes, because the bigger you get they stretch right along with you." I said that'd be a good title for a movie, and sure enough! (laughs all around) . . . He used polyester! So a friend of mine who knew me, knew that I talked to John like this — one of my college professors, he said to me, "Keep ON givin' John your information — let him make money off of it."

(laughs) . . . So you didn't have any problems with *Desperate Living*, I mean, it didn't shock you too much?

No, you know, 'cause we had a private screening and I really thought when I saw myself nude I was gonna be embarrassed, and ... the whole bit. But I had this secret desire inside, when I first got to 400 lbs., 396 then anyway, I wanted to know what I really looked like.

I thought it was a brilliant movie, I think it's his best movie and I . . .

Well you know what, a lot of people tell me that. John don't realize it but you know what? I knew it was going to be a classic. That's a movie that's gonna go on forever, whether he wants to admit it or not. I have hundreds (of letters) and I'm not exaggeratin', every person has asked me — no, over HALF the letters — ask, "Where can I get *Desperate Living*?" But I — the more I look at the movie, 'cause if you seen the calendar of me, did you?

No.

I'm gonna mail ya one.

Okay ... beautiful.

But on — wait till you read the profile, you gonna laugh your ass off. And it says there, "What is your favorite movies?" When they asked me that I said, "Well, I've only gone to see one movie six times, and that's my own." (laughs) I said, "If you call the favorite the one you seen the most, I guess I would have to say my own movie, *Desperate Living*.

You had a brilliant role in *Polyester,* hijacking the bus and biting . . .

(laughs) Well he can tell you in the beginning he asked me to be the maid's part. I said, "John, I don't ever want no reference to bein' a maid again." Because you know you can get hooked up in that stereotype stuff, and I didn't want that. I have always had the opportunities to play diverse roles, and ... I was worried about bein' a maid in THIS movie (Desperate Living), but he INSISTED on that bein' that. Because a lot of people take me — you know in the movie I say I'm her psychiatric nurse, and a lot of people TAKE me for that. You know, as a health-care provider that came to her house and helped her out or whatever. They don't really look at it as a maid. But a friend of mine who's always advised me and advised me right, he said, "Jean, Claudette Cobert started out as a maid, got (typecast), he said, "you just don't get caught up doin' maid roles every time. Because the black people, that's where they make their mistakes, they take the same role over and over, and that's how you perpetuate that chain of blacks bein' stereotypical." I have never had to play that type of role — thank god! It was the same way with the cards: they wanted me to do an Aunt Jemima series. I said, "Look Billy, go and get the masters on that," — let him keep it. "Now if ya'all can't create somethin' stupid, wild, crazy, or shocking — I HAVE no interest in doin' nothin' else."

Yeah, that was a —

Because one of the things I've found with me, I have been fortunate enough in my lifetime . . . and this is what amazed these two people that I work with, they say, "You know we went to the card show and rarely do people call you 'black'." I said, "Because I'm not working to a black audience." When I went up to do "Rock-Shot" cards, they wanted mine to be the opposite of Miss Edie's cards to sell to black people. Well, I know black people don't BUY that many cards. And then on top of that I said, "Why does this just have to be for black people, why can't I create cards" — and this was a big argument. So I told 'em if I just have to do black cards, I won't do cards at all. So then they said, "No-no-no-no, we-we-we-we ..." I said, "Well ya'all ..." that's in my contract, I have to APPROVE it.

And they were wrong too, I mean . . .

They were very proud, and I am very proud of the work that they did, after we agreed. Because I don't wanna be somebody else! I wanna be me. And I was raised by white nuns, then had the opportunity to come home and live with my mother, and in my work I ALWAYS want that to show, that I have lived on both sides of the track. And I had an opportunity to see what the rich life is all about and the poor life is all about. And if those things don't reflect it, I don't want to do it!

Have you seen *Hairspray* yet?

No, but I will. I like it from what I've seen. I really like it. I helped him with THAT! 'Cause he called me up and asked me how do blacks look, how do blacks dress, how do ... I LOVE John, nobody knows that I really love John. But I've found that people can steal from you in the business. But I'll always give him — not only him, doctors, anybody — that I can clarify there is no difference in the races. It's just that ... POOR people have the same perpetual ideas. The only thing that I say — and my mother says this, and this is something that I don't usually believe in ... she said that if a white man don't make it in the United States, he don't DESERVE to make it. 'Cause he can change his name, change his looks, but he can still make it. But a black person, people got to get over their COLOR first, before they will deal with you. You know when I walk in a room I can't say I'm Rockefeller's niece! They would KNOW I'm illegitimate — you understand what I'm sayin'? But YOU can walk in there and know Mr. Rockefeller's ways and sort of convince them that you're Rockefeller's nephew, and you could get over on that. And this is why I say if white people don't make it, I don't feel sorry for 'em. But black people, you don't know —

my race of people, I just say that they have been down so LONG, until, I swear to God in this business I wouldn't take 'em down no further.

So, in Desperate Living, that was the first movie —

— and black people say to me, "John exploited you! You know he ain't never used a black." But honey, I told the little white boy — I'm not rude but it's what I believe in. I believe when you come to ME — I didn't go to John — when you come to me you'd think I'm right for the role, this is one thing I brag on — I never HAD to audition for a job. People send it to me. That's the fortunate thing in this WHOLE business, I NEVER had to write out a resume or nothin'. So, the little white boy said to me (mock confidential/serious tone), John Waters is a very famous man, and you are very fortunate to have met John." I said, "No darling, JOHN was very fortunate to have met me." (laughs all around) He looked at me, he said, "Oh Miss, you're something! Do you know that's a great producer?!" I said, "Well, honey, he came to me so he must have thought I was a great actress." (laughs)

Yeah, I think he described you as "400 lbs. of raw talent."

I *LOOOVE* John. You know what he said to me? When I was tellin' him — I said, "You know, John, with these cards, I bet you I make about $25,000 a year in royalties." He said, "Oh no, Jean! People NEVER make that kind of money." You know how much I made the first year? Eighteen thousand dollars.

For the cards?

Yes! They had to pay me quarterly. They had originally said they were gonna pay me once a year. But then when the cards came out — 'cause everybody laughed in my face — but see, I knew the timing was right because I got to a point, I couldn't go to New York, Washington, nowhere, for people to say, "When you gonna make another movie? When you ..." I said, "Well if I don't make another movie I'll make somethin' in another medium," never thinkin' about modelin', modelin' was the furthest thing from my mind. But I woke up one morning at 38 years old, broke, and I said, "Lord have mercy, I gotta make some money." And I called up there and they told me to come up, December the 4th, and I started workin' in February. Now, when the May cards came out — this is a card that will be around forever ... I don't know whether you ever saw the one with the bag over my head that says, "Happy Birthday From Your Secret Admirer"?

Ah, no.

I have made over $9,000 from that card. That card stayed number one for ... 17 weeks. Now I never knew these things, but I could tell the tension was stirrin' around, and people didn't know — I don't GET a swelled head and shit because I'd already predicted it. So this is what they said, when I went up there they had told me I would only make twelve cards. Well, by the time the May issue was out they had started pumpin' me with cards ... and CALENDARS, and then KEY RINGS. That's when I had this little clause put in my thing that I only make cards. If you want calendars and other things you gotta sign another contract.

So that's good that you've made ... So you've made almost more money off the cards than off the movies, or ...

Oh yeah — all I ever made for makin' them few movies total, was seven — na, I didn't make $1000 ... 'cause John offered me $100 to make *Polyester*, and I told him no, I said, "Honey, you're the one that made me the star." He said, "Well, that's all I have in the budget." So I said, "Get any old fat bitch then." So about two weeks later he called me up, he said, "I had to take some money from somebody else, but I found you $250." So ... that's when I wrote him this LONG, 18-page, letter, and he said he swore that he would never speak to me again. 'Cause I told him how I had broke my teeth and had to spend $300, and that I had spent MORE, and — had never had another new coat 'cause I had gotten too big, 'cause I used my coat and tore it up in *Desperate Living*, and used my own SHOES — oh child, I went on and on and on and on. 'Cause I was hurt because I had asked John to lend me $500. He said when you want that kind of money you — you ask your parents! I said, "This is what rich mothafuckas say! What? "Jean Hill has made it?! Jean Hill now has a little corporation?!" ... I don't have a lot, but I'm comfortable.

And you KNOW they can never find another Jean Hill, so they've gotta pay you.

Well, honey, I said to John, "You know somethin'? You LIED to me a long time ago." He said, "What?!" I said, "You told me people forget people." He said, "Well, Miss Hill, I didn't know you had somethin' people just DON'T forget!" And when I was in the hospital — I have won over one hundred more fans. The doctors were sayin' today, he said he'd go down there and everybody'd know you. He said Sister Kerin asked about, Sister so-and-so asked about you. I had the nurses CRY when I left the hospital, (demure imitation) "We're going to miss you." They say Jackie Jackson has never made friends with NOBODY — she was the vascular lady for my legs? 'Cause I had her laughin' in there.

First of all, when they see fat and black they don't want to deal with you no way. When they see you're on MedicAid or medical assistance that's even worse. ... But see, I'm one of these people ... if you feel like you're hurtin' my feelings, or I feel like you're not tryin', or I feel that I need somethin' and we can work somethin' out, we're gonna have to make arrangements. 'Cause I'm not gonna ACCEPT what you say. ... and, when I left she came up to see me about four o'clock and said, "Oh! ..." and hugged me — "I'm so glad you're here." And told me how I had — "Jean, you changed procedures in this hospital!" 'Cause they LINED the people up, and I turned us around like we sittin' on a couch talkin'. They talkin' about, "Don't hit those wheelchairs against the walls, it'll mess the walls up!" I said, "Are you concerned about the WALLS?!" And see, when I say the damndest things I give you this big grin. (laughs)

Right — but you say what should be said.

Yeah! I said are you more concerned about the wall or our health?! She didn't answer me. So I said, "Turn around everybody!" And all of us started talkin'. So she came up to tell me, "You know that old man that was a grouch?" — and one of the reasons that they didn't make us turn back around: they had a eighty-five to eighty-nine year old woman who actually wanted to die, and she said later, "Oh it's wonderful down here today! I look forward to comin' down here!"

So when did you go into the hospital?

February 3rd, came out Valentines Day and went right back in on the 20th ... and stayed in there until the 14th. No — I came out on the ... 12th. I came out two days ... a DAY before I went to the funeral.

L to R: John Waters, Ricki Lake and Jean.

Ricki Lake and Jean.

28

Right, so you were in the hospital in your bed watching TV when you first heard Divine died?

Yep. And I bust out crying, and I had this black woman in there and she couldn't understand why I'm cryin' over this white woman for. 'Cause my head was knotty — I'm tryin' to tell ya, you could NEVER make the association, that I was anybody but a peon in there. (laughs) . . . 'cause I wore SHEETS . . . 'cause the doctor would tell how I would dress up in a sheet like FROG. (laughs) I felt fine, though . . .

So nobody recognized you?

But the DOCTORS, a lot of doctors know who I am. This is another thing that has really amazed me in my career. And this is what I'll tell people . . . they'll say to me, "Well, I don't know who you are." I say, "Well, evidently you're not a doctor or a lawyer or an educated person, like a college student or something. Because if you were, those are the people that know me. The first day I was in the hospital — here's my hand to god — I had over 150 guests.

So your room was JAMMED with people?!

EVERY ten minutes there's ... the kitchen help, there's the doctors. I had a doctor bring his fiance up. He said, "I don't have a card or anything, but can you just sign this medical thing for me? Just so people will know that I KNOW you?" I felt like a real celebrity there. And then I gave one of the nuns, she wanted one of the cards: "Get Well Dammit Before You Make Me Sick." I said, "You really want THIS card?!" She said, "Oh I just LOVE it!" So I said you certainly may. (laughs) Then up in Intensive Care — here was a real joke — four o'clock in the morning I'm layin' down, finally I'd gotten some rest, there's this woman standin' over me, I look up . . . and it's the nurse. She said, "You don't know who I am! But I know who you are!" (laughs)

Four in the morning?

(Laughs affirmatively) 'Cause see in Intensive Care they move you every two hours. So the eleven o'clock shift — really changes at 12. And, she was

Two beautiful ladies ...

the HEAD supervisor. I said, "Where's Georgette, my nurse?" She said, "I told Georgette I would take this shift. I"m the supervisor up here . . . you don't know who I am, but I know who you are. Your sister is a friend of my daughter, and she's a big fan of yours . . . could you give me your autograph?" I said, "I got the IV in my hand." (laughs) "Oh, I'll wait till you get the IV out of your hand." (laughs) She said, "I'll wait 'cause I want the real JEAN HILL handwritin'." I laughed! And Dr. Ellison? Dr. Mark . . . Oh, just all of them. And then they worried me about the calendars. Dr. Franks said that you would have calendars for all of us." I said, "I got 'em! This is your'all pay, you know!" 'Cause he is so sweet. They won't pay for the operation. He told me today, "Don't even worry about it."

• • •

[Doctors] never want you to attribute things to miracles or god or nothin'. It's always, "You changed

Jean arrives at Divine's funeral.

your way of eatin', you changed ..." Those people was givin' me insulin four times a day. I said to the Lord, I said, "God, I cannot handle all of this at one time, PLEASE," I — I ain't lyin' — in my MIND, and this woman who is very religious, stood over me at four o'clock in the mornin', and she was prayin' over me, and I thought this bitch was gonna try to fuck me in my sleep! I said, this bitch better move AWAY from me, but she was sayin' a prayer and the next thing you know I was sayin' the "Our Father" with her.

Your personality seems to help you get over hard times.

The doctor told me the minute you start believin' in stuff like that [miracles] and God, you'll forget the medicine. But it's not the truth. I told them in the hospital, and the doctor laughed in my face, but he had to COME BACK to apologize to me. I told David, nobody liked him. I liked him. They said, "Jean, how did you get that man to smile?" He would have to come up to me at twelve o'clock at night, he was TIRED, he didn't want to talk, but I held this man's attention. "Do you hear what I'm sayin'? he said, "Let's not go too far off the subject because I got another patient to check on," but we still would go off the subject. And he never got frustrated with me or nothin'. The woman in the other bed said, "I can't stand him!" — the woman down the hall said, "I can't stand him!"

Weren't you you actually talking to the nurses about Divine the very afternoon he died?

I had just said that afternoon — as a matter of fact the people that made the calendars was with me — 'cause we all was bustin' out laughin' in the thing, they had brought down some gift certificates so the doctors could go and eat dinner, and I said," I could take Divine's place!" (laughs)

You said you'd recently seen him on TV and he didn't look too healthy?

No, because when I saw him on "Good Morning America," his stomach was hangin' and that's what happened to mine ... his chest was hangin', and I said to myself, he's got a heart condition, he definitely·can't breathe. And see, when you ... I'm never gonna let this job get me down, 'cause I ain't in it for the money. I've learned that money don't make you happy. YOU got to make you happy. And when you overdo anything — and I really felt, and this is my personal opinion, by Divine bein' what he was, which was — I can't say a transvestite ... an actor playin', an actress, that's what I call it, he had gone as far with this thing as he could go. And I think this is what his WISH was. And this is why he ...

I have this thing — I have been near death more times than anybody I know, but I have never died. I've never died. The doctor even told me, every operation I have had — now you know, big as I am, 500 pounds, goin' through what I went through with a fifty/fifty chance, but like I told the doctor, I got a nurse, nuns and priests prayin' for me — I'm not gonna worry myself I said, and I haven't made my four million so take me on down. (laughs) And then when I had that gall bladder operation, I had that out-of-body experience, so I had seen more than they did. And I KNEW in my heart that I wasn't gonna die. But you should'a seen these people in the operatin' room. I told 'em, ya'all were more scared than I was. (laughs) Because I could remember Dr. Vogler handing the knife to Dr. Vergossa, and they're tellin' me I shouldn't have seen this.

• • •

My first husband would tell you, I used to tell people back in the sixties, there was a song called (in a sing-song voice) "Free looove ..." and I said, all of this, we're gonna pay for it one day.

I slept with 400 men. But here's how I sleep with a person. Number one: I rarely sleep in the dark with them. 'Cause I like to see expressions, and not only that, I LIKE TO LOOK! If my body's too big and ugly to look at, mutherfucka — you don't want this body! Go out the door! 'Cause I'm not sleepin' in no motherfuckin' dark. I don't LIKE to have sex in the dark. If the moon lights up, okay, or turn the light on, or give me a camera, give me something 'cause I need to see. (laughs) Another thing is: if I smell an odor on somebody, they ain't sleepin' with me. Go wash. If they wash and still got it, that person got somethin' wrong with 'em. Another thing about it, if I pull on your dick too much, and I don't think I'm bein' rough and you say "ouch!" — YOU keep it! And I know you goin' home and sleepin' with somebody. You keep your meat. This is why I don't go with married men. 'Cause honey, I want to believe, even if you GOT somebody home, that I'm the only one ... and that you go home and do nothin' to her. (laughs)

Yeah, exactly.

So that's how I told somebody I had the fortune enough to get old without getting venereal disease. And then another thing that I did, I used to screw a lot of guys that were ... a lot of alcoholics. Well I wouldn't say "a lot" — at least eight alcoholics. Out of this eight I have brought at least seven out of what I call "alcoholism." One of em' I called when I wanted to kill myself. You know what that bitch told me?! "I don't fuck with losers — YOU taught me that." (laughs) He makes $700 a week now, selling cars for Mazda-Chevrolet.

But I don't know — it was this thing that I had about men that I like. I LOVE men, and whenever I saw a good man — but I never fucked with a junky. It had nothin' to do with AIDS at the time. Junkies tend to STEAL from you, and I like too many nice things in my house. No matter how CLEAN I keep it, I always kept a little oriental stuff, and I don't want that bitch takin' my shit outta the house. So junkies and me never mixed. But an alcoholic, baby! I knew, number one, that he wasn't doin' but so many people, so I take that bitch in my house, bathe him, wash him, and let him fuck! (laughs) ... never went with the stars. Never. Because they're the ones that think they can get anybody, and they catch ya in their thing. (long laughter)

Yeah, that's where —

I used to tell people this shit, but they always talkin' about ... my sister told me one time, she says, "Keep on ..." — and I fucked every last one of my girlfriend's husbands! But most of the time it was when they were separated from her. When Ernst and his wife separated, I went on the bed with him, and I knew he wasn't sleepin' with nobody. When Maxwell left Maxine, I went to — well they didn't "separate" but I knew they weren't sleepin' together 'cause she was sleepin' with my uncle, and he was in another room.

Uh-huh . . . so you could hear it.

But if you just take those precautions . . .

Right, that's some good advice.

Now people might say that I didn't love myself, but I realize now that I was addicted to sex, 'cause if I didn't have sex five times a week, child, I felt like I was nothin' or nobody. But I ALWAYS WAS selective. My sister used to say, "Selective with THAT drunk?" I said, "But I know he ain't been to bed with nobody, honey." (laughs) And I know when he get up he's goin' right back on the corner and get his bottle. (laughs hard) 'Cause people ain't puttin' up with drunks. But they'll put up with junkies that will rob 'em ... knock 'em in the head, drag their friends — ya ever notice that? I can't stand people that take ACID and — I can't stand em!

And the one thing they'll do is they'll take your prized possessions, baby. They don't care, they just gotta take it outta there. But see, an old alcoholic, you can buy him a 59 cent drink and fall on out . . . (laughs) Cheap thrills, honey.

So you got to know Divine better over the years since *Desperate Living*?

Yeah, last two or three years, really, and like I said, when I saw him at *Private Eyes*, because even his agent said, "Thank you for coming up to *Private Eyes*" . . . I didn't come there specifically for him 'cause I didn't even know he was gonna BE there.

When was this? Recently?

About a year and a half ago.

Was this an act he was doing at a club?

Um-umm.

And you got up on stage, right?

No, I SAT up on [stage] — I got the pictures of it. Joe got the pictures, I don't have 'em. But, I sat on the end of the stage 'cause the stage was very weak, baby. I figured if he and I had been up there together we'd have broken it! (laughs) Because it was one/eighth inch ply-board . . . but he got to the point I noticed he sweat like a goddam pig on stage. I said

he gotta have either a heart condition or the blood pressure's up high — you know once you get blood pressure you're gonna get heart trouble.

Right, and that very day you were mentioning it, and WHAMMO.

But THAT is what really shocked me, because I said, "Now that I got this, and I'm walkin', I'm ready to take his job." And you know with Edith Massey I said the same thing (laughs) I told John I went to the funeral out of GUILT 'cause I thought to myself — all I thought about: "It could've been me, it could've been me."

And so at that time [Divine's funeral] you were still quite sick, but you got up and into a wheelchair and got to the funeral.

Yeah, it — I ain't gonna lie, it had not a whole lot to do with respect for Divine, it was just the idea that I wanted to actually see somebody lyin' in their casket where they could have been saved had they just followed simple health rules.

• • •

I told John one time, I said, "You don't believe this but I'm a very shy person." That's why I said I KNOW John don't really know PEOPLE. John gets leery of people that love him. And I've heard him say to me, "Jean, I'm scared of 'em!" But I have never been afraid of nobody I've been near ... and KNOW that I'm in harm's way with some of 'em — KNOW it. Know that they hate me. But you cannot let that get on your nerves once you decide to go public. You cannot RUN, you cannot let them bitches tire you out. You just have to ease away. And you've GOT to stop carin' about what other people say. This is why you need two or three people that love you in your life, that are loyal to you, that will kiss your ass from breakfast, lunch, dinner and supper. And if you can't have those things you move on to the next thing.

Because John is actually becomin' paranoid. He don't even realize what's goin' on. But I believe with Divine's death — and you don't NEED to run from the public, because the public is what's payin' your bills out there for ya. I'm not sayin' you LIKE everybody or you put up with everybody, or you tolerate everybody. But you need to get out there and meet and greet 'em, or if they get on your nerves, TELL 'em.

Right, but he still goes out to meet weirdos who come thousands of miles to see him.

You can't hold animosity and fear in your life. I mean there's a certain amount of fear that everybody needs, but never to the point — because sometimes that can cause people , if they react to some of the things you're feelin', they can KILL you or HARM you, and I don't want that to happen to me.

'Cause see, I've had three people who have told me they were gonna kill me, or rob me, but I just was never rude to 'em. This one guy kept sayin', "You big [unintelligible], you got money!" and he wound up

31

Thinking of you!

hear me say nothin' about it. And I tell people, when people are really close to you: the first one hurts, the second one gets a little less, and I have had two or three people come back and tell me that.

So how old was Michael when he died?

Six weeks old. He died right in the house my mother bought. This is how I see death, of people that you swear you love. God forbid if your mother should die. The first year you're gonna go through anger, you're gonna go through grief — you NEED to go through these stages 'cause you're questionin', "Why, why, why?" You're questionin', "How can I live without you? Especially because I loved you." Then you go through the grievin' period where you start missin' that individual 'cause you remember him as a tangible person. But you don't realize that his spirit and his soul is here. Then you start sayin' to yourself, "Damn . . ." — that's when the resolutions start comin' in. But people you love you never get over, you never really get over.

But here's where they come to serve a purpose. If you truly believe that there is a higher bein', be it God, be it nature, be it the DEVIL if you worship that. That individual, I guarantee anybody, will in three days time serve a purpose for them. There has not been when I actually needed, not outta war, not outta greed, — but NEEDED somethin' to hold me over, that I haven't called on my son, and I never realized this until I started gettin' sick. But one day I started doin' what I call this "death thing" and a "positive thing," and one Mother's Day, about three years ago, that was when I had got to a point where I couldn't bear myself anymore — I even stopped likin' myself. And I took all these pills, wantin' to get rid of me and everything. I was in the hospital, and it came to me that this little boy had died for a purpose and all the time I said to myself, "I've never asked

stayin at my house, and he told me he had killed this guy before — matter of fact he told me he had killed two people. But it didn't frighten me. Because I got to know him real good, and right now if he sees me he says, "Anybody botherin' you? 'Cause you know I don't mind gettin' rid of 'em." When that man raped me — I seen that man walkin' out my back door lookin' for the motherfucker. And I knew who did it, but I said, "If I let you kill that man, it's gonna be on my conscience, not yours."

You know in my lifetime I've gotten the opportunity to meet EVERY kind of person that I ever wanted to meet . . . a oriental, Ku Klux Klan . . . mass murder killers. I know one guy who's killed six people. He told me, "Jean, when you kill the first one, that's usually the one you remember, but the more you kill, the easier it gets. He says it's the same way with death. Now he told me this when I was fifteen years old. But when my first son died — do you know Michael's been dead since 1962 — and it still, it doesn't traumatize me like it used to, but I'm talkin' to you now about Michael like he died yesterday. But the twins died a year later and you don't hardly

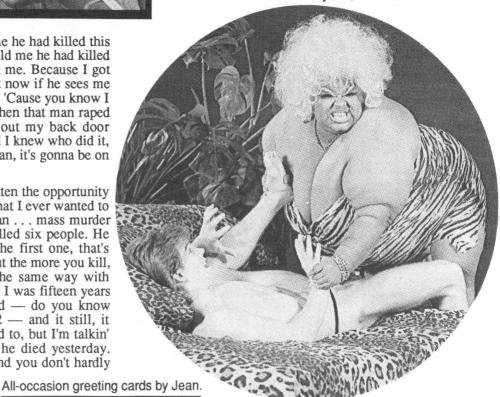

All-occasion greeting cards by Jean.

him — and he's closer to god than I am — I keep askin' a hundred people up there, and HE can get to that man quicker than I can. And I said to him, "I don't want to die." 'Cause I called four people and they all talkin' about now, Jean — you were such a strong person . . .

But you know, the older I get the weaker I get? I used to have a ego one time that was so big, but all it was was ego! And I never dealt with none of the problems. But when I got sick, become immobile, couldn't hardly move anymore, what could you do but sit back and say ...? And then I never had resolved anything in my life. So what happens? I'm constantly in conflict with myself, constantly in conflict. When my son died, and the twins died, two weeks later people said, "Ya'all was out partyin' just like nothin' happened." 'Cause I said, "I can't FEEL like this." But I had never sat down and RESOLVED nothin' in my life.

So did you talk to John after Divine died?

Oh, a couple times. I talked to him the day before yesterday, I said, "Look, I know you still goin' through a grievin' period, but I need that letter!" (laughs) So he said he'd get it out.

What letter's that?

I need a letter to send to my lawyer about the money that I lost, because when he sues Comstock for my leg he's suin' for lost wages, the attorney's fee and everything else that he can get. He told me to try to have all that stuff up here 'cause he wants to finish everything up by November.

So who is suing who?

Rockshots is suing me, the first card company — they said that I was supposed to work for them exclusively. 'Cause he called me a couple days after I got out of the hospital, and told me that if I come back to work for them they'll drop the lawsuits. But it's not my suit anyway! It's between (four unintelligible names). I'm — like the lawyer said, "You're just in the middle of it."

So it was another card company you did stuff for?

Yeah, Comstock, the new company.

But Rockshots treated you better?

Oh, they fucked around on me too. But they still send my royalty checks. Everybody's shocked about that.

And you said one card was your very favorite, called, "I get lost in your love."

That's one of 'em. I have three of 'em. It's ah, "If you want my body I charge by the pound," "I am woman and don't fuck with me," and "I get lost in your love." I like those.

Yeah, I'm gonna have to try and pick those up. When you went to Divine's funeral, what was that like? You said the priest talked about . . .

Oh, the minister was WONDERFUL. He talked

about the fact that when he first met Divine, and ... how Divine and his mother had first joined the church — I think Divine was around seven or eight, and he talked about when Divine wore this red coat and they had to exchange coats. And how so many years he pondered over Divine and how Divine was BEFORE HIS TIME. And one thing he admired about Divine: he never changed. Because he knew all his life that he was Divine. He knew what he wanted to do and that's what he did . . . and he talked about the mother being alienated for a long time but these last eight years they got along great. It was like, everything had moved into perspective for him.

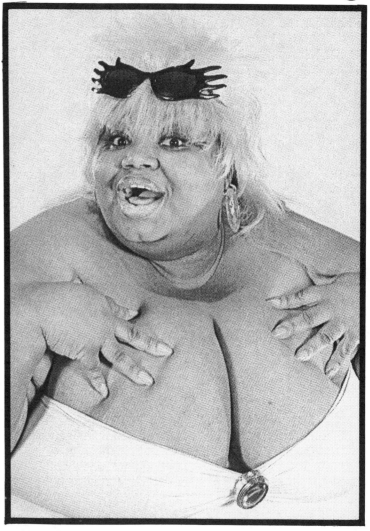

This story, when Divine was young and wearing this red coat, now was he like an acolyte in the church or something?

I think he was supposed to speak that day or something. And he (the minister) told him, "You can't wear that red coat before the assembly, it's too LOUD." So Divine insisted that he wear it — called him "Glennie" — that Glennie insisted that he wear it. So finally the minister said, "Look, if you gotta have a jacket on, your mother and you are about the same size, why don't you put your mother's black coat on and let her wear the red." (laughs) I know nobody else in the church took it like that, but I said,

Divine and Jean Hill at John's 40th birthday party.

'That's the first time he went in drag." (laughs all around) . . . had his mother's coat on. But they let him speak at the assembly there, with her coat on.

And then the minister was talkin' about how for years he PONDERED over what to do with Divine. But there wasn't nothin' he could do with her — he did exactly what he wanted to do.

And John talked about the pranks, and the things that they did. I'm tryin' to think of some of the things that stood out in his mind. And how KIND he was, and he said Santa Claus couldn't have been a better person. But he looked life Alfred Hitchcock in his casket.

Did he look peaceful?

Very peaceful, very restful. I mean ya can't look but so good after a whole week dead. And . . . even the makeup. But that whole silhouette, when he died, it was like — even though it was like Alfred Hitchcock, it was like a STAR. You understand what I'm sayin'? He could've lost the weight or somethin' and looked like nobody. But you see he resembled Alfred Hitchcock. I wish that I could have got a picture of it. But nobody hardly took pictures in the church. They wouldn't even let the camera people in.

Was it like a movie star's funeral? Or very quiet?

A very quiet funeral, peaceful funeral.

Lot of people, though? Right?

It was about three or four hundred people. They filled all the pews up and they was standin' in the back of the church and on the sides, near the back — some motorcycle people and the WILD lookin' people. But the ordinary people . . . I think Fran Liebowitz was there. And Whoopi Goldberg sent flowers, Tab Hunter sent flowers. I mean there was FLOWERS galore, you couldn't ask for more

flowers. ALL of the stars sent flowers for her . . . but it was just great seein' . . . I don't know — nobody knows how I like the transition of life. And I have watched John and his crowd from "just makin' it days" to "arrivin'" days, the following year I met him, to . . . nothin' as sad as Divine's funeral. But it became sad first when Edith died, but it was like — it hit US, 'cause Edith was old, but it hit the basic crowd, like Pat, myself, Judith, Mink, John, and it was like "that could've been us." And the proudest thing like I said, I'm glad it wasn't drugs, I'm glad it wasn't any of the Hollywood bullshit that people think. It was the man seriously ill needing a work-up. A medical work-up.

Yeah, there was no scandal or anything. And when Edith died, did she die in California?

Uh-huh. They just had a service here for her, that people got up and testified, and, they showed a film. But, ah — she was cremated. Ashes thrown over in the Venice waters somewhere.

So you met her first on the set of D*esperate Living*?

The first time I met Edith she was down in the hallway, and I was comin' through the doors goin' upstairs to the apartment. And, I seen this little old lady sittin' out there, and she was rubbin' her feet. She said, (extreme Edie imitation) "I haaaate rehearsals." I said it's gotta be somebody that's in one of John's films. So I said, "You goin' to John's apartment?" She said yeah. So I said, "Well I'll be there too." 'Cause that was my first day comin' down to rehearse with them, because he likes to rehearse so he won't have to use a lot of film. But I'm one of them people if you tell me what you want me to do, you won't have to use a lot of film anyway.

You did some acting before you ever met John, right?

Right, community theater. And then I use to do children's plays with Wally Sanders.

When you were on the film set of *Desperate Living*, do you recall one time when you knocked one of the actors against the wall and knocked him unconscious?

Hm-hmm. 'Cause you know what: I don't act. In my first pay, called "Land of the Golden Apple," I played Mrs. Apple, and one of my scenes was to push the individual — 'cause I was very mean to my "husband" until the end . . . well we finally get the children through Apple Valley, and we had searched long enough and hard enough, and then I tell him, "I love you and I'm gonna bake you your own chocolate chip cookies." — well I had to take that part out and tell 'em "vanilla" because it '69, '68, there was still a lot of racism here. (laughs)

But, ah, one day we were down at Delaney Valley and they had the stage so slippery, until when I pushed him I had pushed him almost out in the orchestra pit, and the orchestra pit had to be at least six feet down. 'Cause he used to always say, "Jean, don't push me so hard!" I said, "I don't know no other way to do it."

Then I was playin' in a play called "Little Ham," and in order to get the reaction — 'cause see: I LOVE reaction! — in order to get the reaction that I wanted I actually choked this guy with a scarf. (laughs) Every night he used to hate that scene, because it was a woman on one end of the scarf: "No, he's my man!" and I said, "Take your hands off him — he's my man!" — so I'm snatchin' the other side of the scarf. And it's not a reaction, BELIEVE me, he's really chokin'. (laughs all around)

And then John (Waters) said, "Well, fight, I'm just gonna let the cameras run and you fight." I'm sittin' there, "Now supposin' this bitch can really whip my ass?" Honey, I fought for all I was worth! (laughs)

And which scene was that in *Desperate Living*?

That was the fight scene with the policemen. And I was worried about gettin' out of breath anyway, and then I actually shoved one of 'em through the house and he really went sailin' through there! (laughs) But I don't "act" when I do those parts. No! If somebody says "slap their face," they get a real slap. When they told me to lay over on Mink, Mink said that she was so scared!!! (laughs) . . . she said, "Jean, no one's actin' — all I thought about was your big ass comin' down on me!" (ongoing laughter) And I'm trying' to raise up on the bed, and the bed would go up in the air! . . . I don't act! I'm tellin' you, I DON'T ACT! Anything you see me do on stage, it's for real. From the grunts to the groans to everything. It's just me.

John told me, he said, "Get up there and drive the bus." I got on the bus . . . can't smile 'cause sometimes I be thinkin' funny thoughts too. And one of the ways that we got the people to react in *Polyester* was, I was on the bus and the brakes went off, and the people said, "Jean, stop the bus!" I said, "I don't know how to drive no bus." (laughs) They really got John saying, (screams in panicked imitation) "That's what I want, that's what I want!"

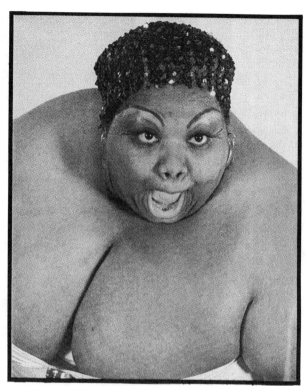

"Anorexia ... where do I get it?" — greeting card

And he was shooting all the while! Didn't somebody make you another sort of offer to be in a sex version of *People's Court*, to act as the "Sex Judge"?

Yeah, the "Love Judge," and I'm to determine whether these people should be separated or divorced or stay married.

It would be just like *The People's Court* except they would come up before you with their sex problems and then they wanted you to . . .

Well, basically he said, most of these people are separated because they have sex problems. "My husband doesn't kiss right," or "He doesn't make love right," or ... somethin' like that. So I'm to listen to it and determine whether they can resolve it or should they get another bed partner.

And he, like, wanted you to open up full blast on these people.

Uh-huh. He said, "What would you say . . ." Like if it had to do with kissin' I guess I would say, "Well, let me see how you kiss and maybe I could supervise that." And I asked him what the outfit would be and he said just a regular black robe. I said, "Well, I would have to have a LARGE gavel!" . . . "Oh yes!" he says, 'That'd be great!" He said, "They told me that you probably could do that." (laughs) But he said it would be run like *People's Court*, and the Supreme Court, only it'll be real funny, and these are real people ... real people's cases. He said if you need any help we can give it to you but from what I see I think you could do it by yourself!" (laughs)

So what are your plans for the future? Probably first just get yourself back in shape?

Well, I hope — I'm prayin' and I'm crossin' my fingers — that by, maybe ... six months from now somebody offers me a film role, or I go and make the rest of these all-occasion greetin' cards, or hang that up and then try to get into the movies, or a series or something'. But my LOVE is really wantin' to be on the screen. I'd really like to make a couple of commercials. Now the guy from Amsterdam told me that he POSSIBLY has a — that wide-body commercial for TWA, he said because they have been negotiating, but he hasn't really cleared anything up with 'em. It's somethin' like, "If Jean Hill can ride wide-body seats, then ANYBODY can." TWA said that they wouldn't pay me but that they would defer the cost of me comin' over to Amsterdam. I said, "Defer the cost?" They need to pay, too! They got the goddam money. But I'd settle for residuals from it.

As far as movies go, I think a lot of people who don't know what John's films are, they think all he does is porno films and you do porno, but it's not that at all. People that don't know John, have never seen his films, have always made that mistake with him.

But he's only made one X-rated film! *Desperate Living*. The rest of 'em are Rs. And he ASKED for that X.

But the films are so wild, and people think that (porno) is the only way things can be wild and shocking, when actually most porno is slow and very standard.

Well, you know a lot of people just don't understand shock humor either. I was tryin' to explain to somebody what it's all about: When a child shits itself and the shit is runnin' out the drawers, nobody says anything — they come in and change the pants. But John would have a grown man doin' the same thing, and hopin' that people find it funny. And nobody says to him, "Come change your drawers," 'cause he would have to change himself. You see what I'm sayin'? A child might eat their own shit, and you would just say, "That's not what you're supposed to do." But for a grown man to do it ... And that's what shock humor is to me. It's acceptin' what a child do, or acceptin' something at a certain age, but when you reach another age it's not supposed to be.

Right, and his movies are a lot more shocking and funnier than porno movies.

Right! You know, where would you find a fat woman, NUDE, in the movies, except in a porno movie? But I wanted to be the first nude person in his film — that was another reason I wanted to be nude. I told him I really didn't care, because I said, as long as it's not pornographic, it didn't make no difference to me.

Right, exactly. And being in this magazine, *Jumbo*, I think people don't really know how to take you. I think you —- and all your photos in *Jumbo* are done so tastefully — and strangely — that people just can't understand. I think you blow their minds a little bit.

But they really liké it, but it's like, "Tease us with more," or "Where can we find more revealin' photographs?" I said I GOT to see what's in this magazine! *The End* 🐀 🐀 🐀

Jean Hill at John's 1988 Xmas party

GEORGE STOVER

The original Buddy Deane with George Stover on the set of *Hairspray*. (John flew Buddy in from his home in Pine Bluff, Arkansas to play a TV reporter in the film.)

Peggy Gravel (Mink Stole) NOT on the road to recovery as she confronts her husband (George Stover) while reaching for medication in *Desperate Living*.

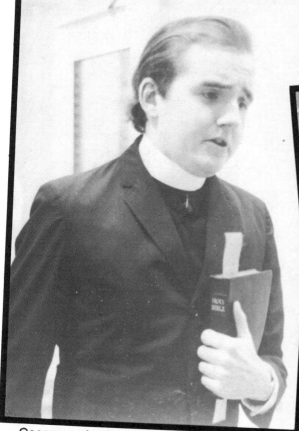

George as death row priest in *Female Trouble*.

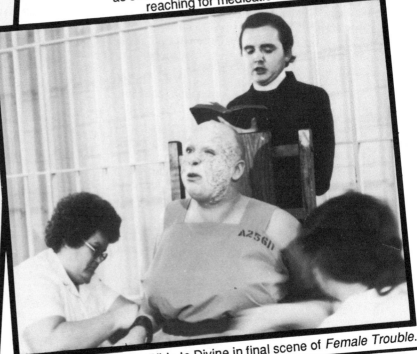

George reads from the Bible to Divine in final scene of *Female Trouble*.

You knew John Waters in high school. What was he like back then as best you remember?

John and I first became acquainted in eighth grade homeroom at Towson-town Junior High School. Although John usually attended Catholic schools for some reason he was enrolled in public school that year. Students were assigned to homeroom alphabetically and since the first letters of our last names are close together in the alphabet, we ended up in the same homeroom. As I recall, John was rather quiet and shy like me so we got along okay. *The Twilight Zone* was on network television in those days and I remember that on Monday mornings we would occasionally discuss an episode of that show that had aired the previous Friday night. I don't believe we were in any classes together, however, and we didn't spend any time with one another outside school.

Were you from the same neighborhood as John, Divine, and Mary Vivian Pearce in Lutherville?

No, I wasn't. I was from Towson, which is close by, but I never met Divine or Bonnie until I became involved with John's films. Divine and I were at Towson High School around the same time, but our paths never crossed until the evening of our rehearsal for the prison scene in *Female Trouble*.

Your first Waters' role was as a cop in *Pink Flamingos*, right? Do you remember much about the filming of that movie? Any weird inside stories?

I wasn't in *Pink Flamingos* at all. **(Editor's mistake: At least one of the cops looks very George Stover-like.)** After junior high school I lost all contact with John. In fact, I wasn't even sure if the filmmaker by the name of John Waters I would read about in the newspaper was the same person I went to school with. In one newspaper article I read that John had trouble finding "normal" looking people because most of his friends were on the bizarre side. So I ended up sending him my picture and resume and was cast as the prison chaplain in *Female Trouble*. When I went to rehearsal, I discovered that John was the same person I had known from eighth grade homeroom. My first part in a movie was in *Female Trouble*.

In John's films you've played a priest, a husband and a reporter. You seem to have the look of "authority," of the "establishment" that plays counterpoint to his raving grotesques and maniacs. Do you feel an affinity for these "straight" roles? Do you enjoy them? In other films as well, such as *The Private Files of J. Edgar Hoover*, you play an FBI agent.

In addition to the roles you've mentioned, I've also played a scientist — another authority figure — in two Don Dohler films, *The Alien Factor* and *Nightbeast*. I guess I do feel a certain affinity for these types of parts now that I've played so many of them. Of course, I like just about any role because I'm grateful to be doing it. I think many of these "establishment" types of parts that I get are due to typecasting. An actor is often cast in certain types of roles because he has a certain look about him.

In *Desperate Living* you played the part of Peggy Gravel's husband. Whose house was that opening shot in? Do you remember anything about the filming of that movie? You refer to it as the high point of your Waters' film work. Is it your favorite?

That was John's parents' home. I remember that they left for the day which was a smart thing to do since there were so many people traipsing around. All of the scenes at that house were shot in one day except for a few retakes which were done a week later. My scenes on the front porch were filmed in the morning and then the rest of my scenes were shot in the late afternoon and evening. My largest role in any Waters' film was in *Desperate Living*, of course, so that makes it my favorite one in a way. Story-wise, however, I think I liked *Female Trouble* better.

Do you know Jean Hill personally? What's she like?

I haven't seen her in a couple of years now, but Jean and I were pretty friendly and we got along just fine. She's so sweet and down to earth and she has a wonderful sense of humor. She's always saying funny things and making people laugh. She once invited me to one of her parties and I went and had a real nice time. I bought her 1988 calendar and collect all the greeting cards she's modeled for. Next to Edie Massey perhaps, I think that Jean was the person I was closest to of anyone I met while working on John's films.

You recently were pictured in *Fangoria* for your role in the upcoming *Dracula's Widow*. What sort of role did you play in this film and what is it about?

I play the coroner who supervises the removal of several bodies from the scene of a grisly mass murder. I have two brief lines of dialog opposite actor Josef Sommer. Sommer has worked in a lot of films and received third billing in the Harrison Ford movie *Witness*. I don't know too much about the plot of *Dracula's Widow* except that it centers around Count Dracula's widow who goes on a killing spree after arriving in Hollywood from Romania via the Hollywood Wax Museum. Sylvia Kristel of *Emmanuelle* fame stars in the title role and the film was directed by Chris Coppola in Wilmington, North Carolina under the auspices of the DeLaurentiis Entertainment Group. However, none of the film was shot inside the studio gates so it should have an interesting location feel to it.

Considering the deaths of David Lochary, Edith Massey, and now Divine, perhaps a certain Waters era is really over. Between *Polyester* and *Hairspray*, John wanted to make a movie called *Flamingos Forever* but

gave up on it after Edith Massey died, saying that "audiences would never go for a fake Edie." Now with Divine's death, perhaps he will have to change his approach even more drastically. What are your opinions on this?

Actually I've been aware of many "eras" in the life and career of John Waters. In a way, *Pink Flamingos* ended one era and began another because that was his first color film and his first to be blown up to 35mm for wider distribution. I'm sure that to some people, *Polyester* marked the end of an era and the beginning of a new era because that was John's first R-rated movie after a string of X-rated films. On the technical side *Polyester* ended the era of 16mm films and began the era of 35mm features. It was also the end of an era when David Lochary died and the end of another era when Edie died. As a matter of fact, it was sort of the end of an era for me when Edie moved to California because I missed not being able to visit her in her shop in Fells Point. *Hairspray* was

the end of another era because that was John's first PG film and his most mainstream movie to date. And now another era has ended with the death of Divine. Certainly, Divine will be missed in future John Waters' films and if I know John, he will not even try to find a substitute for Divine just as he wisely chose not to film *Flamingos Forever* with a "fake Edie." People like Edie and Divine are one-of-a-kind originals and it would be foolish to even try to replace them. I don't know what approach John will take in his future films, but as I pointed out, there have already been numerous changes along the way.

END

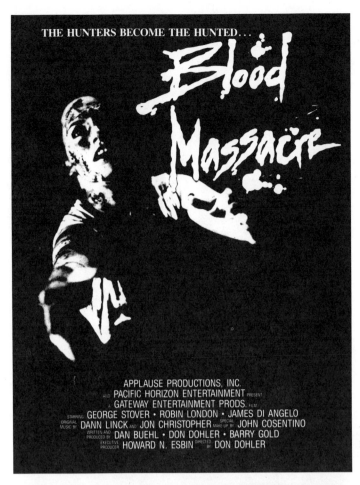

THE HUNTERS BECOME THE HUNTED...

Blood Massacre

APPLAUSE PRODUCTIONS, INC.
AND PACIFIC HORIZON ENTERTAINMENT PRESENT
A GATEWAY ENTERTAINMENT PRODS. FILM
STARRING GEORGE STOVER • ROBIN LONDON • JAMES DI ANGELO
ORIGINAL MUSIC BY DANN LINCK AND JON CHRISTOPHER MAKE-UP BY JOHN COSENTINO
WRITTEN AND PRODUCED BY DAN BUEHL • DON DOHLER • BARRY GOLD
EXECUTIVE PRODUCER HOWARD N. ESBIN DIRECTED BY DON DOHLER

George with Edith Massey on the set of *Polyester*.

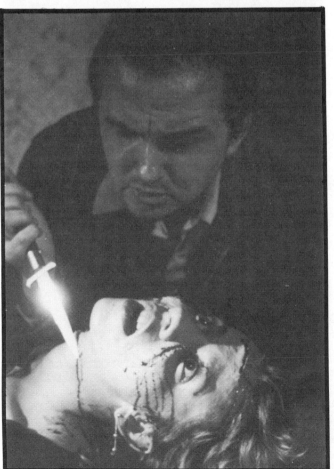

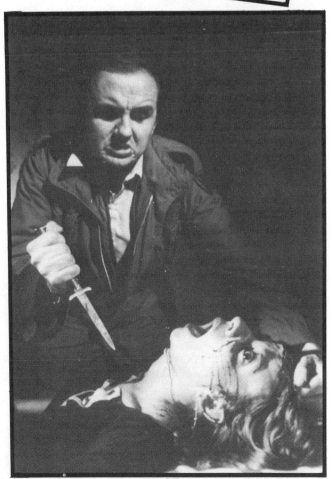

Blood Massacre (1988), a Don Dohler film, features George Stover as "Rizzo," a crazed Vietnam vet who turns to violence and slaughter.

40

JOHN WATERS INTERVIEW OF SEPTEMBER 30TH - 1988

by J. Stevenson

This interview's going to be a little bit different. You're going to be in this third issue with a whole new cast of characters and I'd like to get your point of view on some of these folks for the sake of some insight or friction.

Some of the people are Johnny Eck, Jean Hill and Mary Vivian Pearce, among others, so it'll be something like a Baltimore homecoming issue.

(laughs) You should get Spiro Agnew.

Johnny Eck, now he lives in Baltimore. Have you ever had any communication with him?

I've never ever met him. I saw him recently in this movie called *Painted Screens* which is a documentary about this phenomenon in Baltimore, and he is actually one of the most famous painted screen artists.

I guess he lives with his brother, Rob. Do you know what part of Baltimore he lives in?

I think they live in East Baltimore — I'm sure they do.

He is famous here for the painted screens. I'm sure that most of the people that know him don't even know that he was in *Freaks*.

And painted screens is strictly a Baltimore thing?

Yeah, it's like Folk Art. I mean, it's in a lot of the houses in East Baltimore where I've certainly filmed a lot of my films, including *Hairspray*. What they are is they're all these like, I think kind of corny scenes of DUCKS, and that kind of thing. But they're all on the screen so that you can have your windows open and look out but people can't look in. For those hot summers here.

This movie that he was in, was this a local documentary?

Yeah. I was in it but they cut me out. (chuckles)

Did it receive play anywhere else?

Yeah, I think it's gonna be on PBS — I think it WAS already on PBS.

Was it a mondo Baltimore type of thing?

No, it was a serious PBS type documentary ... and that's how he's known in Baltimore, painted screens. I mean, film people know [of *Freaks*], but I think for many, many years he has refused to discuss *Freaks*. And this new breed — they don't know what *Freaks* is.

Do you remember the first time you ever saw the movie *Freaks*?

I probably saw it ... I saw it in New York, at a theater on Times Square ... and I saw it in about '64. But then you know when underground movies first came out they played it a lot. I think maybe that was the first real revival of it, and I think that was when it was THE most popular ever, then. And then I showed it to my prison class ... they liked it. (chuckles)

Do you think a remake of *Freaks* [proposed several years ago by a major studio] would be a feasible thing?

Well, it's feasible. I'm against the idea personally, but financially it could work.

It seems like freaks have totally gone out of style, though.

You know I used to always go to the freak show, I was obsessed by it. Last time I went it was with Pat Moran, her husband and her kids. And I remember the guy came up and stuck a nail up his nose with a hammer and said, "You think it's fake but it's not!" And then Pat caught her daughter trying to shove a nail up her nose. (laughs) I think that's a reason they don't have it anymore.

But, there were no REAL freaks — most of it was all kind of fake. There was one guy, that was like — flippers he had. Seal Boy. But mostly it was just bad tricks with the most PITIFUL costumes that needed to go to the cleaners so badly!

I think, also, a sort of social consciousness type atmosphere has taken over that says "these people should not be exploited."

This one, there was the barker out front, and you went in, and it was SO HOT — that's all I remember. See, I could never go to state fairs because all I can think of 'em is BEES and TRASHCANS ... it was like 110 degrees in there, and believe me, this was NOT a highbrow audience.

The midway always had a freak show. That's where I saw my first fat lady, too. I used to go and look at her every day. She sat in a polka-dot dress eatin' a peach and she'd just GLARE at you. And I'd just stand there by myself.

Speaking of underground films, we also have some material from George Kuchar. In speaking of your teenage years when you were coming up to New York City to see some of the underground films, you often mention George's film *Hold Me While I'm Naked*.

Yes, and *Sins of the Fleshapoids*, which I think is Mike's. BOTH of 'em — they made me want to make films, THEY are the reason. Because they were like — and I hadn't even seen Douglas Sirk yet — they were the first people that ever idolized Douglas Sirk, they were so ahead of their time. And their films were that LURID color, and they were the biggest influence on me, of the underground filmmakers.

More so than Warhol, and ...

Yes, because ... I saw them first, and the Warhol movies then were just like *Sleep* and *Eat* and stuff,

---

◀ Opposite page: John Waters in the old days — poses in an electric chair during the shooting of *Female Trouble*.

know what I mean? That was before the Superstar thing. Then, of course, the early Warhol — I saw the Warhol premiere of *Chelsea Girls*.

But I had seen some before that like *Couch* and *Harlot* and — you always had to go see them in churches and stuff, and weird — well, The Bridge Theater, that's where they had a lot of that stuff.

As for the lurid colors, you certainly used that yourself in *Female Trouble* and *Desperate Living*.

Oh yeah. And just all their ... I don't know, I still love their stuff — I still visit them when I'm in San Francisco. You should see their apartment. They have the BEST portrait of themselves, it's an oil painting that I've always wanted to break into their apartment and steal!

But George, I've seen his new stuff — you know he still makes movies all the time. He still teaches at the Art Institute and all the students that sign up for his class HAVE to be in his movies, (chuckles) which I love!

And George is also obsessed by tornados, you know. And so we talk about that and he's told me all these great books to get on tornados. *Those Terrible Twisters* — that's my favorite one, where you had to send to some post office box in Oklahoma, and make the check out to "Those Terrible Twisters" — I love doin' that! And he made this video about — every year he goes and sits in this motel and waits for a tornado, and I think when one finally came he ran and hid. (laughs) I'm not sure, he might have been joking. But that's his vacation every year — he goes by himself to a sleazy motel in Oklahoma and sits and waits for a tornado.

He's done a lot of video recently, too. You've never been inclined toward video yourself?

No ... PORNO looks better on it. But, ah — no.

Speaking of porno —

I knew THAT would get you going! (laughs)

Yeah, (dryly) my favorite ... subject. What did you think of his collaboration with Curt McDowell on *Thundercrack!*?

I liked the movie very much. I thought uncut it was a little long. But I think it's SEXY. I think the sex scenes really are sexy for real. And I think it's funny and I love how it looks — I liked it very much.

If you ever shot a porno film ... but you've never been inclined to take that up ...

No. No ... it's too limiting. (chuckles) If I ever shot one I'd keep it for my personal use.

Yeah. I think they might've been trying to expand the boundaries of what's a very narrow form.

But they DID, but it's very hard, though, to make a good porno movie and be FUNNY because they're sort of the opposite. Good porno isn't funny. It's DIRTY, you know ... to ME at least. You know, I'm not interested in, ha — finding a "meaningful rela-

tionship" (chuckles) — I don't think it's what most people are lookin' for in pornography.

Well, speaking of "dirty" pornography and pornography that has a dirty look to it, did you know Curt McDowell at all?

Yes, and I saw *Loads*, which I was SHOCKED by. That was a little more (laughs) "self" ... what's the word I wanta use for that one? Well, I kinda was AMAZED, especially in interviews when he talked about "these are the tricks that I got," and filmed them! ... You know, I though "GOD!" Maybe I didn't want to know that, I think maybe that's how I felt.

Yeah, George said his (Curt's) calling in life was pornography, and that's why God put him on earth.

(chuckles) Well he knew him better than I!

George has referred to *Female Trouble* as "a quite magnificent and sweeping saga, worthy of Edna Ferber."

Oh! That's nice, so BIG! (laughs) I think I have a biography of her called, ah ... George wrote me the sweetest of all the notes I got when Divine died. And I really got a lot of 'em. And his was maybe the MOST touching.

Print made from color snapshot of Divine performance
mid-1980s

What was his star's name? He had a GREAT star.

Donna Kerness?

THAT'S the one! She's my favorite — I had a picture of her from *Film Culture* magazine in my apartment for many years — wonder where that is — in a prom dress. She was great. You know there was really great stuff in *Film Culture*, they really covered them [the Kuchar brothers] really well. That was the BEST underground film magazine. It was really good in the Warhol years and underground film years. It was really the only magazine that ever wrote about them. And it had GREAT stills and really, really good stuff — I have a lot of them.

And I think maybe the reason *Film Culture* went out of business was because that whole scene ended in a way.

Well yeah, it did. People saw too many movies with colors jumpin' around, you know. That wasn't what they had in mind for underground movies.

Speaking of that period of the underground, did you ever see any Kenneth Anger films?

Oh yeah! The premiere of *Roman Candles* which we had during the Flower Mart in the afternoon in a church, and the Flower Mart then was a thing that all the lunatics came to. It was really a flower show for old ladies but it was a big BEATNIK scene at the time, too. We showed *Roman Candles* and Kenneth Anger's *Eaux d'Artifice* because we wanted to use his name but we didn't want to show anything TOO rude in a church, then, because ours was rude — we didn't want to be out-ruded. And, we used his name to lure people in.

In the best tradition of exploitation ...

Yeah.

And *Scorpio Rising*, did you see that one?

Oh yeah! I mean, I loved it. Kenneth Anger was the very first person — and I don't think anybody ever did this before — that used pop music the way now every movie does. I copied him — everybody copied him.

Yeah, like *Blue Velvet* ...

EVERYBODY copied him, he did it first.

Do you know him at all, personally?

I met him once, I don't know him, no.

You've read his books (*Hollywood Babylon I and II*) though, of course. Bonnie was reading a copy of *Hollywood Babylon* on the bus. [The opening scene in *Mondo Trasho*.]

But she was reading the REAL one, the one that was banned. That wasn't the — the two *Hollywood Babylon*'s that came out in this country — that is different. That was the French one, that was published underground.

Can you ever envision a *Hollywood Babylon III*?? Because he has said that maybe in ten years he'll need more money, so he has to ...

The PROBLEM with it is — you know I sort of feel bad because I gave *Hollywood II* a bad review. (chuckles) Well I think that if you're gonna tell gossip you have to act like you're upset about it and not glad.

Bonnie's "Magic Feet" in *Mondo Trasho*

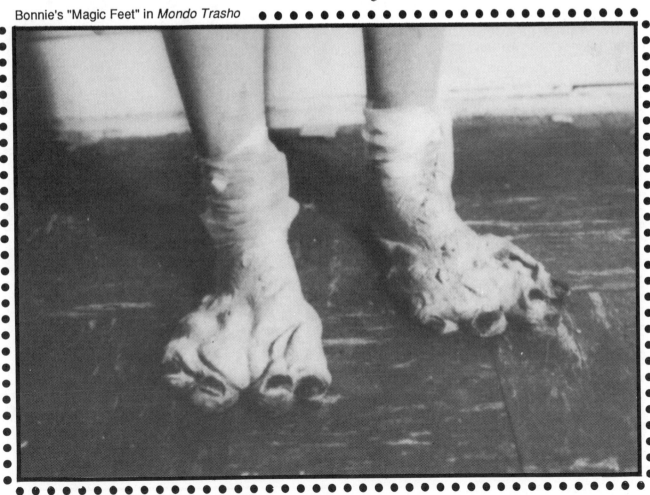

And I just read the Clara Bow biography, which is really, really good, and it disproves every single thing that he ever said about her. So, I'm not sure how much you can believe a lot of it. Which, I'm sort of against the idea that when you die you lose all rights. I even know that when I've written books, when the lawyers go over it and they go berserk ... With *Shock Value* when the lawyers first read it they almost had a heart attack. But, if someone's dead they don't care what you write. You could make up every lie and there's not one thing anybody could do, so, I'm against that.

Didn't you have a line in your review of *Hollywood Babylon II* that the book was so bad nobody should pay for it with cash?

No, I didn't say it was so BAD — I said it was the kind of book that no one should pay cash for, everyone should charge it on their "MasterCard."

I'm not saying it was BAD. I thought the TONE of it was different that the first ones, I thought it was TOO mean. And I think you can be mean, more mean, if you're not as happy that these horrible things happened to these people.

I'd like to talk about Hubert Selby, who is also in this issue. You've read some of his books — in fact you turned me on to *Requiem for a Dream* in 1980 — what do you think of him?

Well, MOST of 'em are GREAT, there's a few I don't like. *Demon* I didn't like. Certainly *Last Exit to Brooklyn*, *Requiem for a Dream* are good ... I liked his stories [*Songs from a Silent Snow*].

I think he's really great, and I'm happy they're doing this movie [*Last Exit to Brooklyn*].

Yeah, I wanted to ask you what you thought about the idea of this movie.

Well, I'm dyin' to see it.

Do you think there will be any problems bringing unvarnished Hubert Selby to the screen? I mean is it possible?

Well, certainly less problems than there would've been when the BOOK came out! I can't wait to see who plays Tralala!

Did you read *Last Exit* when you were young?

I read *Last Exit to Brooklyn* when I was in high school — it was a MAJOR, MAJOR influence. And I like his books very much. I like the IDEA of Hubert Selby, Jr. because everything I've read about him ... I still have never been able to figure out what he's like.

Just theoretically, how would you shoot *Last Exit to Brooklyn* if you were going to do the movie?

Well you know, I'd have to re-read it — I haven't read it in twenty years. And somebody DID make it, I mean Ricki Lake's in it — I mean there's a 7-page ad for it in this week's *Variety*. It's a German-American film.

It seems to me like it would almost have to be shot in a grainy documentary style.

Well I don't know, you know Cronenberg's gonna make *Naked Lunch*. In *Variety* this week it says that. So ... maybe these kinds of things, everything comes back. (chuckles)

Also, I think Charles Bukowski is another example; there are three movies out about him but they're all like, art movies, they're all shot by Europeans.

But I LIKE the movies, I liked all three of them a lot. I really loved *Love is a Dog From Hell* — it's my favorite movie of the year practically. And I like *Tales of Ordinary Madness* and I liked *Barfly*.

You always run into these Bukowski fanatics who just bitterly HATE those movies, because — I think they take him as some sort of ... saint.

Well anybody who loves a book that much, they're NEVER satisfied with the movie. A movie is a different thing than a book, and it can never be what

French poster of Marco Ferreri's 1983 film, *Tales of Ordinary Madness*, based on the autobiographical writings of Charles Bukowski.

they expect. That's why I don't have much desire anymore — I used to want to make *A Confederacy of Dunces*, but I think that would've been a mistake because that book has SUCH a following that it's never gonna be what they want.

I think *Naked Lunch* will be ... it'll be very interesting to see how that's filmed.

Well Cronenberg could do it.

Jean Hill is another star of this issue. She was in community theater before your films. Didn't you go to one of her plays at one point?

Yes, it was called *Little Ham*, and that's how I met her. The guy that works the desk in my building — 'cause it's a highrise — I kept saying, "I'm lookin' for a fat black woman that weighs 200 pounds," and he said, "I know one that weighs 400 and she's in this play." And so, she came over and then I went to see the play. And she was TOTALLY — I mean no one had a CHANCE when she walked on stage. And sometimes she forgot her lines and it didn't even matter 'cause she'd make up new stuff that was better than the play anyway. But the actors (laughs) looked like they were scared of her.

Yeah, she says she never really "acts" — if you ask her to do something, choke somebody, she will DO it — she WILL choke them.

Well, she did knock somebody unconscious in *Desperate Living*.

And so she lived in your building for a while or was staying with somebody there?

Yeah, that was the guy at the desk. But no, I don't think she ever COMPLETELY lived here. (chuckles) Her presence was felt heavily.

But that's rather astonishing that she was living in the SAME building ...

Yeah, I was lookin' all over everywhere for her when we were casting *Desperate Living* and she was LITERALLY right in front of my own nose. (chuckles) But I had never seen her before.

Jean lives right in your neighborhood today, doesn't she?

Yeah, she lives the closest to me of anyone I know in the world. And she ALWAYS has.

Have you been to her house that she's in now?

Yeah — it's very tastefully done, very pretty, it's a very nice apartment. She always has people LURKING around in the background but I'm not sure who they are (laughs) ... usually her house boys.

Not to pry into personal matters, (mutters) which of course is absolutely what I'm about to do ... but, ah, she mentioned some notorious 18-page letter of some years ago that she wrote to you. Do you remember it?

Yeah, I remember, but she actually didn't give it to me until way afterwards, so, you know ... it was like a moot point kind of. And I don't remember everything in it. It was right after *Desperate Living*, I think. And I think that Jean maybe at the time thought everybody that was in a movie made millions of dollars, or something. I'm not quite sure if she quite understood the independent film world I was in at the time.

What was your first encounter with Jean's mother like? To quote Jean, she said that her mom can be hell on white people. Jean told us to ask you about her, ha ha.

Jean's mother in my mind is a racist. She said, "How

A still from a Waters' Christmas card.

• Edith Massey •

from a Waters' Christmas card.

• • • • • Divine in *Mondo Trasho*. • • • • •

On the set of *Desperate Living*, L to R: Pat Moran, soundman Richard Ellsberry, John Waters, director of photography Thomas Loizeaux, Van Smith's back, Mink Stole.

dare you exploit my daughter," and I said, "Jean made more money on that movie than I did." That shut her up.

But her mother CONSTANTLY was against me. And a lot of people's parents have been against me in the beginning with the movies ... so I'm used to that. But her mother was so rude to me — her mother basically doesn't like white people. Usually parents don't like me because they find the scripts, or they see one of my movies, but usually not because I'm white. I guess also in a way it's good for white people to feel that prejudice. But it was the first time anyone was really so blatant about it.

You know, she might have changed, because a friend of mine is in the hospital, who is very white, he has long blonde hair, and she was on the same floor and he said that she was absolutely lovely and they really got along. And I did see her once at Jean's birthday party. But now I kid her when I see her: (yelling) "Oh, Mrs. Hill! It's so GOOD to see you!!!" — and she even laughs, so I think over the years she probably calmed down about it. In the beginning she was ... not exactly a stage mother. (laughs)

But I guess Jean has always had white friends.

She ALWAYS has! And I think her mother's probably always hated that. But in any case, I haven't seen her in a long time. Her brothers and her father are really very lovely.

Did her mom ever see *Desperate Living*?

I doubt it. (chuckles) Who knows, you know? I don't know. She wasn't at the premiere. And Jean has a very CLOSE relationship with her mother. She goes through all sorts of changes with her, but she's certainly very close to her mother.

... Well you know, in the beginning, everybody's parents were against it. The only person's parents in the very beginning that weren't against it all were David Lochary's. Well, it was his mother — you could ALWAYS go over there. I mean, she loved Divine from the very beginning — we always used to go over there. And David would hook school and she worked, so we'd go over there in the day. But she always was nice. She died a couple of years ago, but I stayed in touch with her way after David died. You know, she went back to art school and everything, she was always very, very lovely.

Jean was featured in the porno mag *Jumbo* a few months ago. What was your gut reaction when you saw this magazine?

Well, she told me about it first. She called up and said she didn't know — suddenly her mailbox had like HUNDREDS of letters in it. And she just gave an interview to one of those magazines like *Penthouse* or *Gallery* — I don't know, one of those kind. But yet, no dirty pictures or anything — it wasn't dirty. And then they sold it to that magazine, and when I SAW the magazine! I mean, the title I think is very, very funny. But I read the letters she got and I felt like washing my hands afterwards.

I mean, there are really a lot of chubby chasers, and SHE is the Marilyn Monroe if you're a chubby chaser. But the letters were like, "I'd like your thighs to crack my neck" ... and stuff. And people sayin', (anguished cry) "PLEASE let me see your ass, PLEASE." Begging, you know. It was like, there are so few magazines I guess if THAT'S what you're into, that, when you finally see it you're just crazed about it. They just were RAMPANT chubby chasers.

And the other girls in that magazine —

— Oh God! But they like THEM, too. A stretch mark is sexy to them.

And those other girls, I mean some of them didn't look too HAPPY to say the least!

Oh, I couldn't even look at it (voice trails off in disgust), I mean, you know ...

And I guess readers of that magazine wanted copies of her "nude film" which boils down to *Desperate Living*!

Well, they probably ASSUMED, not knowing anything about Jean, that she was like the rest of the women in the magazine, that she had a porno career. And you know, there was some black woman called "TV Mama," and there was some other one, a big black woman that has done porno. People get mixed up sometimes.

And I think somebody who reads *Jumbo* probably has never seen any of your movies.

Well, I don't think any marketing team has done a survey of *Jumbo* readers. You know? How much they earn, what kind of liquor they drink, what AIRLINES they fly ... I really don't think that there's been a marketing survey of *Jumbo* magazine.

Jean Hill hands her favorite honky a birthday gift. (John's 40th birthday bash held at the Waxter Center Old Folks Home in Baltimore in '86.

Correct me if I'm wrong, but sometimes *Desperate Living* seems to be your least favorite of all your films.

Yeah, probably is. I LIKE it, though ... but, ah, I think it's the least joyous. And I wrote in the screenplay book that really maybe it's a film to watch if you're crashing from a glue high. (chuckles)

Well, that makes it sound more negative than I feel about it — no, *Mondo Trasho* is by far my least favorite. Every year I'm tempted to snatch that one off the market!

Did you actively try to get away from a "midnight movie" style after *Desperate Living*? Or was that just something that happened?

Well, midnight movies were over, you know? I'd be a FOOL to make a midnight movie now — there's like one theater in the country that shows 'em. Video is midnight movies now. See, you go into a movie with your friends and say, "look at this hideous movie," and THAT'S what a midnight movie is now.

So certainly ... I know the business well enough now to know that that would be like saying I want to make an underground movie. You know, the TIMES are different.

Some people have said that *Desperate Living* lacked a little because it didn't have Divine in it, but I always thought that any movie with Jean Hill and Edith Massey didn't need Divine.

Well you know, Divine was supposed to play the Susan Lowe role (Mole McHenry — lady wrestler and botched sex change) and everybody assumes it was supposed to be Liz Renay's part.

Well, it's easy for me to think that was some of the problem of it, because there is something not very JOYOUS about it. Maybe I was in a bad mood when I wrote it. (chuckles) You know, in Europe they like it a lot, and some of the really hardcore fans like it best. So, I don't know that — I can't really tell. I probably like it least because it did the worst at the box office. That always colors how I feel about one of my films (laughs) ... in hindsight.

Jean said that she knew Divine a long time ago, the early '60s or something, at a place called Eddie's Bar in Baltimore. Now, is it possible that two future Waters' stars could have collided before you came into the picture?

YES. I know what Eddie's Bar is — I was in there once in my life, too. And I'm sure that Divine had been in there in his life, yes.

And very possibly Jean, too?

Oh yeah, well Jean I'm sure was.

Did you ever go to the Royal Theater back then?

ALL the time, you know, it was my favorite. And I would go, and I'd always be the only white person and I'd get beat up and it'd be worth it. Because I saw, like, Little Stevie Wonder when he was 12, I saw the Jewel Box Review ... The Marvelettes ... I saw Tina Turner when she still had a moustache. I mean, it was quite good.

And it's really a shame, because after the riots they tore that whole neighborhood down, which was really stupid. 'Cause that really was the Apollo Theater of Baltimore. EVERYBODY played there. Ruth Brown said she played there a lot — it was really a FAMOUS black theater.

How's your relationship with Jean been over the years? She's pretty feisty sometimes, isn't she?

Jean can be difficult, but I think my relationship's been good with her. Oh ... yeah, we've had some ups and downs but never anything I'd think of as serious. You know, I love Jean, I mean she's great fun to go out with because no one ever looks at you. (chuckles) She's better than wearin' a camouflage outfit. And Jean, you know, underneath it all, is ... can even be conservative. It's hard to see what she's really like because she can be so aggressive ... but underneath it she's a good Catholic girl. (wry chuckle)

It's ironic that *Hairspray* was a "black movie" for you but was made without your only black star. Surely there would have been a part for Jean in that movie?

She broke her leg, though. You know? Really, a month before we started shooting it. So, and — the insurance people — there was no way. I mean I even talked to her doctor and he said "she will not be able to walk." So right up to the last minute I tried every possible way to get her in it.

We also have your old friend Mary Vivian Pearce in this issue. Now, your parents and her parents are back on speaking terms again?

Oh, they're best friends again. (in a tone of bemused chagrin) Her mother asked me for my autograph at her father's funeral, to give to some friends of hers ... so times DO change. Her mother's very lovely to me now.

I've known ... well, BONNIE is what everybody calls her. Mary Vivian Pearce is her name in movies, and you know, she just had her first published article that came out in the paper, about being a clocker and it's by "Mary Pearce." So she's "Mary Vivian Pearce" in the movies, "Mary Pearce" in the press, and "Bonnie" to everybody that knows her. And this piece in the city paper is very good.

I've really known Bonnie since I was born. Our fathers were friends in college.

You know her sister?

I know all of 'em — she has a million sisters.

But there are lots of things in all my movies that come from growing up with Bonnie. We weren't allowed to see each other for a long time, by the POLICE I think, for a while. Well, at least they threatened that, I don't know. We ran wild together as teenagers.

In those early movies, did you pattern Bonnie's character after any particular Hollywood star?

No, she came up really with that look of that white hair and bright red lipstick before anyone I'd ever seen in my life wear bright red lipstick. That's what she really looked like.

I remember when we lived together on 25th Street where we made the movie — that house she walks out of — (I think she walks out of a basement apartment, but we lived upstairs), but in that house was also, on the first floor, a plumbing school. And you had to walk right through it. Plumbers would sit there working on pipes and we would walk through with, like, Divine in DRAG, you know, and I remember the head plumber came to the movie. We were making *Eat Your Make-Up* there and the whole beginning is this girl just going (in a breathless panting grunting moan) "make-up, make-up — Oh God — make-up!" moaning about make-up for about three minutes, right? We had to try to synchronize it on a tape to the lips, which was impossible ... but I didn't know that then, so we did it for like four or five DAYS, she was up there going "make-up! make-up!" and the man in the plumbing store finally said to me, "Well, I heard that up there but I just thought it was one of your friends havin' a baby so I didn't say anything." (laughs) I couldn't believe that.

But Bonnie lived there then and she looked like that, and I remember her just walkin' out of the house and people would go CRAZY!

Do you remember back when she used to hang out at Windy Valley?

Yeah! She used to hook school and I used to meet her there. And I remember mostly meeting her when I lived at my parents' and she lived at her parents' and the quickest way for us to meet was walking up the railroad tracks. So we'd both walk up these railroad tracks and see each other in the distance. (chuckles) It was very ... Tennessee Williams. (laughs)

Bonnie is the ONLY one — Bonnie is in *Hag In a Black Leather Jacket* . She's the only one of all the people that was in ALL of them. None of the other people were. At the end of *Hag In a Black Leather Jacket* she was doing the "Bodie Green," which was the dance that was later used in *Hairspray*.

Oh, the Bodie Green was in *Hairspray*?

Yeah, they do it in the record shop. The "Dirty Boogie" — it's the same thing.

Now, did you guys invent that or was that an existing dance?

No, it was the one dance you weren't allowed to do. And Bonnie and I used to go to a Catholic Youth Organization — it was the only time we could see each other — and steal pocketbooks and do the Dirty Boogie and be asked to leave. No, it was a real dance. We carried it to unheard of lengths. (chuckles) She was REALLY good at it!!!

Yeah, I remember when you were in Boston, here at your show, and somebody asked you to do it up on stage and you said you weren't ABOUT to do it by yourself —

(tone of dry conviction) Well, I CERTAINLY wouldn't. I did do it some with Divine when we were teaching Ricki Lake to do it, in rehearsals. Divine could really do it, too. Matter of fact, one of the first memories I have of Divine is him doin' it. At a swim club.

But yeah, Bonnie was even in *The Diane Linkletter Story* with a very limited cast (Lochary, Pearce and Divine), so she's been in every one of 'em.

And I think she was really impersonating her mother in *The Diane Linkletter Story*. It was the same stuff her mother was saying to HER at the time.

Now, "Miss Cotton" in *Pink Flamingos* — she was the "traveling companion" and I think psychologists have debated and studied this role for many, many years ... what exactly was her relationship to them, was she RELATED to —

No, she was Cracker's ... ah ... girlfriend, but they never touched. So she was Divine's friend and Divine's son's girlfriend. So I guess Divine in that movie was a common-law mother-in-law. (chuckles)

And in the sequel you see Divine has married his son and had a baby. And Cotton is MORE of a voyeur in this one 'cause it's fifteen years LATER. So it's all the same character — Cotton, Crackers.

In some of those early movies, I think even *Pink Flamingos*, a lot of people used their own names, like COOKIE (Mueller).

Well, Cookie may have been the only one, and that was because she was new and I wanted people to REMEMBER her. (chuckles) That's how we did it in the beginning, to BREAK 'EM IN.

But the main characters ... well, Bonnie's name wasn't COTTON! God knows where that name came from — maybe her hair looked like cotton.

Yeah, Cotton and Crackers — Crackers was a brilliant stroke. And NOODLES, I mean this is like, ah ...

Well, that name came because Cookie WAS going to name her baby Noodles, because her last name is Mueller, it was gonna be like "Mueller's Noodle," and the hospital people told her she couldn't. They wouldn't do it.

And that IS her baby in the movie. He's now seventeen.

And the baby that Divine has in *Female Trouble* is Susan Lowe's son, who is now sixteen.

I even saw "Taffy" the other night at the movies, and she's in her twenties now. You know, the one that played "Little Taffy" in *Female Trouble*? She looks great. I said, "Does anybody ever recognize you? And she said, "No, but my boyfriend and I rented it (*Female Trouble*) the other night and he was SO APPALLED, (laughs) he said, "That's you??!!! OH MY GOD!!" — he just couldn't believe, like, what was her life like? and her parents? at the time that she was in this movie. (laughs) ... She's very pretty.

Those first three films: *Eat Your Make-Up, Roman Candles* and *Hag In a Black Leather Jacket,* do you EVER show those anymore?

I showed *Eat Your Make-Up* to some friends a couple of years ago ... the problem is that *Hag In a Black Leather Jacket* is 8mm with the sound on tape and you need a reel-to-reel tape recorder. My 8mm projector is broken and I don't have a reel-to-reel tape recorder. *Roman Candles* is three of 'em shown at once — like an obvious rip-off of *Chelsea Girls* — and same thing — I need a reel-to-reel tape recorder. And both of those, there are no prints, they're the originals. *Eat Your Make-Up* is 16mm, black-and-white, filmed at 16 frames a second, 'cause I didn't know the difference, so you could never put it on video ... and it also has a very, very closely synchronized soundtrack on a reel-to-reel tape recorder but I would be the only person who could ever ATTEMPT to show it, to make it sync right. And I did show it to one of the stars (in it), Marina Melin, a couple of years ago when she came down to visit — and I hadn't seen it in a long time, and ... it's fun to show — it's like showin' home movies to your old friends. In my apartment, to people I've known for twenty years, it's fun to watch. To put it in a theater, or in front of an audience, I'm sure that ... there'd be a few people that would enjoy it. But basically it's much better to imagine it. (chuckles)

What's the condition of these movies?

Hag In a Black Leather Jacket is really bad ... *Roman Candles* is, literally IS, home movies. I mean, it's random shots of people, there's no story or anything. And it's got Mink in it, praying at some grave, SOBBING, it's got ... I really haven't seen this one in ten years. It's got Alexis eating an apple. Alexis was this other huge girl we knew at the time, who was really good friends with Divine. It's just random shots (chuckles) *Eat Your Make-Up* is the only one that SORT OF has a story. (laughs) SOME would call it a story.

And *Mondo Trasho* is one that you —

Every once in a while I'm tempted to take it out of distribution. But ... what the hell — it's already out there. And there are parts of it I like. It should be twenty minutes long but it's ninety, you know? I think if you've seen all my films it's okay to see that one.

It played here recently, in a theater, and the audience ROARED all through it, so, I don't know.

It always struck me as having the most COMPLI-CATED plot in the history of cinema or no plot at all — I can't figure out which.

(laughs) All my plots are complicated, but I remember one reviewer in the very beginning said that all my plots are mere clotheslines to hang my dirty wash on. And I even think of that today when I'm writing a script, I never forgot that one. (chuckles) It's maybe true.

So John, I guess the last question is more just directed at you. I just figured I had to ask it ... in our last issue I asked you if as a movie director you ever employed a casting couch, and you said you never slept with anyone in your movies except one person, and —

No, I ... it was one person and it was years AFTER the movie. I've never slept with anybody before a movie and I still haven't.

Who was it?

Ah, I won't tell you that one.

(laughs) That's what I figured.

Did someone else tell ya — I'm tryin' to think of ...

No, people just always ask me, they say, "why didn't you ask him WHO it was?" — that's the LOGICAL question. I guess then I have to ...

Good try! (laughs)

John Waters

~~sidewalk~~

gutter

stroll

of

stars

Cookie Mueller in New York City, 1981

Cookie Mueller in 1981.

EAST VILLAGE EYE   JULY. 1983   2

ASK

DR. MUELLER

By COOKIE MUELLER

Intro art for Cookie's medical advice column that appeared in *The East Village Eye* in the early '80s.
JON MATTHEWS

Cookie Mueller, circa 1988.

Reprinted from *Details* magazine, 1989

Patrick McMullan

COOKIE MUELLER

**John Waters and Cookie Mueller
at the *Torch Song Trilogy* reception
at Lincoln Center Performing Arts Library**

Cookie at John's 1988 Xmas party

MINK

STOLE

Mink Stole in nun's costume, 1988

Publicity shot from the Christopher Durang play *Sister Mary Ignatius Explains It All For You*, starring Mink, Summer of 1988.

Mink Stole and Joseph Casarona, 1988.

56

Caged and enraged Edith Massey in *Female Trouble*.

JOHN WATERS' *Female Trouble*
DIVINE · DAVID LOCHARY · MARY VIVIAN PEARCE · MINK STOLE · EDITH MASSEY
A DREAMLAND PRODUCTION FROM SALIVA FILMS, INC. A DIVISION OF NEW LINE CINEMA CORP.

⭐ *Edith Massey*

EDITH'S SHOPPING BAG   ☞ "a thrift store"

AS FEATURED IN JOHN WATERS'

FEMALE TROUBLE

PINK FLAMINGOS

MULTIPLE MANIACS

OPEN LATE FRIDAY & SATURDAY NIGHTS

NEW & OLD CLOTHES – JEWELRY – NICK NACKS – CANDLES – INCENSE – DISHES – TOYS
HATS – PURSES – PICTURES – BOOKS – SWEATERS & ETC.

EDITH'S SHOPPING BAG
726 S. BROADWAY
"FELLS POINT"
BALTIMORE, MARYLAND 21131

Flyer, circa '83, for Edie's thrift shop.

...ovesick Blues and Only Won... ...eed (yes, t... Alice Cooper nightmare) — and the results are refreshing. But the street says she's even better in person.

Next week the Horseshoe is importing another big American mama: movie star **Edie "the Egg Lady" Massey** of *Pink Flamingos* notoriety. (You don't remember *Pink Flamingos*? Well, the Horseshoe will also screen it for you at 8 p.m. each night she's here.) Anyway, tired of being "the motherly type," she has played a "nympho-fascist queen" in another movie (*Desperate Living*), and put together a punk rock group called the **Enfants Terribles**.

This time we in Toronto will be among the first to experience this, um.

The Toronto Sun, Monday May 8, 1978

Edith Massey conquers Toronto, May 1978

And live like a flower   ...are booked into the El Mocambo for four days in June.

EDIE THE EGG WOMAN and her band coming to the Horseshoe next week.

57

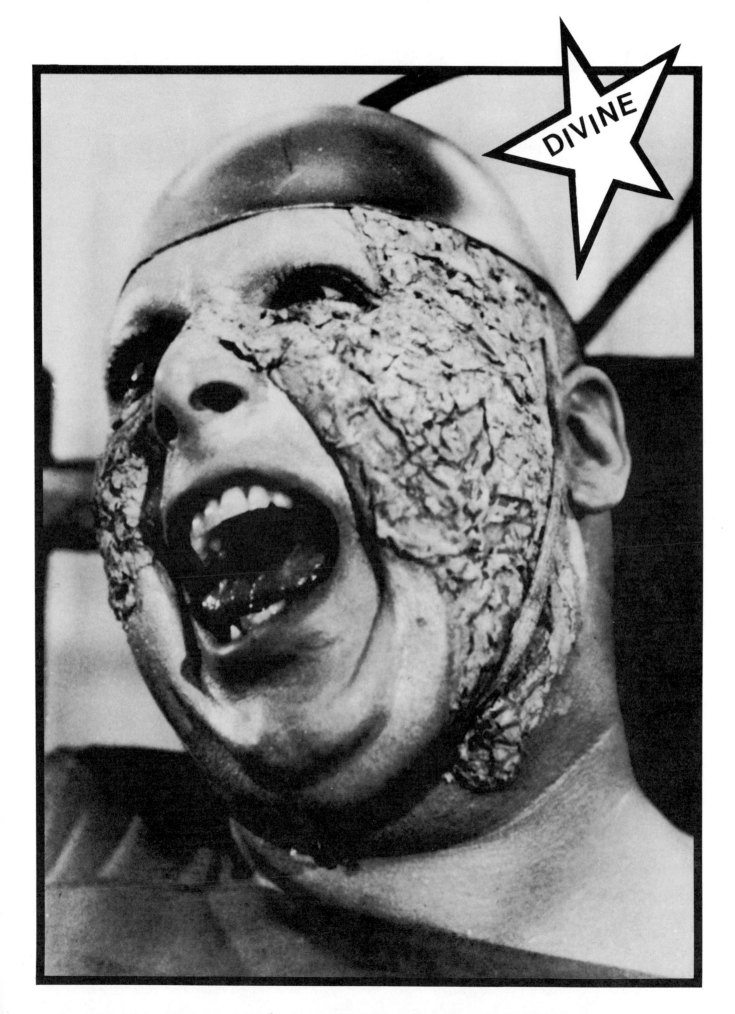

GEORGE KUCHAR

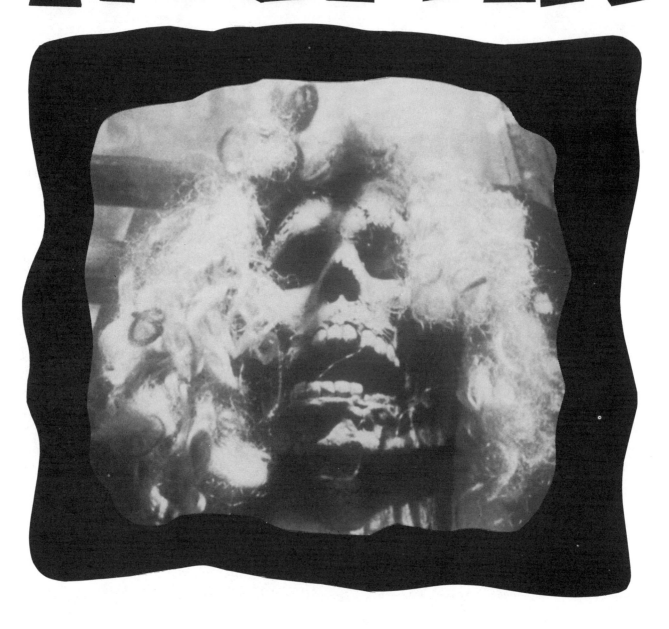

What follows is an interview George taped for us while staying in the Reno Motel in El Reno, Oklahoma in May 1988. We had supplied him with several pages of written questions. May is the peak of tornado season in Oklahoma. George is a regular guest at the Reno Motel and the setting figures prominently in his *Weather Diary* video series as well as his film, *Wild Night in El Reno* (1977).

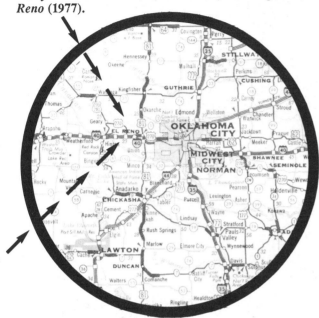

Describe where you are at the moment, the decor of the room, what activity you are engaged in: drinking? eating? smoking? How do you feel about this interview, talking to yourself into a tape recorder?

I'm here in Oklahoma, I'm at the Reno Motel here in Oklahoma — maybe don't mention the place ... I don't know WHY, but ah, maybe ... don't get anyone else trapped here.

I'm sittin' on the sofa, which they had re-upholstered in kind of a ... Virginia design, Virginia water-wheel? On a MILL. The kind of activity? I'm just sittin' — I thought of doing this because I'm gonna fall asleep. Not that it's late, it's just that for some reason I get hit with tiredness here in the middle of the day, and then in the middle of the night I wake up. My hours are all screwed up. Anyway, I wasn't drinking coffee, I was drinking "Postum," because I had already had two cups of coffee — that's enough for me, two cups of coffee today.

I feel okay about this interview ... talkin' to myself, I'm used to that, I talk into a video recorder all the time, so ... I'm constantly acting, in fact I'm here working on *Weather Diary 3*. I turned the air conditioner off in this room and put it on in the bedroom, it's a two-room "suite," let's call it, because it's kind of hot and humid out, and I don't want the buzz of the air conditioner, the ROAR of the air conditioner to interfere with the interview, so ...

Now, you started making films at about 12? Back in the 1950s? — with your brother Mike?

Now I did start making movies with my brother when I was — before I was a teenager. And people

seem to nowadays "admire" or "respect" or "envy" somebody that was a teenager in the Fifties.

Of course it was a usual time of pimples and gang wars, and ... other kids beatin' you up, and — I don't know, feelin' like you had to go out on dates and stuff like that, so it was a typical ... hell period. I wonder if kids got it better now? I don't know, I see the kids in San Francisco: they're kind of awful. But that's because they copy the adults that are out there. And the adults are terrible.

So, I started makin' pictures when I was ... ah, a preteen.

Where did you show these early films and what was the reaction?

Now when I used to show my pictures, I used to show them at friends' houses, at parties. You know, I'd go to a friend's house — they'd be the cast and then a week later we'd come back and they'd be developed, and we'd show 'em the rushes and then maybe a week after that I'd edit them, and come back and show 'em the thing and we'd shoot some more, and then we'd have a party and show the final finished film. I used to show them in Queens, and they were regular 8mm. But I used to work in CASSETTE at that time, they had 8mm cassettes, only they called 'em "magazines" (metallic magazines) in those days. They weren't plastic, they were made out of metal, and they fit into a DeJur camera, I had a DeJur 8mm, magazine load camera.

And, ah — then I used to show 'em at an old fuddy-duddy club, The 8mm Motion Picture Club. In New

Edith Fisher in *I Was a Teenage Rumpot.*
(co-made with Mike Kuchar). 1960. 8mm; 12 minutes; color.

Opposite page: A scene from *Reason to Live*

Still of George's graduation picture from *Eclipse of the Sun Virgin.*

York. It was run by fuddy-duddies; everybody got dressed up and they showed their vacation footage … and there'd be old ladies there and there'd be old men, and the ladies'd be sitting next to the men and their stomachs would be … acting up, and making noises. And the old ladies would get offended, and … you know, people would get offended at my movies because they were "irreverent" I guess. I was looking for … I don't know … SUBJECT MATTER, and I'd pick anything out of the newspaper, and at that time — I remember one time the Thalidomide scare came out where ladies were taking Thalidomide pills and giving birth to deformed babies and I made a comedy out of that, and that was the last time I was at the 8mm Motion Picture Club, and it was the only time they ever gave a bad review to a movie.

Where *are* these earliest films today? Like *The Naked and the Nude* ('57), and *Pussy on a Hot Tin Roof* ('61), etc.?

Now those early films are … I think they're in my mother's closet in the Bronx. The originals. I have copies in San Francisco, I made copies. Some of the copies are good, some of them are not so good. They just made an untimed print of all of them. Ah … the originals are still in my mother's closet, I think they're still holdin' up.

The SOUNDTRACKS, unfortunately, are falling apart. Although some are still there. But they're beginning to flake off the tape, the magnetic particles are flaking off the tape. So, I probably gotta get that fixed sometime.

What was your childhood like? You used to LIVE in the movie theaters, eh?

My childhood? It was … well I guess … torture, except I was a nature lover, since I was born in a city and lived in a city, New York, all my life, born in Manhattan and then moved to the Bronx at an early age so, I worshipped nature and storms … anything that came into the city and disrupted it, in a "nature way." I liked sunsets, and the colors of the sky, … a different series of weather events. And going to the park 'cause I did live near the Bronx Park, and the Bronx Botanical Gardens and they had waterfalls, and water running over rocks. And there were animals in cages — I didn't much visit them, that was sort of the boring part of the park … the WILD part was a turn on for me as a youth.

And … I was a tortured youth I think. Miserable a lot. And I took solitary walks. But I was "social" making movies. It was my one connection with other people. The fact that I was able to interact with them, and we were all doing things together. I had friends, but I wasn't that much of a party-goer.

I used to go to movies a lot. That's for sure. And I

FILMOGRAPHY

EARLY 8MM COLLABORATIONS BY GEORGE AND MIKE
★ ★ ★ ★ ★ ★

The Wet Destruction of the Atlantic Empire (1954)
Screwball (1957)
The Naked and the Nude (1957)
The Slasher (1958)
The Thief and the Stripper (1959)
A Tub named Desire (1960)
I was a teenage Rumpot (1960)
Pussy on a Hot Tin Roof (1961)
Born of the Wind (1961)
A Woman Distressed (1962)
A Town Called Tempest (1962)
Night of the Bomb (1962)
Lust for Ecstasy (1963)
The Confessions of Babette (1963)
Tootsies in Autumn (1963)
Anita Needs Me (1963)
The Lovers of Eternity (1963)
Mom (1983 – George alone)

16MM PRODUCTIONS BY GEORGE
★ ★ ★ ★ ★ ★ ★ ★

Corruption of the Damned (1965)
Hold Me While I'm Naked (1966)
Leisure (1966)
Mosholu Holiday (1966)
Color Me Shameless (1967)
Eclipse of the Sun Virgin (1967)
The Lady From Sands Point (1967)
Knocturne (1968)
Unstrap Me (1968)
House of the White People (1968)
Encyclopedia of the Blessed (1968)
The Mammal Palace (1969)
Pagan Rhapsody (1970)
Portrait of Ramona (1971)
The Sunshine Sisters (1972)
The Devil's Cleavage (1973)
Back to Nature (1976)
A Reason to Live (1976)
La Casa de Chorizo (1977)
Ky Kapers (1977)
Wild Night in El Reno (1977)
Forever and Always (1978)
Mongreloid (1978)
Blips (1979)
Aqueerius (1980)
The Nocturnal Immaculation (1980)
Yolando (1981)
Cattle Mutilations (1983)
Untitled Musical (1984)
The X-People (1984)
Ascension of the Demonoids (1985)

SAN FRANCISCO ART INSTITUTE PRODUCTIONS

Destination Damnation (1972)
Carnal Bipeds (1973)
I Married a Heathen (1974)
The Desperate and the Deep (1975)
I An Actress (1977)
The Asphalt Ribbon (1977)
One Night a Week (1978)
Prescrition *(sic)* in Blue (1978)
The Power of the Press (1979)
Remember Tomorrow (1979)
Symphony for a Sinner (1979)
How to Choose a Wife (1980)
The Woman and the Dress (1980)
Ochokpug (1980)
Boulevard Kishka (1981)
The Oneers (1982)
Ms. Hyde (1983)
Club Vatican (1984)
The Legend of Thelma White (1985)
Motel Capri (1986)
La Noche d'Amour (1986)
PRC Musical (1986)
Insanitorium (1987)
Summer of No Return (1988)
La Verbotene Voyage (1989)

FILMS AS PERFORMER
★ ★ ★ ★ ★ ★

Foster and Fester (1973, d. John Thomas)
The Hole (1974, d. Paul Marioni)
Thundercrack! (1975, d. Curt McDowell)
China Moon (1976, d. Barbara Linkevitch)
Nudes (1976, d. Curt McDowell)
Weiners and Buns Musical (1976, d. Curt McDowell)
The Wicked One (1979, d. David Michalak)
Undertow (1979, d. Virginia Girithan)
George Kuchar: The Comedy of the Underground (1982, d. David Hallinger, Gustavo Vazquez)
Web of Fire (1983, d. Mike Rudnick)
Screamplay (1984, d. Rufus Butler Seder)
Sparkle's Tavern (1984, d. Curt McDowell)
Palmer's Pick-Up (1984, d. Christopher Coppola)

George in leather in *Eclipse of the Sun Virgin*

loved going to the movies, my brother and I used to go spend hours, whole Saturday afternoons seeing pictures over and over again. We had our favorites. Got to know movie film scores and who the composers were. In fact I would go to the movies just because a particular composer was on. Bernard Herrmann was in his heyday. And Franz Waxman and Alex North and all of them were ... grindin' out stuff. My brother and I would sit through movie after movie, sit through the SAME movies, and *Written on the Wind* we used to go, I don't know — I've seen that eleven times when it came out ... and spent a lot of time in the movie theater and made games, used to crawl under the seats, and ... well, it was a house of activity — a house of activity.

Didn't you shoot most of those first movies on Bronx tenement rooftops?

I did shoot a lot of early movies in the Bronx on the rooftops because we needed bright light. We didn't have light at that time, in the beginning, you know — artificial light. We weren't into that yet so we needed the sun. And we needed black backgrounds so that you couldn't see that we had no sets. This way you could INVENT — see the black background and maybe invent in your mind an imaginary set. And that was a current trend at that time, on television they used to have the actors act with just a step ladder and a black backdrop. I guess it was avant garde at that time in TV of the Fifties. And so, I carried it over into film, but the pictures were — would begin bright but then get darker and darker as stratus clouds would move in. We were always making pictures when a warm front was approaching, and the clouds would thicken and thicken and so by the end of the 50-foot reel of film you couldn't see the finale, it was just too dark. The camera only opened up to ... F-2 maybe? Couldn't squeeze a 1.9. And so the pictures got murkier and murkier and darker at the end.

So what if you had grown up in Los Angeles or ... Orange County? Or Yugoslavia? Would the inspiration still have been there?

Well, I don't know about growin' up in L.A. I probably would've drove, be drivin' a car by now. Had a tan. I don't know ... I didn't get to L.A. until ... late '70s? Mid '70s? I don't know where my inspiration would've been.

In New York there's a lot of trashy novels on the bookstands, and my father was into reading trashy novels, at least novels that were exciting to me — the art work on the covers. That inspired a lot of imagery in my head. I loved the kind of sordidness of what it was like, evidently, to be grown up. It was a turn on for me, I'd get excited looking at those paperback covers. And also the comic books. I think they twisted me also. I remember I used to be real disturbed when the heros were captured and whipped and beaten and ... I don't know ... strange experiences that might have warped me.

You were reportedly first introduced to the New York underground when Bob Cowan suggested you bring your films down to Ken Jacobs' Ferry Street loft where it seems a lot of good shit was going on at the time. Do you remember vividly those days?

Now the early days, I was making 8mm pictures, and I did meet Bob Cowan, and I was making 8mm films with him. I met him through Donna Kerness, she was my big star, we went to high school together. I started putting her in movies — she had big bazooms. And she had a very nice face, and she could ACT — she had a style about her. And so I put her in movies, and all my Bronx buddies were all excited about her. She was a big sensation. I had regular Bronx buddies — they worked either in the Post Office or they were furniture polishers, or they were going into the Air Force, or, later became transit patrolmen on the subway. And, ah, they really got excited about her and thought her a great talent, so ... I MILKED her. I went over to her house, and we began to put her in bathtub scenes where she wore a bathing suit of course, the straps were pulled down. We simulated the tawdry stuff that I used to see on the screen. It was very nice, I met a lot of girls that way, she had girlfriends that were dancers — but I didn't particularly care for them, they were snooty, a lot of them. Except for Donna, she was kinda down-to-earth, and probably troubled also.

So, we got along well, but it was only via pictures. We got along in personal life, also, but personally we, ah ... well I never used to get involved with anybody personally making pictures, it was always "make the picture." And ah, well that later ... changed. But then ya have to, I don't know ... you get tired of doin' one thing all the time, you know.

Now Bob Cowan took me down to Ken Jacobs', and we went to the loft there, my brother and I, I remember we came in suits, and these were all the underground people. But we came in suits and we showed 8mm movies, and I guess I was kind of a bit square lookin', but the movies took off. Ken Jacobs liked them and played them the other week, and Jonas Mekas came and he wrote about them in the *Village Voice*. And then they began to be on the "circuit" — whenever they had an 8mm show, my brother and I, our work was on there, and it was shown to the public, and I got to meet a lot of the other underground filmmakers. Some are dead. A lot of them are dead now I guess. Ron Rice died early ... Warhol I met a few years later when I was doing 16mm. Dead. Who else? Gregory Markopoulos went to Europe ... oh I don't know, a bunch of people.

And I used to SEE movies, the Brakhage movies ... Kenneth Anger movies, *Scorpio Rising* when it first came out. That was kind of an exciting period. It seems like a past life. One foot in the lobby, one foot in the street. The street was full of people, they'd be in business suits and they'd be comin' in, and there'd be more ... bohemians inside ... it was kind of an interesting time in New York.

And I do remember them vividly. I wasn't always LIKED at that time, I know. Because I guess I appeared kind of SNOTTY sometimes to some people.

Donna Kerness and boyfriend in fabled shower scene of *Hold Me While I'm Naked*

I wasn't, I was just ... callously irreverent, maybe? But they were kind of snotty, too, some of the people.

It seemed like a great time to be alive and working with film, like the whole "underground" movement was taking malformed shape. John Waters always mentions *Hold Me While I'm Naked* **as an early influence on him when he was a no-good teenager coming up to New York City.**

Now it was kind of an exciting time, and there was — of course we had been making movies way before, 8mm, and our friends were paying attention to it. And now this underground movement, got to meet a lot of other people making films. And then we saw these 16mm movies and said, "Oh, wow, you can see so much more detail, you can put the sound on the film also" ... and 8mm didn't seem like too big of a deal. I had to get a new projector so I said maybe we're gonna rehaul and just get 16mm.

It was nice to be in New York at that time. Although New York ain't always that nice to be in. But when you're THERE, it'll probably eventually get WORSE, so, enjoy it now, then forget about it, leave it, you know.

Yeah, *Hold Me While I'm Naked* was my most popular film. I think it took about six months to a year to catch on, and then when it caught on it was played a lot. I had liked it myself very much. But, ah ... I never met John Waters in New York, you know. I met John Waters later, in San Francisco.

Is there anything similar going on today? Anything that can be called "underground" anymore?

Yeah, there's plenty of that going around. But you gotta be in the big bucks a little bit now, to afford that damn film. Of course you can make it in Super–8. There's tons of stuff goin' on. People workin' and makin' real, ah ... trash. Interesting trash, and making kind of elegant stuff. And then of course there are people making kind of "politically correct" stuff, and ... that kind of trash, too. So there's still a lot going on, a hell of a lot going on. In San Francisco a lot. And New York. New York you're supposed to kvetch a little more than San Francisco. New York is always kvetching, kvetching, kvetching! At least that's what the filmmakers there tell me.

Did any of these other early NYC filmmakers like Jack Smith or Warhol or Ron Rice influence you or was it mostly the stirring Hollywood epics?

Now I got influenced by everybody. And probably a lot of my work has scenes in it lifted from other things because, ah ... they just imprint on me, and then when it comes time, just cough it up. Sometimes I don't even know I'm doing it. Anything will influence me. Therefore ... I think it's fine. Just keep watching things and doing things and getting involved in things, it all influences you and you don't dry up. Cough it up, you cough it up in your work. Of course the Hollywood stuff influenced me a lot, but then also Warhol, JACK SMITH ... all of it.

You knew Jack Smith — he was in your 8mm film *The*

Lovers of Eternity. **What is he like and where is he today?**

I did know him a little bit when I was in New York, because I made a movie, my last 8mm movie at that time, with ah ... Dov Lederberg who lived next door to him. Dov Lederberg used to make 8mm pictures, and he used to take the 8mm film and put it in his oven and cook it. It looked like, ah, ... texture of an eggplant, when you projected it, you know the emulsion was all cracked. And he lived next door to Jack Smith. Of course Jack Smith at that time was like King of Underground pictures in New York. And you would think maybe because he was king he would act like "nobility," but he didn't — he was crazy as a coot which he probably still is now. I guess you can call him mercurial? And I don't really relate to him too much, goes up and down too fast, too high and too low probably. I always admired his work, though. And I put him in a picture, and he was fine in the picture. Gets outta control once in a while, which is fine — let him get outta control. You want to get away from him anyway, so let him get out of control so you got a chance to get away from him.

Jack Smith stands in bedecked glory in Ken Jacobs's
—— *Star Spangled to Death*. ——

You worked as a messenger for a greeting card company back then. What was that like? Did you lead a "normal existence" — whatever that is?

Now I did work for a greeting card [company] in New York, it was Norcross Greeting cards. And it was mainly run by women, although Mr. Norcross was the big deal — I never met him, though. But it was run by women. And they were ... amazons. Large, frightening, terrifying amazons, that walked the halls all made up and smelling of perfume. Madison Avenue type women, clacking down the halls. Frightening, terrifying figures. I don't know what was wrong with those women but ... I DO know what was wrong with those women, they had ulcers, some of them were eaten up alive ... they were like men with wigs on. Wigs and make-up. And in fact some of them looked like Glenn Strange as the Frankenstein monster, because, the faces were horrid. It was — severe amazons.

I worked at that job many, many years, and then I left that job — thank God — I can't remember how. And I was leading a normal existence, that you come home with a big cake, after work you come home with a big cake, you have a big meal and then you come home with a big cake, you eat it and you bloat, you get fat. Look like 40 when you're only 25. And that's ... the normal existence.

From the Bronx you ended up coming out to San Francisco where you now teach at film school.

From the Bronx I came out to San Francisco, because I met Larry Jordan, teaches film in San Francisco, I met him in Cincinnati. It was some kind of a festival, and I stayed an extra day and we flew kites together in Cincinnati, and he asked me if I'd ever like to come to the San Francisco Art Institute to teach for a summer. I said yeah, I went, and then, I guess ... I was a "visiting artist," or I was something. I came there and they hired me. I did a summer course maybe? I can't remember. But the students, and my very first student, Curt McDowell, circulated a petition to get me there. They said the school needed new outside blood, or someone from New York, so I got on the payroll, at the Art Institute.

Were there any scandals or infamous episodes or wild times in between, that the prurient voyeuristic scum that comprise our readership would be interested to know more about? Or any shameless dirty secrets, very personal, about ANYBODY ELSE that you can tell us?

Well at that time ... (thoughtful silence) ... I don't know, there was, of course. But the shameless dirt never comes out until, like, you're in your thirties. It's there, it's forming. But it's never that DIRTY I think when you're in your twenties, at least in my time. It was developing, a developing dirtiness that exploded, I guess, when I hit 33.

In the early 1970s (?) in San Francisco you became good friends and a collaborator with Curt McDowell, right?

Now Curt McDowell was my very first student. In fact he was sitting in the room when I came in, sitting on the desk I remember, it was ten to nine, and there he was, and he looked healthy ... he was swingin' his legs, sittin' on the desk ... and ... he ... (voice trails off) I don't know how much I should go into this. Well, he was a strange person. Strange in a way ... ah, maybe I ought to turn off the recorder. (laughs)

Didn't he shoot *Thundercrack*, the hilarious porno flick with people incessantly talking as they fuck? What about that movie?

Curt McDowell had at that time been going to the Art Institute, he was originally a painter and got interested in film via Bob Nelson, who turned him on to film. He saw some movies and then switched to the film department.

Curt McDowell's main calling in life, ... God gave

Curt McDowell during the shooting of *Thundercrack*.

him a calling in life, and that was to make pornography. Sex pictures. He was mainly interested in homo-erotic, and MEN, he loved buns, men's buns, and he loved that kind of stuff. That was his calling in life, and his early pictures he would do it in a round-about way and he'd also throw in women so it would be a more ... rounded picture. He was interested in heterosexual sex, watching it. He was interested in heterosexual men humpin' them.

He was a strange person. Sometimes he had very low self-esteem, but he used to ... get, I think, power by eating men. And, I guess it was a form of probably, sex magic. And he was a very loving and a very giving person. Like he was very, very giving. And I'll always remember him, the image that stays in my mind of Curt McDowell is him one time when we went to the North Country by the beach, and he was standing in a field of flowers with his pecker dangling out. He was shirtless and his pants were unbuttoned and his pecker was dangling out and he was smelling a flower. It wasn't a hippie type image, it was just, I don't know what you'd call it, it was just ... weird, but sweet. He did have a strange ... sharp edge to him at times. Probably a lot added to it ... drugs maybe. But, he was a very giving person. He gave a lot, let's just say that.

He did work on *Thundercrack*. That was funded by two other guys, John Thomas and Charley Thomas, they were the producers. They were rather handsome guys. Charley, I always remember him — he always sweated under the armpits, his armpit area was always wet. And he was very stocky and kind of muscular. And John had a bit more of an elegant face, although he had a little problem with his back — he was stooped over, and then he went for rolfing and they straightened him up.

But they were rather handsome guys, contemporaries to Curt, they were students and I was their teacher.

And, I think their dad used to own Burger King, or something like that, then he sold it. So they had a lot of money and they were dabbling in the arts. It was sculpture and painting, and then they were doing filmmaking — they had money and they bought a lot of equipment.

I guess Curt asked me to write a screenplay of *Thundercrack*. I labelled it *Thundercrack*. He wanted me to do a sex picture — all kinds of mixed sex in it. And, I wrote it, and he wanted to make it because he made a lot of money on another film called *Lunch*, that he starred his friend in, Mark Ellinger, who later did the soundtrack for *Thundercrack*.

I remember I just saw one shot of *Lunch*, and it was Ellinger ejaculating, and he squirted clear across the room … almost practically missing the head of the girl who was lying down whose name was Wendy. Wendy was kind of a chunky girl, built like a "brick shithouse" or maybe built like a refrigerator. She was a student also. Those students used to make sex pictures, because in those days it was fashionable to show your chakra.

So, those were the Seventies. Anyway, Curt asked me to make this movie, and he was sure we would make money because *Lunch* was making money.

And I had a feeling, no … usually whatever I work in doesn't make money, would be a disaster. Sure enough, the picture never made any money. I think the audience was repelled by it, the porno audience. Ah, they didn't want to see black-and-white I hear, and they don't like talking, and they go to see specific sex acts. I think if you mix 'em up too much they get turned off. It offends them. I don't know if that's still true today.

But the picture got very good reviews in the magazine *Sight and Sound*. John Russell Taylor, I remember he had a whole thing, he wrote about John Waters, he wrote about the TRASH movies. And he called that one a genuinely erotic and genuinely frightening picture. That was a very nice review.

The picture was later cut by the producers — it played at Filmex, Buck Henry liked it a lot. The other judges wanted to turn the thing off after 15 or 20 minutes. But Buck Henry said, "If you turn this picture off I'm leaving the film festival, I won't judge." So they sat through the whole thing and it got on. Thanks to Buck Henry that picture was — we had a big L.A. premiere in Century City. Very nice. I look at it as my big Hollywood premiere where we arrive in, like, a limousine, and there's search beam lights outside. So, I did that already, I

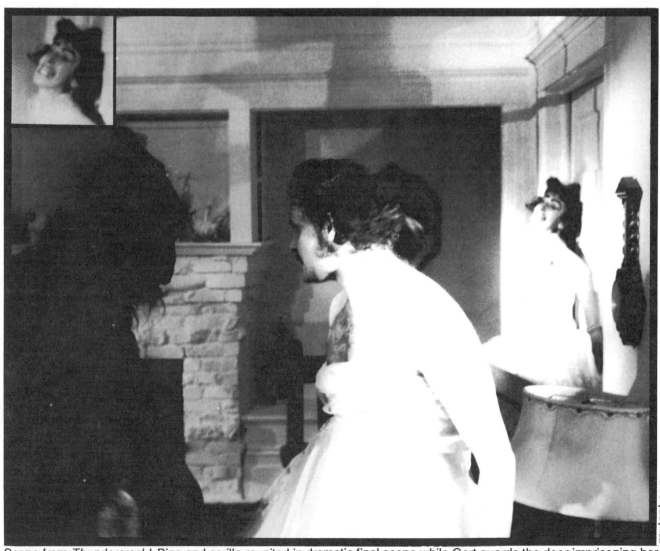

mutant son.

Scene from *Thundercrack!* Bing and gorilla reunited in dramatic final scene while Gert guards the door imprisoning her

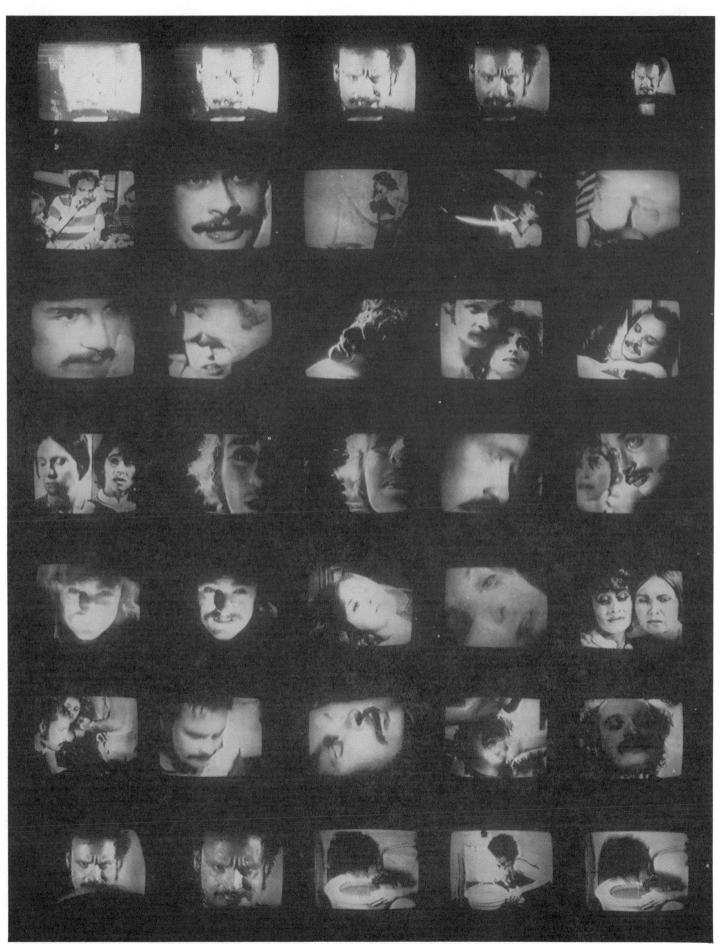

Thundercrack!

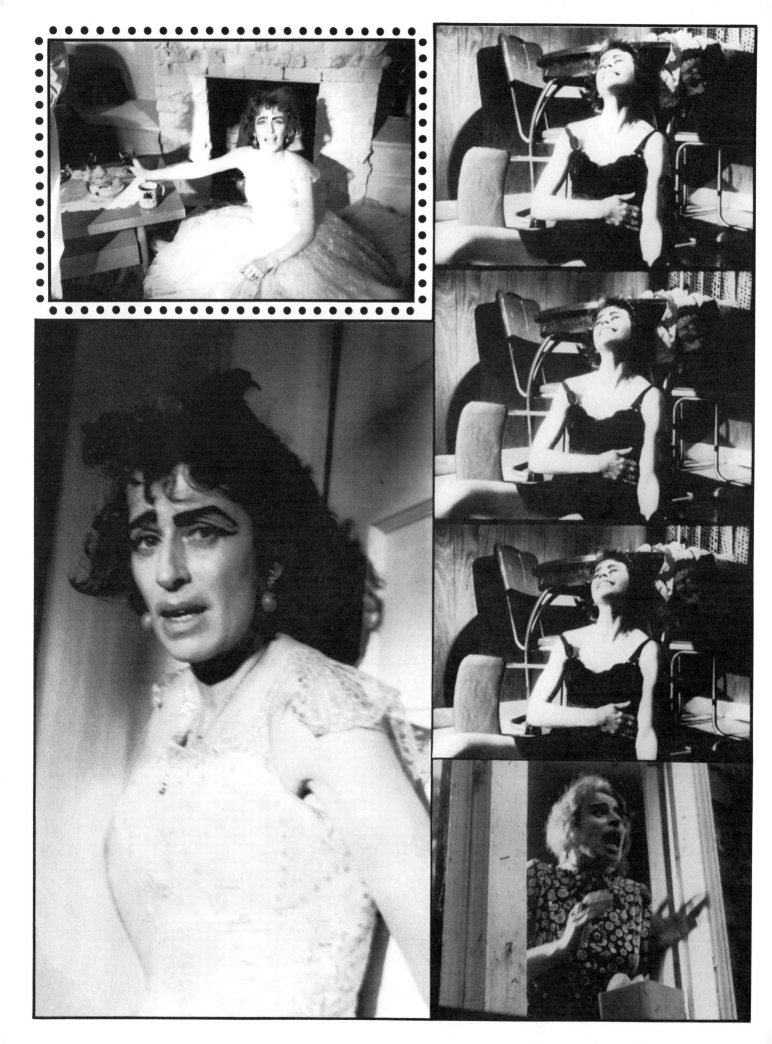

Opposite page, top left: Marion Eaton relaxes between takes on the set of *Thundercrack!* — Lower left: Beyond Baby Jane, beyond Blanche Dubois ... Marion radiates melodramatic alcoholic dementia with hairstyle and make-up by George Kuchar. — Upper right: "Is that YOU knockin' at my door, Mister Maple Tree?" ... Gert Thomas, lonely (and drunk) (and crazy) widow of Prairie Blossom hears a human voice at her door. — Bottom right: Flashback, Gert watches in horror as husband Charley staggers in from the field covered by devouring locusts. Charley is reduced to bloody gristle that Gert pickles in large jars and saves.

Top left this page: Bing, prodded by voyeuristic companions, recalls a dark past. — Top right: Bing and Gert against the world in *Thundercrack!* — Bottom right: Flashback, George as Bing, carnival gorilla keeper in Matinee idol pose ⟶

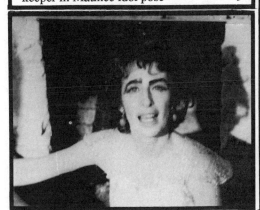

Billy Paradise as the gorilla trainer *Mrs. Harlan.*

Thundercrack

Directed by Curt McDowell. Script by George Kuchar. With Marion Eaton.

"THUNDERCRACK starts out in OLD DARK HOUSE style with a dark and stormy night, an assorted group of strangers stranded in a remote Victorian mansion, and a crazed hostess with her husband pickled in a jar and her monstrous son locked in the spare room. From there on it is a series of test situations which manage to get everyone together, sexually and socially, with everyone else before dawn brings everything to a rousing conclusion."—J.R. Taylor, *Sight & Sound*

Ken Scudder and rubber sex doll in *Thundercrack!*

THUNDERCRACK Curt McDowell (U.S.A 1975) (116 mins) with Marion Eaton, George Kuchar, Melinda McDowell, Rick Johnson

The plot is gloriously camp. Employing the B-film format of people seeking refuge in a haunted house on a stormy evening in the middle of nowhere, THUNDERCRACK opens with a credits sequence reminiscent of those creepy black-and-white Paramount pictures of the Forties. Into a dilapidated mansion occupied by balmy widow in a black slip who keeps her deceased husband pickled in half-a-dozen giant jars on the kitchen table and her 'diseased' son (a victim of gargantuan sex organs) locked in another room, enter an assorted group of strangers: four men, three women and a love-crazed gorilla

In the course of the film's 116 minutes we are witness to a succession of episodes involving interspecies communication — a homosexual tryst between a circus gorilla and his trainer: voyeurism — the widow masturbates with a huge ripe cucumber whilst peering through hidden wall holes as her guests enjoy such sex props as inflatable rubber dolls with arses greased, giant vibrators and dildos, jack-off suction tubes. French ticklers, etc: and sexual (gay and non gay) couplings — in bed, propped up against a refrigerator, inside an overflowing bathtub, etc. And it all ends, convincingly — given the 'crazy' logic we've been successfully seduced into accepting, in an orgy of sexual liberation.

Directed by Curt McDowell and scripted by underground moviemaker George Kuchar (whose previous works include A TOWN CALLED TEMPEST, HOLD ME WHILE I'M NAKED and ECLIPSE OF THE SUN VIRGIN), THUNDERCRACK is the funniest film I've seen in years (I literally fell from my seat at one point). It's Trash film of such raw imaginative power and originality that it deserves a much, much wider viewing than it's likely to get. That's because THUNDERCRACK is also the hardest of hardcore pictures — the most sexually explicit movie I've ever viewed in Britain: solo, lesbian, heterosexual and mixed male couplings are viewed with a camera that remorselessly catches every drop of semen, throbbing organ and stiffening nipple.

This is, in short, a steamy spoof filmed with a sure and witty grasp of genre conventions whose prevailing mood is one of buoyancy and exhiliration. But it's also strenuously subversive in its eroticism. THUNDERCRACK is, simply, pro-sex — of all sorts: Try it, you'll like it — that's its theme.
Jack Babuscio

N.B. The above review contains a graphic description of THUNDERCRACK. Please read it carefully, and decide beforehand whether or not you may find it offensive. It is certainly not recommended to those with tender sensibilities.

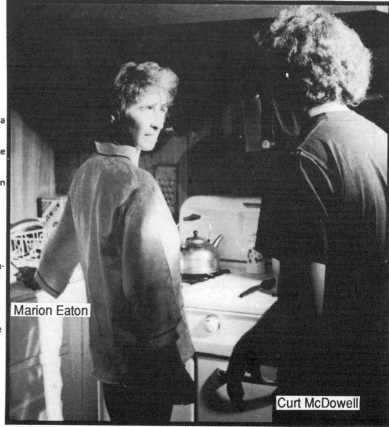

Marion Eaton

Curt McDowell

don't feel I missed out on anything. Thanks to Curt, the Thomas brothers and Buck Henry.

Curt found the picture at the end was too sour or something. Or maybe ... one of the gay actors wound up with a girl? A gay guy — I don't know what it was. I guess it was like a "bitter-sweet" or sad ending, and he was more into sex as a jubilation or something. But, ah, I felt ... the thing was tragic. And I guess my view was sex as HORROR in people's lives. OBSESSIONS they have, fetishes, urges that they don't know where the hell they got these but they can't understand it and many times they can't control it, so it becomes a horror in your life. So that was my outlook on the thing, my outlook on sex. Of course as I look back on the film now I realize I was in serious trouble, probably. There was something WRONG somewhere, but, ah ... I don't know, you just forge ahead.

What was Curt like? Describe some of his other films — I know nothing about him.

Curt had ... appetite. Insatiable appetites. Some of them I guess were spurred on by various substances. And others ... your libido sometimes goes crazy in this (California) area of the country — know what I mean? He was originally from Indiana, that was a turn on for him because of all the guys smoking with their rolled-up shirt sleeves and stuff. Well, he was hungry. And he also did very good artwork, he was an excellent artist, a wonderful painter. And had a wonderful sense of Smut cinema, I guess.

Actually he loved ZOOMING, his movies always had a lot of zoom shots and they were kind of over-exposed and he loved raw looking stuff because he was turned on by pornography, and he incorporated all pornographic movie techniques into his pictures. That was his calling in life.

He had a sister, Melinda. And Melinda finally wound up on the West Coast. And, well he used to use her as bait to attract the men. She was a very voluptuous girl. And they'd be shooting footage of

Melinda McDowell, sister of Curt and star of *Thundercrack*, poses in front of scenery painted by George Kuchar.

her with Arabian ... grocery clerks, you know, three of them, they're all humping away, and Melinda's there, the object of their ... affection I guess, and they'd be squirtin' all over her. So, Melinda had her San Francisco experience. She's still there, she's a mother now. She married kind of a nice looking guy — at least he was nice looking when I saw him which was maybe 10 years ago. But I think he has troubles. He's a Vietnam Vet and he flies off the handle now and then. But she's got two or three kids now. Lives across the Bay.

George during the shooting of *Thundercrack!* "I realize I was in serious trouble, probably."

● ● ● ●

George, you've always had a deep love of tornadoes. In *A Town Called Tempest* (1961) there's a great special effect of a tornado destroying a town, while the more recent *Weather Diary* (video) seems centered on tornado lust and longing.

Yeah, I did like storms, and TWISTERS, tornadoes. I don't know why. I think in the Fifties a big one had gone through Worcester, Massachusetts. And I guess there was talk about it in New York, and it was in the news, and for some reason it excited me. The great storm smashing up towns, and blowing into people's lives, and changing it. Not so much that I was interested in the carnage, but the fact of ... whirling clouds and big winds and stuff like that.

It was weather on the rampage, it was nature unleashed, nature loosed. It was dramatic. From all descriptions the sky is a weird color, the clouds are BOILING, and etc., etc. It struck my fancy. And I think most people that are interested in meteorology are fascinated by that particular character in meteorology, the tornado.

When you first met John Waters, didn't you get together and talk about tornadoes?

Yeah, John Waters came over to the house and I showed him my tornado books — I collect literature on tornados. Any visual material I can get. We discussed this. He's got some of the books.

You shoot a lot into TV sets. Plus you seem to like to spy on, watch, observe people ... sometimes from behind the curtains. This sometimes gives your work a voyeuristic feel. In previous interviews both Rosa and John have said they possess voyeuristic inclinations (me too!) Society in general seems to treat this tendency as some evil or perversion or character flaw. What do you think about one of the most important issues of our day — voyeurism?!!

Voyeurism? Well ... you know I was a voyeur way back because nobody used to look at me, so I'd be looking at everybody, you know, look at people, and, nobody would really pay any attention to me so it was like being invisible. So I'm very comfortable with voyeurism.

I used to go to motels and put the drinking glass against the wall and put my ear to it and listen and hope there was some action in the next room. And sometimes there was, and it was sweet to listen to a couple exchanging talk, and how they got around to the intimacies. It was something very interesting, something very — touching — I thought. It was also something very exciting.

My father, who was a truck driver, used to belong to a little film exchange group, he used to bring home the "red reels", red plastic reels of 8mm pornography. And I remember — I think it was via my father I got interested in pornography 'cause he had some pornographic books stuck away in his drawer, and when I was a little kid I used to find them, and look, and was amazed and would laugh ... these adults, the world of the adults.

And then later when I was older, in my twenties, and he would bring in those movies — 'cause I had an 8mm projector, and he would want to borrow it, and I said I'd like to see the movies, so he would leave them with me after he was finished lookin' at 'em. I would get a chance to see pictures. But I was very much repressed, ah, very much ... secretive, and ... probably ... well, I was hungry also.

It's getting dark here, I think I may stop this and start tomorrow. But, ah, last word on voyeurism — I guess 'cause I was invisible anyway, nobody bothered lookin' at me — I was not that attractive, I was ... kind of quiet, bland dressing, hair stood up ... in fact I looked like that character in *Eraserhead* only a skinny version with a skinny neck. Ah, but my hair was the same — it stood straight up, the type of hair the wind blows and it just sticks up, like a toilet brush. And that's why I like so much the David Lynch movies, because *Eraserhead* was like my New York living experience, and the new one, *Blue Velvet* is exactly like my California experience. That's it in a nutshell.

(Next day)

Alright Jack, it's a new day, and I'll start answering from page 3, question 20, **"Do you like your job today?"**

HENRY [ERASERHEAD]

I do like my job today, in fact ... I don't really like saying I like it because sometimes I feel if I say I like it I'm not really doing that good of a job, 'cause I think there has to be a certain kind of TENSION, teaching.

But I am pretty lucky, because, I thought about it last semester — which ended a few weeks ago — because we're working on this movie *Summer of No Return*, it's a "teenage picture." The male lead was extremely beautiful and so was the female lead, they were like real movie star material. I found myself on a makeshift bed with most of the cast, and I looked around at them in various stages of undress — they were in various stages of undress 'cause we were doing a sleaze scene, the students wanted to do a sleaze scene. And so I said "fine, let's have a "sleaze director" 'cause I don't want to be blamed for these sleaze scenes. And a girl said she would do it, but then she told me when it came time that day that she was tired, she didn't get much sleep, she'd been taking too many drugs, so she was going up to the library to rest. So I said fine, so of course I was the sleaze director, and ... I found myself on the bed lookin' at these beautiful skinned people. Life had not smashed them, they were like wonderful things of beauty ... great, ah ... living things of beauty. And really ... I guess arousing, but when I'm with the Bolex, you can get aroused now and then but not that much, you know what I mean? — it's the picture, you think of the picture. And suddenly I real-

L to R: George, Hrayr Eulmessekian, Christopher Anderson and Haluk Kecelioglu in biker cap and fake tits

L to R: George, Cliff Hengst and "Doctor" Hannu Van Hanen

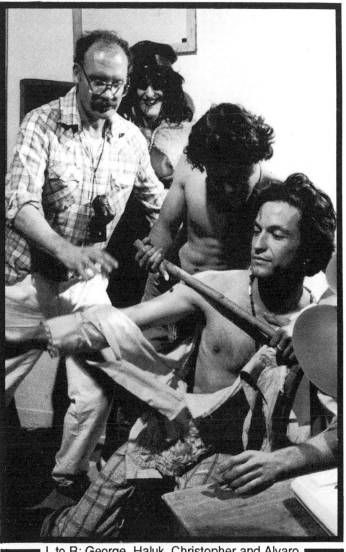

ized how lucky I was, that this was like a dream come true: I was in California surrounded by semi-nude beautiful people. The male lead was extremely beautiful and he was layin' right there in front of me, and they were tellin' him to pull his underpants down more, and I ... thought this IS a dream come true.

So, the job is pretty good.

(Tape runs out.)

Okay, here we go, Side Two. I was talking about this personality split the character was supposed to have in *Summer of No Return* ... straddling the fence — one side of the fence was the seedy side, the other side was yuppie heaven I guess. And the character was walking on this fence. Falling over onto the seedy side, then managing to scramble back to save his girlfriend who was ... hurt in a fire. She had her

L to R: George, Haluk, Christopher and Alvaro

SUMMER OF

Top right photograph, L to R: George, Beth Friedman and Christopher Anderson. Left photo, L to R: George, Christopher and Alvaro Múnoz. Lower photo, L to R: Alvaro, George and Francis Kohler.

NO RETURN

All "SUMMER OF NO RETURN" photos taken by David Hallinger.

face scarred. You see we had to get rid of her because she didn't trust me, the actress — she's a very nice girl but she thought I made dirty movies. And she thought I was trying to show her underpants. And I said, "I'm not interested in your underpants, I'm really not, if you don't believe me, take 'em off — I don't care." So, she thought I was tryin' to get too much ... FLESH from her. Whereas the male lead, he was pretty much all for it. He knew I had an eye for ... this type of beauty. I knew that we were creating a sex symbol, a new sex symbol was being created. He was to be a new one and she was to be one. But she balked at it and he didn't and that was fine with me, we just had to put her out of commission, because, ah, I didn't know quite how to work with her anymore if she didn't TRUST me that much, so we had the character burned in a fire and put in a hospital, and THAT advanced the plot because we now knew that her beautiful young suitor was to try to be a plastic surgeon, fix her face up. And he had to get the money so he delved into the UNDERWORLD ... became a hustler, was addicted to drugs, then had to clean up his act, all to make money and to clean up his act to fix her face. So, thanks to her the plot advanced considerably.

What's your advice for a kid who wants to make movies? Go to film school or do it on your own like you and John Waters did?

All I can say is, this is a kind of strange transition time. If you have money, go ahead. Best of luck, make your movies, and ... have a nice time. But if you don't have much money I'm afraid you may want to pursue another medium. There's many things out today, and many things in plastic that are lightweight — I'm talking video cameras, Camcorders. I bought a Sony 8mm video Camcorder three years ago, because I was having difficulty financing pictures. It's outrageous now, the cost. It was always kind of high but you were able to do it. Now I'm afraid it's ... they've discontinued stock like crazy, and the cost is preposterous. So ... I hate sounding negative, but — if you've got money go right ahead, 'cause it's great to get your dreams and fantasies on the screen.

(Sometime later)

Now of course I'm talking in terms of 16mm movie making. You can work in 8mm, and I'm sure you can still finance THOSE things. But every time I go to a Super-8mm festival at the school it's like demolition derby. They put it on the projector, the projector's rippin' 'em up, the splices aren't working, the SOUND goes out, and it's truly disaster time. The projectors all seem like meatgrinders. And there is great hurt to the filmmaker. They see their work butchered while the public views it. Butchered on stage.

So I'm sure if you have nice equipment, go ahead and do it. But ... I think what's happening now, electronically, pay attention because it may save us ... and I'm talking about ... how can I phrase this? I don't want to sound negative, but negative does enter into the picture because you've got to shoot negative nowadays. They don't want you shooting reversal film anymore. You have to shoot negative stock. And that'll cost you I estimate $40 every 2 1/2 minutes. That includes buying the negative, getting the work print and stuff. Forty dollars for ... 100 feet. And what's that? 2 1/2 minutes? You'll throw away two thirds. So, with this already you might as well be in the big time, and thinkin' about Dolby sound, and — maybe you better look for a job in commercial movies. Because they're doing very good work in the commercial movies and they got all the big technological advances.

I guess what I'm getting down to saying, this is a transition period. Please be careful. And please look around at the electronic media, what's happening in the electronic media. They're doing a hell of a lot. Sorry to sound this way, but don't get into trouble. You'e got to get into something that's not gonna be a 40 lb. monkey on your back, it's GARGANTUAN, whatever's gonna be on your back. So, lighten the burden, see what's around.

Are you "famous" today? Recognized?

I'm not famous. Well, visually once in a while somebody spots me who's seen my movies. Usually they spot me in some place I don't want to be spotted, like in the dirty bookstore. Although that doesn't happen too much, it used to happen in some seedy houses I used to frequent. That was always a bit strange. You didn't know if you should twist your personality back to your, what you were supposed to be instead of what you are now.

But ... I have a REPUTATION, 'cause I've been at this long enough, like 30 years or something, grinding out stuff, so ... I guess I have a reputation in certain circles, like movie circles, which would be the festivals ... in Athens, Ohio, and places like that. And perhaps also in other "spheres" that widen out, sometimes in Los Angeles. But I can still walk the streets unobserved and no one pays attention, nobody really cares, either.

My friend, Virginia, went down to L.A. She said, "In the underground film world it's what you MADE that makes you important, what you made in the past, and in the commercial film world you're only as good as your last picture." See, she had gone to the Art Institute and now she went down to L.A. and she's hardcore junior executive with Bud Yorkin Productions. And she said that, and I think there's wisdom in those words ... I think. (She's now laid off from her job, though.)

Do you think TECHNICALLY video will ever replace film? Will "high-definition" video soon be perfected and shown in theaters, making celluloid obsolete?

I don't know. I LIKE film, I like big pictures, I like going and I like seein' big pictures, and I like Dolby sound. I like going to the movies. But I'm not a real ... in other words I don't BATTLE for motion pictures anymore. I see no reason to put up a boundary, 'cause I like going to the movies and I like watching television.

Sometimes what disturbs me is I've found that a lot of people in the filmmaking community were very provincial and bigoted and narrow-minded, and this was in the supposedly avant garde. And I can understand if you go to school and you were trained in motion pictures, or trained that this is an art form. But if the thing gets so damn expensive that you can't afford it, and you're paying big companies like Kodak tons of money, and you're paying other places tons of money in order to rent machinery so you can edit your sync-sound pictures — when you eventually did try to get sync-sound equipment. And then you go to labs where you're paying high cost to make color prints of movies that have no color in them because you couldn't afford the stock and therefore you had to scrounge around and get outdated film stock, and yet you're paying high prices to get a color print ... I think it's like, come on, you should be fed up already. And if this is what's happened with movie making, the hell with it.

There's a lot of things out there in the world. I also like watching television. I was raised on television, and ... I enjoy painting and I enjoy writing. I'm not gonna get stuck in one thing and then go down with the ship when the ship appears to be sinking. Or maybe it should be sunk already. Maybe, let it go down, you know. Certainly, putting I didn't know how much money into movies, and trying to make talking pictures also, and you get soundtracks nowadays with reversal prints that you can't hear anything — you made a talkie that's completely unintelligible. After a while you can get completely fed up.

So there's a lot being done. See, in 16mm there's no technical innovations being done anymore. In other words stock is being cut, you can't get the kind of stock you used to get. The technology is all going into video and they're getting some amazing things. Pictures, in the big commercial pictures, they're doing wonderful things with technology. You know, they got the Dolby sound, THX sound, they're also thinking of changing the shutter speed, make everything more realistic, and stuff, so there's advances in that, but you need a lot of money for that. I'm afraid if you want to be — I'll use the word "personal," or an ARTIST, so called, an artist using a medium, if it gets where you can't afford it, I see no sense in going with it. Sorry to say that.

Of course you can work in Super-8 and 8mm, and I worked in 8mm and I had a really good time doing it, and also in Super-8. But I also wanted to make pictures with sound. And, things on the market today, where you can get sound and pictures together, electronically, and you can edit in the camera ... you can undermine this whole system that's been built up on money, because movies mean money. You hear the magic word "movies," it's money, and costs are escalated. Movies mean you pay a lot of money, you know what I mean?

Movies are also big things on a big screen and you get a big reputation at a big festival, and — bigger than life. So, I don't mind shrinking it, pulling the plug and shrinking it down, boob-tube size. Maybe it got a little too big for its own good.

What do you find are the AESTHETIC differences between film and video?

They are different, of course. One is smaller and the light is coming from the back, unless you have like in a movie, "rear screen," you don't get that kind of effect. Also it is small, and it's a DESPISED medium, video, 'cause it's related to the TV which is a despised medium.

I got attracted to video because it WAS a despised medium, and because film got to be too puffed up financially for me. So, I thought it might be interesting to try something new in a different medium — maybe it would change my approach and subject matter. Because in film I worked in a certain kind of language and it was kind of a short-hand. Film, I tried to squeeze the essence out of each scene because each scene was expensive. I don't really know if that was on my mind while I was making it, but I did know I had a certain language in film. And that was like, do away with extraneous scenes like coming and going out of doors and telling people where you were and who these people were. Just have them go around doing their business, and their business, while you're photographing, should be very high key, at that moment. Emotional peaks. So that became my movie style. And in video, I look at the medium or the tape as not something small and cheap — although that's what it is, it's really cheap stock — but it creates pictures and it's just as valuable to me as a roll of film, it's just in 8mm, it's smaller. Therefore, there's nothing that's that expendable.

See, when you make movies you throw it away. You take strips of film and when you're editing you're eventually sitting on a pile of film, it's all your rotten scenes are at your feet and you're steppin' all over them and you're keepin' just the cream of the crop, which may be out of 100 feet is maybe ... 20 feet? You're lucky if it's 25. Sometimes you get three sequences out of a 100-foot roll — maybe it'll go from the floor to the ceiling, and meanwhile you're sitting on a mountain of film, you threw it in the garbage.

So the material itself never really mattered to me. It was eventually just put on a projector — you didn't look at the material — and thrown onto a screen and you saw that. And the tape to me is the same way. I look at it as — you know, it's STOCK, and, ah, you slip it into your cassette player and it gets thrown onto a screen, and the screen's a hell of a lot smaller, but, it's fine with me.

(Later)

I will always enjoy going to the movies and I love going to the movies. And I enjoy making movies ... I don't know if you can use the word "enjoy." There are many stages to go through, and there is great enjoyment, and great work. Like, I love the work. But ... you see, I made a lot of movies and I don't really know how I made them. I don't know how I put all that effort into making them. And I've been sidetracked so often, I've been hit with such terrible vices ... that I don't know how I managed to pull off the pictures. But, for some reason, maybe in order to overcome my vices, or, maybe that movie-making WAS a vice on my part, I was able to turn out these things and go through all the steps that you have to go through making a movie. And I would wind up in the editing room and say, "I've been here before," and these were like great markers of my life, this was the "editing room." And it was like, "my life either had significance?" or it was like, "I'm alive again and I'm here in the editing room and this is the final stage."

And then you go into the lab, you bring it in, you get your movie and there's the premier and people look at it and ... of course it's like, how did this horror ever get made?

So ... making movies is a very peculiar thing. But if I have difficulty ... am paying $600 or $700 for a 20 minute movie, you know, that gets shown on a screen and gets pooh-poohed because it's either not "politically correct" or, for some other reason. And I could make something that's even more offensive for $6 or $8, and that's so offensive it would even offend the filmmakers — because I'm workin' in VIDEO. I would option for the more offensive medium.

Makin' movies, see, sometimes you see a very beautiful person. And the first thing that comes to my mind is I want to make a MOVIE of that person. I don't say, "I want to make a VIDEO of that person." I WOULD say that if my camera broke, my Bolex, or if I didn't have access to any film. But in the classroom, when I see a beautiful person, I want to make a FILM about that person. 'Cause I like putting gauzes ... ah, cheap — it's a black cloth on the lens with a rubber band, and creating these, what look like 1940s movies, or movies of a beautiful Hollywood style, and blowing these people up bigger than life and making them into gods and goddesses. And I think in the movies that's a wonderful way of pushing them on the public, and infusing the public with great objects of desire, and DREAMS, and things of great beauty ... living human beings of beauty.

So, unfortunately in a lot of underground pictures and, art film schools, if you have people in your movies, you're considered ... not very avant garde. They're very "anti-human." They're more like ... conservationists, probably. Hate the rotten people that pepper the landscape in the park, make all that filth amongst the trees and nature, you know the bears walk around and they're okay, but people stink.

So, in a way, I say if I really want to really create a star I want to do it via movies. But video's fine too, in creating a, ah, god or goddess. For the masses!

You say you've fallen from favor, or "fallen from grace" with the film people since your recent conversion to video? What sort of flack have you caught in this newly erupting holy war?

Well I know when I started making video, I did in a way disappoint, or ANGER some people, or they thought I was making CRAP. Of course I was beginning making video so I was just trying to develop my style, get a feel for it, and learn how to edit

George in motel room.

VIDEO-OGRAPHY

"Me and Babeth Van Loo, my European agent at that time, being interviewed at the Rotterdam Film Festival."

in the camera, and do everything in the camera. And very few people encouraged me. But there were those people who did encourage me, after seeing some work, and told me to please go on. Which I would have ANYWAY, but, ah, very few people did encourage me. Very few FILMMAKERS encouraged me.

Would you ever want to shoot a big-budget 35mm feature movie? What does it strike into your heart, the idea?

What it strikes in my heart? Well ... I don't have very good working habits. When I'm working on a movie, I sometimes only work ... 4 hours a week? I'm not really very good at MEETINGS. I don't like getting together with a bunch of people and we discuss the project.

I do that at school 'cause we got sometimes 28 people in the room, that's our cast and crew. And I explain the project and we get feedback, and I like doin' that, but that of course only lasts about 15 minutes, and then we get right down to working and see how we can bring this, ah ... subject, or theme on the screen. Or bring these performers that we think are nice looking onto the screen.

And then of course the movie develops its own style, when you see what you have and you see the limitations, and you work with the limitations, the style begins to develop. So sometimes meetings mean absolutely nothing to me because when you actually get right down to doin' the damn thing it's a totally different story. So we have a fast meeting and a general idea, and we think we want the picture to look a certain way. And so we do it, but then of course it can detour into other areas.

So, I'm afraid of working on a big picture, I really wouldn't want anyone to sink their money into a project of mine and then LOSE the money, so, my working habits are not that good for the big-time, 35mm production.

Do you ever get homesick for Queens (sic).

Now, getting homesick for the Bronx, I may get sick for the Bronx, like a certain area of it, in other words the LAND, maybe the rolling landscape which is wooded. There are sections like that in the Bronx. Or the look of the clouds, and that certain kind of feel to the air, and that shade of color that would be "Bronx sky." Ah, that would perhaps make me a little homesick.

As for anything else, no, it's all changing, you know what I mean? I don't have that many friends there in the Bronx anymore. I have my mom and when I go there I revert back to my old self, I lay around and say, "What's to eat, Mom?"

And ... I get back my old self and it makes me stronger for a while. But then of course I've always gotta leave home, and I go ... into the world that I have to DEAL with 3,000 miles away. In California. And that sort of changes me a bit.

Are you still in touch with any of your early stars? Where today is the ravishing Donna Kerness?

I am still in touch with my old movie stars, like Donna Kerness — she's in Texas. San Antonio, Texas. She had married the guy who she was in the shower with in *Hold Me While I'm Naked*. They had a very tempestuous marriage, with three children, I think. Or two. And, I think when he eventually threw an open container of lye at her, I think that was the end of the marriage. And divorce came, and then she got a job in a ... discotheque or cocktail lounge, where she wore scanty clothes and did belly-dancing, for jocks. Texas jocks.

Then she was KIDNAPPED, I hear, or there was an attempted kidnap, and she was in the papers and stuff — I don't really know the details of the story. But, she got away from that, and now she's settled down. She married a kind of heavy-set man who looks very comfortable and nice, and they're living in San Antonio, Texas. I write her now and then, and get letters from her also.

How do you get along with Mike (Kuchar) today? Where is Mike?

Now I get along with my brother Mike very well. We have our ups and downs, and once in a while it's turbulent, most of it is my fault because my brother is much more even-tempered. I mean he's got his ups and downs, but I'm more ... jagged-edged sometimes. He's smoother. And much more leisurely. We get along fine though.

You made a movie in 1986 called *Ascension of the Demonoids*.

Yes ... that was my only — no, I was funded one other time — but that was my big N.E.A. funded picture. I got $20,000 to make that picture, which is hard to believe. $20,000 is an awful lot of money. I got it in two $10,000 installments. And I finally opened — I had a bank account, finally. That was able to last.

So I put the money in the bank, and then I took it out to buy the film stock, to buy all the props. I went to Woolworths, and I went to boutiques and head-shops and bought all these little items 'cause I wanted this to be a spectacle. I wanted to make miniatures, and also have space ships in it, Big Foot, etc. So, I wanted to do all the special effects by myself, I didn't want to have a crew. So I did them in my ... bedroom. With these little dolls and miniatures, and attachments for the lens, to make sparkle effects, etc.

I like that movie because I said with $20,000 I want to have a nice time. With my last picture, before that, *The X-People*, I enjoyed making that also, but I couldn't really get a fine print of it. I spent $700 to get an awful print out. You couldn't hear the sound, it was like there was a waterfall in the background, there was this horrible roaring hiss. And, the colors looked like they put the strip of film onto a mimeograph machine, and just gave it one print and sent it out. It was an atrocious thing and yet it cost $700.

So a filmmaker friend of mine complained to the lab, he saw how distressed I was when I viewed it on his projector. And the lab brought me down, fixed me up. They said, "Of course you know we can't do reversal film anymore, as you know we can't get good prints." And they re-did the whole thing for me in an inter-negative without charging me the money. Very nice of the lab. Thank you, lab.

So after going through that, suffering that, then suddenly getting all this money I said, "Wow, I don't have to worry, I got money now. I won't shoot a negative now because I don't wear gloves when I handle film." I like to actually handle the actual film stock with my fingers. Get a lot of myself onto the film.

So I work in reversal, and then with this thing I was able to make an inter-neg from it and not even worry, then make beautiful prints from that, where the colors come out STRONG. I was able to do that since I had the money. And also I said, "I'm gonna have fun on this picture" — I do have fun on the other pictures also — but this one especially, I'm gonna make it like a big unusual treat. Tons of color. And superimpositions, because I had been working in video already and I couldn't do superimpositions in video — you press the button, you get the image and the sound exactly there, which was ... fascinating to me.

But this, now, I said, "Wow! With film I can run it through the camera three or four times, so I'm gonna make this my big superimposed movie." So, I turned that into the way it looked in *Ascension of the Demonoids*.

And then my friend, David Hallinger, who was acting in it — his girlfriend lives in Hawaii. I had the money so he asked me if I ever wanted to come and shoot there, he was going there to visit her, and I said fine, and I went there and I got a TAN ... ate good food, went to the beach, swimming, snorkeling (first time in my life), shot our footage ... and, was able to shoot in Kodachrome which was $50 every hundred feet. Two and a half minutes was $50 — I think $25 to buy the film and $25 to develop. No worries — I had $20,000.

Has it played in many theaters?

It hasn't played in that many theaters. It's a strange picture in that you have to relax when you see it. It was the last, supposedly the last in my series of U.F.O. films. And I wanted to look away from the subject, so the movie looks away from the subject toward the end. In fact it completely DROPS the subject, basically ... goes to Hawaii and examines the scenery, forgetting about what had previously happened or what the picture was about. That was my intention. I wanted to get off the subject.

So the movie was constructed in that particular way, and also it was a movie focusing mainly on colors, and ... attractive combinations of colors.

Ascension of the Demonoids dealt with the cults and true believers waiting on signals and visitors from space. Do you find these people of interest?

Now the subject of U.F.O.s, flying saucers, had greatly interested me. All my life I have been interested in them. It's like Halloween — you want to believe in the witches and the ghosts, and you read so much about it and you think it would be nice if it's true.

Well, in the mid-seventies I found out that the U.F.O.s are true, they actually ARE U.F.O.s. Whatever they are, I don't know what they are. But there was a big rash of them and they were in California. And in San Francisco, I happened to fall into the mess ... or the mystery, by viewing what were U.F.O.s.

So they came in different colors, they came in a series that lasted about a year and a half. And also different sizes, shapes ... and they have strange mental effects on you. In other words, they're not just phenomena out there that don't seem to relate to you. You can actually communicate with those things, whatever they are.

This was a big revelation for me, because if these things actually did exist, what *else* was around that was not supposed to exist but also was for real ... in some fashion.

So I got interested in this whole parapsychological ... U.F.O. ... monster, Bigfoot area of life, etc. And all these weird rumors. So I investigated it and the investigation is still going on. It's been over ten years.

The movies I made, there's about 5 or 6 of them, deal with different aspects of the enigma. *Ascension of the Demonoids* was to be the big *mural*, at the end, after going through the other movies and hearing about the rumors, and hearing about strange visitors and strange craft and strange animals, and other things associated with the U.F.O. mystery ... you finally get to see everything in a big, wide, broad mural, which focuses in here and there in bright colors on certain aspects of it, and pulls back and you see more.

The whole U.F.O. thing is a thing of great interest for me. It still is. I find it very fascinating and potentially explosive. It'll probably change our views when we find out what the hell they really are. It's an important thing, even though it sounds like comic book material. But it's really WEIRD.

I find the people who are waiting for space visitors, I find them sweet. They're gentle people and I too would like to believe in space people, and — in fact it may be true, maybe that's what they ARE. But they seem to be something else, something much stranger. 'Cause they interact with you in too much of a personal way, I think. I can't see how an extraterrestrial would have that much interest in you. Plus they seem, while very much advanced, they seem very old fashioned. And from the stories you hear and from my own experiences it's very personalized and BIZARRE. It's a bizarre, archaic mish-mash that's totally new or baffling.

George in the early 1970s on the bank of an Indiana river. ●●●●

Marion Eaton (make-up job by George) in *A Reason to Live*

Do you trace your artistic technique back to the surrealists? The Russians? The …?

I don't really know. There IS one thing that greatly affected me. I remember when I was in … elementary school, we had to read the literature, some of it was a little high class literature. Short stories.

Then there was one short story, I forget what they called it, but it was ABSURD, an absurd story. And it told in great detail — it was this dramatic story — of how this woman came down the staircase, she was dressed for a party, and she had doilies hangin' from her ears on strings. That sort of attracted me very much. The fact that such a revered form of expression like writing, LITERATURE, was actually composed for this ridiculous kind of tale, or this story that had ridiculous elements in it. This revered medium was used for a totally preposterous tale. Not a preposterous tale — the tale was rather mundane — but a preposterous RENDERING of a tale … I think that greatly affected me. Suddenly it seemed all alive.

It's the same thing like classic cinema. There's a great classic cinema and I enjoy it very much. It's HEAVY … it has significance, and it's a joy. It has value. But I also like the junk, like you don't know why these people made it, and why did they ever get these actors that are so lousy? and the special effects are hideous. Why was this thing made in a medium that can be so pompous at times. Or so "revered." And I think that's also what attracted me to film.

As for "comedy" … there is a lot of sterile, soulless one-dimensional comedy coming out of Hollywood and

the studios today, facile, shallow "light entertainment," "trend movies" that you forget as soon as you walk outside, production line product. Your comedy seems to draw or twist from deeper, often darker urges and experiences like failure, frustration, death, jealousy, ugliness, out-of-control sex, slavish blind belief ... Is there a connection?

You know, when I'm making a movie I never think of my movie as a "comedy." Its always a "movie," and even though there's funny things in them — in fact the whole thing may be funny — it was never attempted to be a comedy. Not that it was an unintentional comedy or unintentionally funny, it's just that it's ... usually about horrible ... feelings, or feelings that either I had gone through, or urges ... but it turns out in this way it's transferred into this medium in this style, which is ... funny. Or it turns out funny.

In fact, when my movies were playing at the Film Forum in New York, a lady that I knew from Los Angeles — she was a friend of David Hallinger — she said let's go to your show, they're having a night of your movies. And I said no, I don't want to go because I don't want to relive all the pain. And I realized my career has all been based on pain. And those movies, even the funniest ones, had this horrible pain behind them. And I know exactly why they were made. And I didn't want to go because I didn't want to relive that. I didn't want to relive the main motivations of those pictures.

But then I went and there's people LAUGHIN', and I was even laughin', havin' a good time. And I forgot about the pain.

You draw comics, don't you?

But yeah I did draw comics because I met Art Spiegelman and he invited me over to his house 'cause he found out I knew Ken Jacobs. So I went over, I knew he was a comic editor — he asked me to do a comic and I did and I had a comic career that went on for, I don't know, maybe two years. And it's printed, so it's in existence, and, I don't know if you can get copies now but go to comic book stores and look for Short-Order Comics, and they also did one, a big format comic, *Arcade*. I did some work in *Arcade* comics.

What do you cook up when you're at home? Any recipes for readers out there? I hear you once made spaghetti and didn't have any spaghetti sauce so you used mushroom soup. George, is this true?

Now as far as cooking I don't remember ever using mushroom soup with spaghetti. It's probably true though. When I was trying to begin to cook I would make weird mixtures.

I have no real recipes. My brother cooks much better than I do, and he stays at home and COOKS. And sometimes he makes very good stuff, but sometimes he makes awful spicy garbage. Greasy junk. Like eggplant that would wreck your system. He's had guests over and the pain evidently registers on their faces just before they have to go to the bathroom.

HEAVILY INTOXICATED...RUEBEN GIVES HIS AUTOGRAPH WHILE OLGA INDULGES HERSELF ON CHILI AND BEANS WITH FLUFFED EGGS AND GINGER ALE.

LIKE HER ANCESTORS...OLGA'S BREADBASKET WAS MEANT TO BE SEEN AND NOT HEARD... SO SHE RUPTURED TO DEATH FROM REPRESSED FLATULENCE. *THE END*

Arcade, Spring 1975.

THE LABOR THEORY OF VALUE

by DAVID COHEN
© 1975

"GREAT ART IS NOT A NARCOTIC. IT IS MEANT TO STIMULATE LIFE NOT SUPPRESS IT."

illustrations by GEORGE KUCHAR
© 1975

Comics (excerpts) from *Arcade*, Summer 1975.

Sometimes they're rather distinguished or continental people and they eat his food and then splatter up our bowl. They have to run to the toilet and really let loose, so that it splatters on the rim of the bowl.

So his meals are not always that good either.

Didn't you once do an interview with Al Goldstein of *Screw* magazine?

I don't think I ever DID do an interview with Al Goldstein of *Screw* magazine. I did used to BUY *Screw* magazine, I used to read it for the ads in the back, sometimes I used to answer the sex ads in the back. This was in my youth. And I met ... strange people.

You say the British Film Institute loved your *Weather Diary 2* video, that only a handful of people have ever seen yet. What's it like and why do you think they liked it?

Yeah, I sent the British Film Institute my *Weather Diary 2*. They like it very much. They liked it better than *Ascension of the Demonoids*, which I sent them a video copy of. I think if they had seen *Ascension of the Demonoids* on the big screen they would have thought differently, because PHYSICALLY it's quite an overwhelming picture.

But they liked very much the Americana in *Weather Diary 2*, which is a LONELY work. With *Weather Diary 1* I went out more and I interacted with the people around the motel. And I was a little more friendly, the DOGS I met were friendlier. And in *Weather Diary 2* it was me alone in the room trying to keep things going ... when nothing was happening. It does ... get the feeling of this place here, this motel in Oklahoma.

I think they liked the Americana part of it and also it was kind of a tribute to Jim and Tammy Bakker — I used to watch them on cable television here in the motel room, and ... I liked them because they were real "show biz" people, and made-up, and they were fun to watch. So this was a little tribute to them after their fall.

Their fall was fun to watch, and I think it made for good television. Good news headlines also.

Give your instant response to these words:

Sex: Well ... sex is a fun thing, it's an escape thing. It's not really fun, but it's fun to think about. And it's fun to try to use it as an escape.

Death: I don't really know what death would be like, and it'll probably happen soon enough, or,

The early years: (L to R) Mike and George.

maybe too soon, and I don't want to think about it ... I do think about it, though. And I do hope that I die in a — not in a circumstance that ... I would rather not be dead in.

Douglas Sirk: Douglas Sirk was a big inspiration for me. I used to go see his movies and they were movies made by adults who seemed to know what they were doing.

Douglas Sirk and his cinematographer and the script writers and actors were like adults working in a beautiful form: the Hollywood motion picture. And the narrative kind of Hollywood approach, and they were making beautiful works.

So, Douglas Sirk was a big inspiration for me. In fact, I could've met him one time — he was in the San Francisco area and my friends were going to lunch with him and they asked me if I would like to come and I said sure, but that night I was workin' on one of our class movies, a real schlocky class production, and I was up all night and I didn't get finished until eleven o'clock, and then I didn't go to the lunch because I would've been too bleary eyed. It really didn't matter probably because Douglas Sirk at that time I think was losing his vision.

But they apologized from me to him, and he said, "Movies are more important than lunch."

Pornography: I used to enjoy going to pornography. I enjoyed going to pornography when it was hard to get — to see pornography. But when it's easily available you don't feel the urge so much to go and

see it. That's why I think pornography should always be around, so that you don't feel starved.

I think an element of pornography is boredom. 'Cause boredom will help you conjure up ... sexual feelings? Or, you're so bored you can only think of sex to try to stimulate yourself. So I think boredom is a part of pornography, in film anyway.

Freak Shows: I haven't gone to any freak shows, but come into my neighborhood in the Mission District in San Francisco — you don't have to pay money to see a freak show.

The U.S. Naval presence in the Antarctic: SOMEBODY'S got to be there, I suppose.

The death of a butterfly: I haven't seen a butterfly die in a long time. MOTHS I've seen die. So ...

Pizza: I love pizza, and I hear it's good for you. So after I work out I try to keep my body in shape in case I get called on to do any nude scenes. After a workout I go get a pizza 'cause I hear that it builds your body up.

The National Debt: I ... don't know what that is.

Sharks: I saw last night on the TV *Jaws 2*, and it was very suspenseful. They took their time trying to make the characters seem like real people. So when that big shark, which looked real most of the time, came after them there was a lot of suspense.

A vicious hail storm: There was a vicious hail storm in the next county here. I took video pictures of the thunderheads blossoming.

85

Photo by David Hallinger.

"Me eating a Mexican breakfast in my neighborhood. David Hallinger shot it. Me and him eat too much undigestible stuff."

The hail was as big as softballs in Oklahoma City. And it came in on 80 m.p.h. winds and stripped the leaves off the trees. Somebody took a video of it, it was quite impressive. It looked like a giant, noisy blizzard.

Mother: My mother's getting better. She went to the hospital, she had her pancreas taken out and then they also accidentally threw her teeth out. But now they got 'em back in her mouth, they made a new pair.

Angels: Angels probably do exist but they may not dress the way they do in the religious literature. I think they probably wear suits, and, ah, they do walk around, and, they're interchangeable with demons. I think it depends on ... I don't know what changes 'em into a demon, but I think that angels change ...

Beautiful music: I don't know ... I like all kinds of music, and the thing is ... I used to buy these records, joke records. They used to be symphonies that were off key, and they'd play classical pieces of music. But after awhile I would get into the record and I would accept it that that was the way the pieces of music were. The way they were composed, the way they were SUPPOSED to sound. So I stopped buying those records.

Beautiful dreams: I HAVE beautiful dreams, I used to remember them, I used to keep a dream diary. They were rather interesting dreams — some of them used to come true.

Then I used to train myself to stop and actually try to see what exactly was in the dream, and there would be like this frozen silence. As you look around the room, and it would seem like a real place. I was aware of myself lookin' around the room and gazing at the furniture, and the lights.

But then I stopped, because I was paying too much attention to my dream world, and I think the real world was slipping away.

Last question: Quickly sum up your philosophy of life, art, creation, eternity ...

I don't know if I have a philosophy, I just want to get THROUGH it. In other words, I would like to get through it and do what I'm supposed to do. So every night I pray that ... I do what I'm supposed to be doing, because I don't want to waste the time, or not do what I'm supposed to be doing. So I do pray that I am going ahead on the road that I'm supposed to be.

What will happen with eternity, I don't know. I read books about weird things, other planes of existence ... people that died and came back. And I have friends that died and then came back, and they said it was pretty nice, dying. Seemed like a nice place, so, ah ... since I have first-hand information of people that did die already, I don't know if I should worry about it that much.

The end.

END of Reno motel interview. Next: up-dated interview where George talks about past films and narration by deaf people and foreign speakers, followed by three short written pieces.

I'll talk about a NEW film ... we're workin' on a picture now — in fact it's all FINISHED ... the class ended three weeks ago and we got out the remaining footage. It takes two weeks to develop — we send the black-and-white to Los Angeles, the only place that develops the black-and-white reversal.

I wanted this movie to be like *Loveboat*. It's a *Loveboat*, only it's, ah, bound for disaster. The ship is full of disturbed characters. And they have romantic problems, and other things — addictions and stuff. And the ship goes down but there are survivors, three particularly nice looking survivors, two men and a girl. And they make it to an island.

We shot this picture in Studio Eight, it's an all-indoor picture, but occasionally they went on location. I sent them out to the Fisherman's Wharf, where they shot a big ocean liner. And then they went on their own to the beach, they found a deserted beach and they were washed up on the beach, and they did some nice scenes.

One girl in it, she particularly liked this guy and she asked if I would write in a kissing scene. I said I didn't blame her for liking him, he is really nice looking — he had beautiful long hair. So I wrote them in a big kissing scene and we photographed that, she had a wonderful time with him — she wound up on the beach with him and they did like a *From Here to Eternity* scene with the sea rushing over them ... and they were rolling and kissing. I think the water was FRIGID but they managed to come back looking like they had gone away for a WEEK to a vacation paradise — they came in all rosy cheeked with so much color and life in 'em. It was wonderful to see the young people BEAMING like that.

We had our problems with that picture ... we shot in color and sometimes the color was DAYLIGHT color film, but we were shooting indoors — I didn't want to go outdoors and they didn't have any blue filters to put on the lens to make the color look better so we tried putting blue gels on the lights, but they weren't the proper temperature to make it look good so the film had a kind of orange tint to it. I was kind of depressed about one roll, and I saw one of the students, she made a film and she BLEACHED her film — she brings in a jar of bleach, she puts it in a dish and she throws her film in there.

So I said, "Listen, you think you can do anything with this footage? I'm unhappy with the color." So I gave it to her, and she poured her bleach on a plate, and she put the film in there and it was in there two hours. Then she took a look at it and said, "It's not UNROLLED good enough, it hasn't done much," so she made the film looser on the roll, threw it in for another half an hour, and then she took it out and said, "Looks better — the colors are better now; you got flashes of lavender coming in ..." and other types of colors. So I thanked her, and I have the film in a trash bag. It smells so horrible, I don't know — it's not a bleach smell, it's something else mixed in with the emulsion or something and it's a horrible stink. So I put the whole film in a trash bag. It's just a pile of film. And, um, I'm gonna unwind it, clean it ... I think we SAVED that sequence.

Another time we went outside and we were shooting with 4-X high speed B&W reversal, I think 400 ASA, and we went outside and it was a bright sunlight out there, on white concrete. We couldn't cut down the aperture enough, and we had no ... no way of getting around it so we put sunglasses on the lens. In other words, it's supposed to be a vacation cruise so we actually stuck sunglasses, so you could see the two lenses of the sunglasses and we positioned each actor so that one would be in the right lens and the other would be in the left, and they did their scene, and everything else around them is bleached, but you can see THEM well through the glasses.

This is a vehicle for a guy in the class named Peter. He was in another film that we did a year ago. Peter Van Lengen is his name, he's part Mexican and part somethin' else ... or at least was born in Mexico City.

Anyway he was in a previous film we did about a Sasquatch and he played a doctor who was trying to operate on a ballerina that he kidnapped and intermingle her with a Sasquatch or something to make some sort of hybrid. But it didn't work out, as the character fell in love with her, and eventually it turned out to be like a Romeo and Juliet tragedy.

But, he was always able to read his lines in a very straightforward, serious, underplayed manner which I found charming. I realized that he had a future in these types of movies. So I wrote him a real big part as the captain of this *Loveboat*, Captain Steele. And I tried to give him, also, a more romantic overtone to his characterization. Hopefully this will put him back on the screen in one of our productions. One of our ... "grade Z" productions, maybe?

The budget was one thousand dollars for this one. Looks like it'll be a half-hour long, black-and-white, AND color. I felt like shootin' a lot of black-and-white and then every once in a while we had color film so we had to shoot color, so we'd just shoot color sequences. Evidently these color sequences will just burst on, with no explanation.

But ... what does it matter? We're just scrapin' the bottom of the barrel as far as stocks are concerned.

But we've had LUCK with this picture, and nothing has been terribly RUINED. Except one scene we got out. I saw a note from the lab, and also an extra roll of film came — four hundred new feet of film! And we had sent them two hundred feet. And they gave us four hundred new feet of film and a note, and the note said that they were sorry they had ruined our two hundred feet! Something was wrong with the chemicals or something. And I said, "Oh God, they RUINED it?!" But I put it on the projector and there was an image on there, but they actually HEIGHT-ENED it. They heightened the film by — it was supposed to be a grubby scene that took place in the boiler room of the ocean liner and they put all these blotches on it, so it actually intensified the sequence, so not only did they make the sequence better but they gave us four hundred extra feet. Which I was very grateful for. So we had luck on this picture.

One of the guys in the class just made a suggestion that one of our leading ladies, named Amy, should do a wet T-shirt scene. So of course I approached her — I said, "Amy, how about your wet T-shirt scene next week?!" And she said, "No way! No way am I gonna do a wet T-shirt scene!" So, I tried to coax her, and every session she'd come in with a little tighter blouse on. And I thought maybe she was warmin' up for it. And then it was time and I said, "Amy, it's time for the scene 'Wet T-shirt' and she said okay, and so she had on her T-shirt, and I felt in the back and she had a brassiere on, 'cause I felt the buckle of the brassiere. I said, "Amy ... ah, you gotta take the brassiere off." And she said, "Oh no! No way! No way I'm takin' the brassiere off!" But I said, "Look, if you do that, if you take the brassiere off

and do the wet T-shirt scene, I'll do a WET UNDERPANTS scene." And she still said no, you do your wet underpants scene, I'm not gonna do it. So ... she wore this kind of brassiere, it wasn't like a real brassiere, it was like stretched ... percentage-of-latex-and-something-else kind of material, and so when you did squirt water on it you could see the formation of the breast. And she had to do an exercise sequence 'cause she played a character similar to the one ... Julie? on the *Loveboat*? She conducts exercises, she's the cruise director of activities. So she did her exercises. Actually the sequence turned out really well.

And then she said, "Alright, now you gotta do your wet underpants scene." I said, "No, no, 'cause you cheated — you wore that bra."

So this picture's gonna be edited pretty soon. It's a lot of footage — I had to lug it from the school, it weighs a ton. It's already in the house.

• • •

The picture we did two semesters ago, the one before *Summer of No Return*, was this movie called *Insanitorium*. That was done all with outdated film. All the colors are MAUVE, and green. Not too much color in that thing. We got one print out of it and then made a video copy. And something interesting happened in the video copy; the video transferring machine couldn't quite read the tones of the picture because they were so faded and so the thing turned out looking SOLARIZED. It had trouble reading the

On the set of *Symphony for a Sinner* with student crews and actors.

My favorite Bronx stars: Larry Leibowitz and his mom, Francis Leibowitz (now deceased), plus an oil painting I did of them.

●

← Early photos of George directing New Jersey sex pot Florraine Connors in *Corruption of the Damned*, 1965.

quality of color and the exposure, 'cause the picture was also underexposed. So some scenes have this electric color in them, surrounded by this drab, um ... tonality. So it looks more science fiction-like in the video copy.

We had problems with that thing, too. I wanted the president's [the president of the Art Institute] secretary to play a role as a woman who runs this hospital-type facility that has the Sasquatch in it, and they're doing all these occult and scientific experiments in there.

So I asked her to come about two o'clock, after her lunch period, and I waited and the woman didn't come. She's a nice woman — she does extra work, she's in her late fifties? Maybe. She looks very good, though, she's got red hair ... she used to do extra work for movies that came to town. In fact, she was an extra in a Billy Wilder movie, and she said he was very nice to work with.

Anyway, I had to do this scene and I couldn't just wait around, so I had Peter — who was doing the scene with her — act with a stand-in. Unfortunately the stand-in was much shorter than the president's secretary and had the wrong hair style ... and was also in all the wrong positions. But, ah — 'cause when the secretary, Harriet, came in, we just shot her in extreme close-ups so you couldn't tell where the hell she was, and we just put the script in front of her and she just rattled off the lines. In a way, I guess she was a little humiliated, some of the dialogue was a bit on the HARSH side. But she was a trooper, she went through it, and in fact the rough parts made her eyes water! And so there was more dramatic tension in the scene.

Anyway, you see this big face, and then you cut away to the medium shot and you see this little midget — he's talkin' to this little midget — and they're all in these weird positions. Her head's supposed to be down on the table, and ... it's obvious it's a cut-away. But the effect is — the overall effect is kind of interesting.

So, I was very happy also with that motion picture, which is thirty minutes long.

I don't know who will ever SEE these pictures. I don't know, I occasionally bring 'em around. There's only one print of each 'cause we can't afford the prints. They cost ... almost the whole budget just to print the thing. So we always try to have a benefit show; I show my movies and we invite the public. And try to scrape up money so that we can print the movie ... in some form.

• • •

Of course we've been making these things over the years — many, many years, and so it has a big changing cast, with every once in a while one person coming into prominence over several pictures — 'cause they happen to take my class again. And so we do have certain STARS in those pictures.

They go way back ... and sometimes when there's a

visiting artist at school we incorporate them into the picture. Besides Rosa Von Praunheim, who was in one of the movies, Joyce Wieland, who is a Canadian artist — she does paintings, quilts, movies, she does a bunch of things, and she used to be married to Mike Snow. She's in one of the pictures. In fact she has a major role, she's the person who ties the whole picture together, she plays a Mother Superior. Sort of a twisted hellbent Mother Superior. We took advice from Marlon Brando — we heard that when he does his lines, they're actually pasted on his co-star's face. So we just wrote the script on a piece of paper and pasted it onto our regular star, Joana Zegri, who was the queen of these movies for several years. And, just positioned her so you see the back of her head and Joyce just looked her in the face and just read off from the piece of paper that was blockin' her face. She was quite good in the part.

Now, her ex-husband, Mike Snow, was in one picture that had to do with a female ... sex ... ah ... what the hell do you call them? A Dr. Ruth. Although, this was before Dr. Ruth came into prominence. And this was about a sex therapist who instead of getting her information from books, went out on location in back alleys and other places where things were happening and got first-hand experience in sex matters!

Mike Snow was in that, he played some musical instruments in the beginning of that picture. And the students liked it very much because he had a little combo, he made a little combo with the students and they played jazz and stuff.

Then we had, in a much earlier picture, Cary Medoway. He went down to Hollywood and made a picture called *The Heavenly Kid*. Which I think bombed. Anyway, he was in one of our movies, he played a ... it was an Egyptian — that's what he played. But he had a turban, with a feather in it. And he was on a ship transporting a mummy to Egypt and fell in love with this girl, and the gods were angry; the mummy comes to life. It was a rock-bottom picture. The actual really bottom of the barrel type production, where we only had two hundred dollars to make the 16mm film. Or two hundred and fifty dollars. Ridiculous price for the budget.

I didn't want to make any big elaborate sets 'cause we had a picture done before that had big sets up. So, we made the scenes take place at night on the deck of a ship, and in the dark little cabins below. So it was just a black background. Somebody had a Dixie cup and was throwin' water across the actors, so you'd see this water goin' by so you'd have the feeling they were on a ship. It was actually very successful, the picture, somehow it struck a chord and became a rather entertaining and successful picture. By successful I mean people that looked at it enjoyed it.

Another person that worked on that movie was Meno Meyjes who later went on to work with Spielberg and who had written the screenplay for *The Color Purple*. He was from Holland. In fact, his friend who was also from Holland, this rather statuesque girl, became my agent in Europe. Babe Van Loo. She was queen of those class productions for many, many years, because of her strange accent. Not only did she have a Dutch accent but she had a lisp. I THINK it was a lisp. People said she talked a little like Elmer Fudd. And so all of her lines were charged with this kind of strangeness. It was a great joy to write dialogue for her.

Now in those days James Broughton was teaching at the school, and, always complainin' — he had a screenwriting course and he was complainin' that the class was full of foreigners and they could barely talk English, much less write it. And I was saying, "Well, send them to me!" because I used to love these accents — they gave the picture a continental flavor. They had strange pronunciations of words and they made the screenplay come alive in a weird way. So ... I always encouraged the foreigners to please be in our pictures.

In fact, many, many years ago I was workin' on a picture, *Portrait of Ramona*, my last movie in New York. And at that time my brother was friends with this deaf guy. He could speak fairly well, but he knew this other guy who was also deaf, I think from birth, and he learned how to talk just by watchin' the mouths open, or somehow. And so listening to him speak was the most amazing thing, you really couldn't understand it, but it was an interesting combination of sounds. And I wanted him to NARRATE that movie, *Portrait of Ramona*, but ... some of my friends looked at me with SHOCK, like, "how could you DO such a thing!" But I actually thought it would be really interesting to hear his voice on the soundtrack. And it didn't matter if you understood it or not. Because in our latest class picture I thought of narrating it in German. Because I don't know how I'm going to put it together. I think it's going to make ... some sort of sense. In fact, I know it will, It's a series of big scenes on a boat. But I thought that if they heard a narrator and if it was speaking in German, they would know that the thing is somehow being explained, even though they don't understand it, and so they'd ACCEPT the visual format of the film better. Even if they didn't understand the language that was trying to explain the plot.

Now a couple of years back we worked on another film, also, based on the life of Lupe Velez, the actress who went to Hollywood, made several films, then fell in love with Tarzan. Then eventually committed suicide.

We had a big ICELANDIC girl playing Lupe and she was always getting annoyed at me 'cause she thought there were too many love scenes in the picture. I don't know WHY she would get annoyed. I would be HAPPY if I was in scenes like that. Usually. So she was getting annoyed so she would refuse to do scenes and we had to get stand-ins, and the only ones who didn't complain about doin' those scenes were other guys. And so they would do her scenes, and eventually she didn't want to do scenes so we just had three different guys playing her, these parts. And they did all her raunchy scenes ... with each other ... (voice trails off) other guys ...

Excerpt from *Reflections on Lighting*, a written work by George Kuchar

When I was assigned to light a pornography film, the first thing I did was to blast their buttocks with a high intensity light source as there is not much to concentrate on when you are up close to an exposed rear-end and consequently you search its meager features for protruding hairs or skin eruptions. This does not always inspire eroticism and so I made sure that the buttocks were over-exposed ... technically speaking. As we all progressed on this pornography film I noticed that the general level of acting was much higher when the producer came onto the set, early in the morning, with a bag of donuts for the cast and crew that was fresh and direct from a bakery. When it was packaged crap off a grocery shelf the morale dropped. Drooping is the bane of pornography pictures.

The main actress on the set had delicate features and gentle eyes until I got my hands on them (I was also the film's make-up and hair stylist — going under the pseudonym of Mr. Dominic). Mr. Dominic is sick ... recreating for the motion picture screen the women he viewed in his youth; tremendous creations of endless fascination. Women garbed in fabric coats of dreary tone who straddled the vacant lots of the Bronx, urinating on a kaleidoscope of broken beer bottles. Females who descended between the stone columns of edifices constructed to house the denizens of a naked city revelling in its own shame. Descending the steps with their cheeks all rouged in oval splendor, the circular patterns in the poodle fur shawls that draped their shoulders glistening all black and dead in the sun. Ladies who watched television in the morning with hideous, shrunken men articulating from the screen in a desperate attempt to sell cardboard eyebrow stencils to the frustrated and the frumpy. Mr. Dominic sick? Perhaps he is just temporarily regurgitating the visions of his youth; seeing in the black rainbows that arc above the eyes of that lost race an archway to the magical kingdom of Maybelline and its colorful treasures. Maybe that can explain the splash of candy-apple red that spills way beyond the contours of lip to lap at chin and nostril alike.

And what of the men of that bygone era? The deep, dark, wet mystery of their armpits and the tiny sparks of light that flashed on grease-coated hair? Men who swam nude in city rivers, the water not yet tainted enough to blotch the whiteness of temperate zone flesh. Flesh that hung over trousers in an unabashed display of delicatessen living. Fingers all yellow and brown with the smell of nicotine and that clamping vise of white enameled teeth ... chomping, chewing ... on toothpicks and pierced earlobes; the drab monochromatic shades of their uniforms contrasting sharply with the lightning-white flash of bleached underwear. How could such a creature of filthy promises possess such white underwear?

Opposite page, top photos: Mr. Dominic's living human victims. Bottom photo: George as "Edward Maxwell" in frame blow-up from *Web of Fire*.

"web of fire"

Sometimes I do those student productions in video. One time the budget, a few years back, was cut to three hundred dollars. The school was having financial troubles.

And I didn't want to start a movie with that, I didn't want to be three months with the students on three hundred dollars, not with the prices that were out in those days, you know. This wasn't that long ago.

So I decided to do a video, do a Video-8. The school had a video camera. And it was looked upon as a great shame: here he was, the final humiliation, degraded to using video, workin' on the student productions.

We had about twelve students. Most of 'em were cranky, but there were a few good ones, and I decided since video was kind of a soap-opera medium, we'd make a soap opera about a hospital. And we called it *Calling Doctor Petrov*. I decided to incorporate film in it, by, we sent a crew out to shoot exteriors. When we had that developed we brought it in and projected it on the walls, and had the actors standin' front of it. Then we also took black leader and scratched in it — like there was a lightning storm? — so we had a slide projector projecting a cloud background and then a movie projector projecting scratches on black leader that were in the shape of lightning. Then there was another projector with patterns going on the actors. And so we had this like multi-media show going on, and we were taping in 8mm video.

And so, *Calling Doctor Petrov* is full of special effects of that nature. Nothing was post-production, everything was right there in the studio, on the set.

I actually thought it was kind of a good production. Some of them were kind of mad, I guess, that we were shootin' in video. But there were some good students, and the happy people were the people that I brought in from the outside world ... bring in to do scenes, and they were sort of excited about the whole project.

We finished it, played it and it went over like ... kind of dead.

But then it caught on a year later, there was great interest in it. And it went to Germany, some guy in Berlin. He took it over. His name is Alf Bold. He was crazy about it, so ... It has a LIFE now, *Calling Doctor Petrov*.

We did another one, which was a big dense soap opera, based on the Jim and Tammy Bakker scandal. It was about the Christian network, and it was very FOUL ... I wanted everything foul in it, the language, it's a lot of four-letter words. And a lot of foul visual material hits the screen.

That was an interesting project because it was a crowded class. I went in there and it looked like thirty people. Thirty loud people. And I really didn't want to have a full class because I was warned by my chairwoman that by taking in more people I was depriving some of the other people of students. And

so I felt guilty and stuff like that. But then when I saw that there were these loud people in the class I didn't want to be alone with them. So I decided it would be better if I BUFFER the whole class with just a ton of people. So whoever came up and asked to be in it, I said, "Certainly you can be in it." And I wrote them a note and they went to the registrar and got into the class.

And so we have a big production with a lot of people. And they were having fun being foul. They really got into it and had a great time. It's called *Evangelust*. It's never premiered, I don't know why. I show it occasionally.

• • •

Occasionally I go to a different school and make a production there. This past summer I went to the University of Wisconsin in Milwaukee, and was there for a month to teach video. And I brought along my Sony 8mm Camcorder, and they had half-inch machines there and we made a production called *The Motivation of the Carcassoids*.

It's about a doctor who has a cellulite practise, he sucks cellulite from the bodies of his patients. And it got out of hand it got kind of murderous. There were some errors and they had to dispose of the body, and then it just accumulated, the atrocities accumulated. And the doctor had a bad drug problem. There was a lot of subplot involved in it.

I also went to Cal. Arts and made a production about an associate professor at an art school who has a skeleton in his closet. It's a living skeleton, because he's still carrying on the way ... he shouldn't be.

We also made this big soap opera called *The Hurt That Fades*. I wanted a very Hollywood production. I credited a fake scriptwriter by-line of Edna Levinsky that wrote *The Hurt That Fades*, 'cause I had a feeling that I had over-written the thing and the dialogue was much too florid. And I thought let's blame somebody called Edna Levinsky for that. And I also went under an alias for that 'cause I had an assistant called Scott Shelley so it became "Directed by George Scott," which was me and my assistant.

End

"Me with Richard Plueger ... a guy from Germany who came to study with me in class."

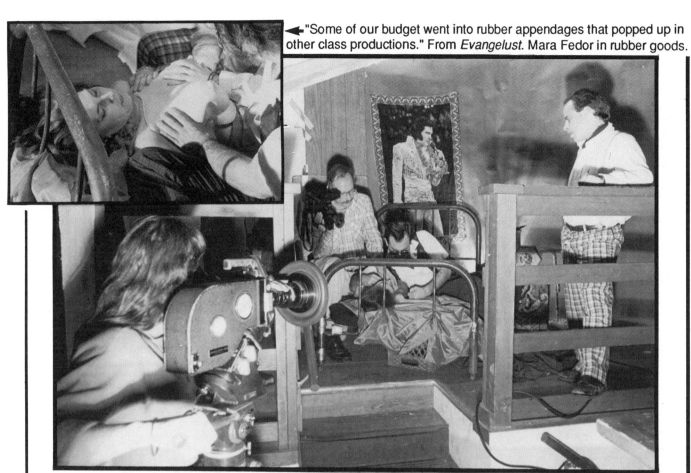

←"Some of our budget went into rubber appendages that popped up in other class productions." From *Evangelust*. Mara Fedor in rubber goods.

The shooting of *Evangelust* — a Christian TV drama featuring violence and vulgarity. Shooting the motel sex scandal scene • George shoots the video version while students shoot 16mm.

George on the set of *Evangelust* with Peggy Ahwesh.

Shooting a fire sequence in Summer of No Return. Note the special-effects man making smoke.

Sound-sync Techniques: Kuchar's Method

Reprinted from *Independent Filmmaking* by Lenny Lipton.

George Kuchar developed this method in several of his films, notably, *Hold Me While I'm Naked*, and Mike Kuchar made use of it in *The Secret of Wendel Sampson*. Although it defies accepted practice, a fair degree of sync can be achieved with this method. Turn on your projector and have your actors speak into the microphone of the tape recorder, while watching the action. You're recording wild. The particular method that George and Mike used was to play all of the parts, or dub all of the voices, by imitating different voices. Have the quarter-inch tape transferred to 16mm mag film, and then fit it to the picture by shuffling it around. How you accomplish this will be detailed in the section dealing with editing magnetic film. You could also record the track at the time of shooting, wild or floating, and then try to match it to the track in editing (short segments, as noted earlier, may be in perfect sync). Either way, if the track is recorded at the time of shooting, or dubbed after, this will work best for very short dialogue segments.

Walter Gutman, now deceased, acted in and produced George's film *Unstrap Me*.

Eugenia Jensen posed with knife above a prone Griff Kiviat in *Evangelust*.

95

L to R: Jerry Teranova, Marion Eaton and George in Curt McDowell's *Sparkle's Tavern.*

Curt, Marion and George on the "Mrs. Blake's Living Room" set of *Sparkle's Tavern.*

Christopher Coppola, one-time film student of George's, cast George in an acting role in *Palmer's Pickup.*

DEVELOPING AN AESTHETIC

You must acquire a finely tuned appreciation of cinema. Don't look at the classics all the time. The classics will be with us till the moon turns blue. Seek out, rather, the neglected works that reveal the world of movies in a bright and blistering light. I write "world of movies" and not "world" period because if you wish to see the world revealed — go out and look at it! Why anyone would spend time in a dark theater searching for reality up on that screen is beyond me, we should go there to forget about reality. People say that black and white movies are more realistic than color ones simply because black and white is not realistic at all and therefore what they are really saying is that they want fantasy disguised as realism by sucking the color out of it. People suck: they suck in beverages with straws while watching films, suck in their breath when the action gets hot and heavy, suck in their tummies to resemble Charlton Heston, etc. Well, all that sucked in air has to come out sometime but our society frowns on its natural expulsion in theater lobbies and that's why you see all those folks exiting cinemas with intense, facial gymnastics, they are trying to hold back ninety minutes worth of sucked in air! Be free to release that air along with your time and money when you go to a movie. Realize that what is seen on the screen is a phony rendition of real life with glamorous dieters playing saints and sinners.

Realism only comes to the screen when the film jams in the projector and the image begins to bubble. An instinctual fear of the dark manifests when the projection light fails ... heightened by the little, furry things with long tails that scamper beneath the seats. The electrical nature of sex becomes apparent as the hair on your neck bristles when that pervert to your left makes knee contact. In these moments of truth, cinema reveals her face of realism. But, she is a two-faced creature, the other countenance being a rainbow palette of dyed coiffures, pancake make-up and pancake bloated guts crammed into costumes designed by cock-eyed midgets. Superstars who beat their children with wire coat hangers and then peddle soft drinks potent enough to rot their dentures. Aging women taking endless enemas so as not to wind up in horror films. Virile he-men doomed to an excruciating regimen of exercises to keep their sodomized posteriors picture-perfect. EST trained actresses showing the world what it is like to be liberated and free of cellulite. Alcoholic celebrities who barf up their past in book form so that all can marvel at the hideous mess that has been cleaned up by a Christian re-birth. Harpies with herpes who rip apart, in print, plump fornicators whose every performance they slander with typeset Ju-Ju curses. Innocent children who sing and dance down the yellow brick road to drug addiction and toxic box office poisoning. This is the other face of cinema ... the side that sells tabloids and makes legends, a trillion dollar heritage of human refuse devoured by a cyclopean eye designed to entertain, to titillate with tit, to teach. THE art form of the 20th century. ○

SCHOOLING

Going to elementary school in the Bronx was a series of humiliations which featured Wagnerian women in an endless chorus of, "keep your mouth shut," "where's your homework," and "spit that gum out." The male teachers were much shorter than the females and whatever masculine apparatus they possessed was well concealed amid the folds of oversized trousers. After school my twin brother and I would escape to the local cinema, fleeing from our classmates: urban urchins who belched up egg creams and clouds of nicotine. In the safety of the theater we'd sit through hour upon hour of Indian squaws being eaten alive by fire ants, debauched pagans coughing up blood as the temples of God crashed down on their intestines, naked monstrosities made from rubber that lumbered out of radiation poisoned waters to claw the flesh off women who had just lost their virginity.

When three hours were up we would leave the theater refreshed and elated, having seen a world moulded by adults, a world we would eventually mature into. At home, supper simmered on the stove, smoking, bubbling and making plopping sounds as blisters of nutritious gruel burst just like the volcanic lava in those motion pictures. Oh how I wanted to grow up real fast and be one of the adults who sacrificed half naked natives to Krakatoa or dripped hot wax on a nude body that resembled Marie Antoinette. Not only were these pictures teaching me about geology and geography, but they were an introduction to giants of history and the joy of creative sculpture.

Religious instruction was supplied once a week by the nuns of a Catholic complex who took students from the city school system into their classrooms every Tuesday afternoon. I loved it, being taught by a pale figure shrouded in black who spoke of life after death and told us not to use purple ink in our ballpoint pens as it was the color of the devil. This was information, that to me at least, seemed of vital importance. Every Sunday morning I went to mass and inhaled the pollution of our lord as frankincense poured forth from swinging urns to soften and mute the tortured features of crucified plaster and bleeding replicas of unviolated women.

Eventually I had to leave the church as one warm, lonely afternoon I found myself kneeling in a pew praying for wild, disgusting sex. I was a teenager with a heavy inclination to explore my own groin and the emissions threatened to put out the fire in the sacred heart of our Lord. I looked around me at the elderly ladies scattered here and there throughout the shadowed house of God and knew that they at least were at peace because they didn't possess a big piece that defiantly poked holes in Christian dogma, demanding lubricated short cuts to the Kingdom of Heaven. I fled from the place of holiness that warm, lonely afternoon and God answered my prayer; a young, suffering Christian was granted wild, disgusting sex. Praise be the Lord! ○

As a youth I yearned to emulate the heroes and heroines of my particular space-time continuum. It wasn't an easy thing to do in those days as television was in black and white and the role models exhibited lacked the neon brilliance of today's electronic idols. There was a noon-time show experimenting in an early color process which featured Yma Sumac but nobody emulated her unless they feared bombardment by cosmic radiation, hoping that all those metal trinkets would repel the deadly rays. Sometimes I found myself wishing that I was like one of the sons on the Ozzie and Harriet TV program, a beefy boy who slept in pajamas and went through life with half closed eyelids. My eyes were kind of stunted and shrunken behind eyeglasses and I couldn't afford to shrink them anymore. As for pajamas, I got fed up wearing clothing twenty-four hours a day — my body having rebelled in a violent display of red and white boils.

As for my parents, well: My mother was a witch (literally) hiding in closets from booming thunderstorms having once seen the devil (in the form of a rat) run into a haystack that a youth had sought as shelter from a coming tempest. Immediately after the devil-rat entered, the haystack was hit by lightning and the boy incinerated. The horror of that spectacle has survived the decades ... the sound of any grumbling cumulonimbus sending her into a panic. My dad, now deceased, was a virile, sex-crazed truck driver who slept all day semi-nude. He lusted after booze, bosoms and bazookas (having served in the second world war). I, as their son, George, was a gangling youth whose hobbies and mannerisms hinted at a future of dark perversions and grotesque obsessions. They fought (alas, in vain) to reroute my path through life but soon realized that their dilemma was already quite well documented in the "Frankenstein" sagas that played on the television every weekend. Out of wedlock they had created a monster — a two-headed one as I'm a twin — and even the holy sanctity of marriage could not undo the horror they unleashed in the tri-state, metropolitan area.

My twin brother, Mike, matured more rapidly than I and he left me festering in a subjective tar pit of self abuse and too much chocolate-mocha cake. He got his own apartment and cultivated a swinging life style. I was swinging at my parent's house ... on the end of a rope which consisted of entwined strands of guilt, gluttony and gargantuan guts.

My best friend in those days was a young Jewish man who was obsessed with cannibalism and bodily mutilations. I'd walk over to his house to view artificial, decapitated limbs and grimacing skulls still in possession of their eyeballs. His mother would make us hot Ovaltine and only once did she object to her son's morbid interests — this occurred during a period of horrific murders perpetrated by someone the press had labeled "the torso killer." The fiend left his victims without arms, legs, or heads. One night she looked out the window and saw her son returning from a walk with a grisly bundle — he had found a battered mannikin torso lying in a vacant lot and was bringing it home as a prop for his 8mm productions. His mom realized the potential for neighborhood vigilante activity if anyone else spotted him entering the house with this thing and so my friend was appropriately chastised in heated Yiddish. My other friend in the Bronx worked for the Post Office and collected Barbra Streisand records. His sister became a dope addict and his dog died of rectal cancer because his family hated to take the pooch out for a poop. This friend became prematurely bald and then bought a wig that looked like it was made from the hair on the legs of a horse fly. With that thing on his head he became so horrible to look at that I stopped coming over to the house to see him.

I hardly ever met anyone in the Bronx streets who wanted to be my friend. If someone did approach it was either to beat me up or else hand out Jehovah's Witness literature.

My main activity on Friday or Saturday nights was searching for new churches with confessionals that had not yet reverberated with the sounds of my sins. At that time the local churches in the archdiocese had their clergy completely glutted with my whispered transgressions to the holy rule. Eventually I took a subway to another borough in search of virgin ears to singe so that the priests wouldn't feel they were victims of deja vu. Before I had gone through all five boroughs of that monster metropolis my faith crumbled into dust and cigarette ashes ... sparing me all that extra subway fare.

Forgive me, dear reader, I have painted a grim picture of my early years in the big apple. There were blinding flashes of great happiness amid the gloom and doom. Unfortunately I was sometimes the only one who thought so as guests who came to see where I lived made harsh, biting remarks, commenting on how the borough of the Bronx resembled a mixture of Miami Beach and Nazi Germany. Of course, their insights were quite true, but this was my home and home is where the heart is. My own heart beat fast at the rolling surface of the land which dipped beneath the surface of Harlem River and then rose in a majestic mound before submerging more extensively under the Hudson where it met the wall of solidified lava known as the New Jersey Palisades. To the east the great Atlantic Ocean spawned storms that roared up the coast causing the window pane in my living room to bulge inward with alarming convexity while outside the metal sheeting on the apartment building was being ripped off and whipped through rain-soaked streets like giant razor blades. Nature swirled past we people of the Bronx as we sat, lay, or squatted in our dwelling units — making whoopee or chocolate chip cookies — living, learning, and lumping it.

Making films was my life and the people who befriended me became the leading ladies and men who populated my productions. In order to finance these motion pictures I had to enter the Manhattan job market. It was thrilling to ride the jam-packed subway trains to work in the morning; discreet perverts would reach out for some sort of stabilizing support so as not to lurch over and fall in the rocking cars and they'd grab onto your private appendages. Full-figured senoritas would mash you against metal partitions using flesh of such abundance that no amount of latex rubber could suppress the meat into trim decency.

Fights would suddenly break out with alarming ferocity but there could be no room for swinging fists and so the squeeze of the traveling mob would suffocate further, violent escalations. In those subway train cars the hot, metallic smelling air was super-charged with the most primitive of living emotions. We would all spill out of these cars (some of us being pushed or thrown out) and climb the stairs into the canyons of dark glass and gargoyled stone which housed the machinery of commerce and coffee breaks, industry and indigestion, finance and fiscal flatulence that smelled of syndicated corruption.

Up in elevators we would go — as if to heaven — not realizing that the next step was a purgatory of clattering typewriters and tortured executives who screamed in fury as their insides were being eaten away by excess stomach acid.

Lunch time came and every grill in mid-town Manhattan would sizzle with greasy slabs of meat ... some of this meat sitting on stools at the counter watching their brethren fizzle and fry. Chinese restaurants administered massive doses of monosodium glutamate in a desperate attempt to curb caffeine jitters. Construction workers could be seen sitting on cinder blocks watching the secretaries stroll by while their hero sandwiches bulged with

swollen sausages; sausages which threatened to squirt juice into the first mouth that clamped down on them.

In no time at all the hour was up and you had to digest that mess in a fluorescently lit working space, the purplish pulses from the elongated bulbs causing to varicose veins on your co-workers to pulsate repulsively.

Things slowed down as five o'clock approached and the concept of a time warp was no longer an abstraction but a living reality as you witnessed the stretching of space-time without benefit of drugs. You need only glance at the clock to see that it was not moving normally toward the desired numeral.

As if in a fever or trance, once again you find yourself crammed into a subway train only this time nobody is grabbing for your manhood, all life has been squeezed out of the beast that lives in us all and it must be resurrected by the six o'clock news, news that will tell us who got pushed down an abandoned elevator shaft after being manicured by a chain saw. Slowly yet surely we will feel a stirring within us but for most it will take something pharmaceutical to bring it completely out, it'll take an Ex-Lax tablet.☐

George during the early '60s in Manhattan when he drew weather maps

WEEKEND WEATHER

DR. FRANK FIELD

"Some of the artwork I tried to get on the air when I serviced the local (NBC) weather show in Manhattan. It was found objectionable at times."

99

The End

Big Man in a Little Town ... George out west in the '70s.

MIKE

Mike directs Donna Kerness in *Sins of the Fleshapoids.*

KUCHAR

Mike
Kuchar
Interview

of October 22, 1988

by J. Stevenson

What are you up to these days? You're recognized as one of the best underground filmmakers of the '60s but it seems you've been keeping a low profile for the last twenty years or so.

No, not really. I been making films actually. Last one I did was — well, I did three in 1984. This half-hour one and these two kind of picture poems in 1984. So it's been a four-year lapse. I do have shows, but I guess they're not publicized.

I was making films through the 1970s. They haven't been COMEDIES that much, but, ah ... maybe THAT'S the reason, you know. But I've never lost my interest in it, I've been having shows. Like last year I had a couple of shows here in New York, both of my old work and my recent work. I had one at the Los Angeles Film Forum last month ...

But no, ah, I still been makin' films. I'm not really in the limelight, but that's alright, I don't care. But I have been having shows around.

You teach film now?

I'm doing a six-week course here in New York, at the Collective, a basic filmmaking course. And also last year, a six-week dramatic narrative class, where I made a film with the students. And other things are coming up.

You're based in San Francisco now?

No, now it's kind of like goin' back and forth.

You yourself never had any formal education in film though, right?

No. No, I haven't. It was kind of like a fun hobby. It's always been that way. Whatever I learned I learned by my own working in film, through the years. So I'm sort of like "self-taught" or whatever, I had to learn. I learned by just working on my films.

You used to do erotic comics or illustrations. Do you still do that?

That's what I did when I was in San Francisco recently, I had to do a 42-page kind of comic book. Erotic nature ... always falls into these kinds of things. They always ask me to do erotic stuff — that's okay, I don't mind it.

Yeah, it was okay. I had no other job at the moment and that kind of helped me get through a couple of months. I got twelve hundred dollars for it. It'll be comin' out right after Christmas, it'll probably get in those more high class gay-lesbian bookshops.

It was a nice job, and at least it got me — gave me a creative outlet to express certain attitudes, and got me back into drawing. I do like to draw and paint — not just film.

Going back in time, your movie of '65-66, *The Sins of the Fleshapoids*, now that was probably your most famous film of that period. How do you look back on this film? Fondly?

Oh yeah. Sure. It's a compete entity unto itself. I hope that's like with every film. For every film, if the chemistry is just right, then I'm able to make it. It's very hard to make a film like that again because they don't fall back into that chemistry. In other words, when the chemistry is right I make the kind of film that I always wanted to make. It was my most successful picture as far as financially. I think it came out too when the camp sensibility was beginning to emerge — it came out right at about that time. There was a need for this kind of camp sensibility. The outside world took it well.

By "chemistry" you mean ...

Where everything falls together. You meet these kinds of people and they're just right to fill the parts that — this film that you've always had in mind.

That's what I find with my work. I have like a few films that I want to do, and they're not really related to each other, but then I'll make them when I meet the right people or discover the right place to film it. It's a matter of chemistry. Then it works, and you know, it stands on its own. And then ... life goes on ... until something else brings out something that you always wanted to make and then you know when it's right and you go out and buy the film and make it.

That's what separates independent films from the film "industry."

Yeah, right. You know, I have to finance these myself, and put the work in it, and I can only do these when I really feel inspired or when I really want to. And to do what I want to do ... What MOOD I'm in determines what I'm gonna do. And sometimes when I do one thing, the next film I usually do something different. Maybe that's another reason why I haven't got a "name" so much now, because you never can tell what I'm gonna do next. So there's a loss of identity, you know what I mean? In other words, you can't really expect the next film to be like *The Sins of the Fleshapoids* type thing. Because I can't do that,

102

Julius Middleman, a friend of a friend whom Mike cast in *Sins of the Fleshapoids*. Julius later became a policeman.

I'm not that way. If you do it where your films have a certain thematic unity, or a certain attitude throughout the whole thing, then you get a kind of a "following" — they know what to expect.

Sort of like John Waters, in a way — people know, or thought they knew, what to expect from him.

Yeah, right. And that's fine and all, but it's just not me, it doesn't occur to me to do that. I just go about my own whims, you know, for better or for worse. I don't care. But then again, I have a lot of people that like these other films that I do, so ...

So each film should be taken on its own.

Yeah. But again it's like, sometimes I could do an abstract film, or sometimes I do these kind of short, hopefully poetic kinds of films, then I might do a comedy. But it depends on how I feel, and also what I had already done. But I've still been making films, so I didn't drop out after the '60s.

Do you look back with any nostalgia on those times of the '60s?

Oh yeah, sure I do. They were nice times. Especially for filmmaking because it was much more inexpensive to make films then.

I resent some of it now, because it's become kind of

like a rich person's hobby. I feel bad for the people who are interested in film now, I feel a little bad because it's become so expensive.

But then my last films I made, I made with all outdated film. I got hundred foot rolls for a dollar each. (laughs) 'Cause I got kind of mad, I said, okay, I just want to make films like the way I used to make 'em. So with these last films there was a little color loss, but I said, "I don't care, it's either that or no film period." But I found that I had some stories to tell, so as long as you're able to tell the story, what does it matter that there's a little color loss? So what? It's the story that's most important. (chuckles)

So that's what I did, so I still keep my eyes open to make it a budget that's my type of budget.

Right, a low budget.

Yeah, low budget.

In a 1967 issue of *Film Culture* there's a quote, you said you have two kinds of actors you work with: "Those who can't act at all and those who overact." Do you still believe in the use of non-actors?

Ah ... yeah ... but [back] then it was what I only had to work with. Actually, my last picture, a half-hour film, two people were actors and they liked my work and they said, "If you have a role let me know, I'd read the script, I'd like to do it." So my last film I used actors — that was real nice ... so, it was depending on who I had to use, who was around, and most of the time it was non-actors.

So you don't deliberately chain yourself to any one philosophy.

No.

Now, Donna Kerness was in some of your films, too.

She was in a lot of our films, both my brother and I ... we met her in school. She's real good, she liked dancing, she was very much into *dancing*, so she had a very nice way of moving ... we made films but they were more like parties and means of expression — she'd be able to express herself and we'd be able to express ourselves. She was very good in films, and she liked films very much.

She's probably the best known star of those early films.

We saw her at a high school reunion, about four years ago ... after not seeing her for about ten, twelve years. She looked fine, still looks fine. My brother

wants to put her in another movie ... I don't know ... she seems game for it.

Those early films of the '50s, like *Town Called Tempest*, and those that you did with George, do you still show those occasionally?

Yeah ... we get good turn-outs, because it's like a novelty, something unusual — 8 mm — it's so antique now. I don't know what it is, maybe it's the fathers and the mothers also used to like the pictures and told their kids to go. But, a lot of new people — I had a show at the Collective, it was like sold out. A lot of young people there, they really enjoyed it.

I didn't know, I was up in the projection booth struggling with this old projector. But when I came out ... they really enjoyed the films, I felt glad. That was about five months ago or something. But the format, just having a show of old 8mm films from the '50s and '60s, people are interested.

How did your film style differ from George's back in the early days? Those collaborations.

They weren't too different, our styles blended well together ... but as we went on we each got our own ... his films are not like mine and mine are not like

Red Grooms with his then wife, Mimi Gross, stars of George's film *Encyclopedia of the Blessed*. Red Grooms also starred in Mike's early film *The Secret of Wendel Sampson*. ■

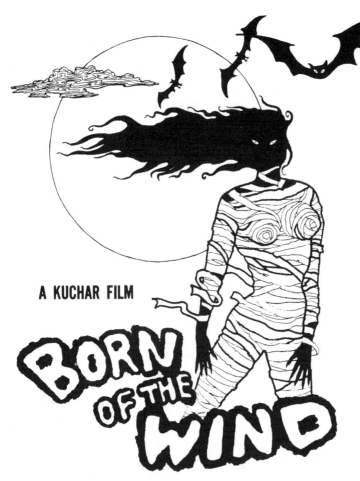

A KUCHAR FILM

BORN OF THE WIND

his now — he's got his own personality, I got mine. Sometimes we still have shows together, 'cause of the name, the "twin brothers."

Right, exactly — "The Kuchar Brothers."

Yeah, right ... but our films really are different. It's like ... another person, another temperament. He does a lot of turgid dramas and all (laughs), sometimes I don't, ah ... some of mine are kind of meditative, they're quiet, they're ... kinda like poetic, and, ah, different. Even technically, too. They're a bit slower. There's a different temperament involved.

And then you started making your own films at a certain point after you branched out into 16mm?

Yeah, we had our own projects to work on, so we just shared the equipment, really.

***Sins of the Fleshapoids* was your first movie on your own?**

Actually no, back in the 8mm it was *Born of the Wind*. That was the story of a scientist who brings a mummy to life ... a half-hour 8mm film ... it was my story, sorta my idea — kind of very romantic, with camp elements in it. Very LUSH. *Sins* ... was my first 16mm film.

Actually we began together on a project, a 16mm film called *Corruption of the Damned*, but then I sort of abandoned it 'cause I wanted to do this kind of color science-fiction film and George picked up and finished *Corruption of the Damned* which he actually did eighty percent of it. So that became like his first picture.

Ever since then we sort of, ah, each have our own projects in mind. And we'd just pool together our money and share the equipment.

You helped Rosa von Praunheim work on his film *Red Love* (1981), which he says you did very good work on. How do you remember that film?

Well, I like to travel, I really enjoyed Germany, and I love cinematography, so ... and anytime I'm behind the camera I enjoy it 'cause I love to photograph people, do lighting, whatever.

That was a very beautiful, lushly shot film.

And the pay was good. (laughs) And I made friends with a lot of the crew and some of the actors, which I then saw afterwards — 'cause I had a tour a couple of years after that in Germany, where I brought films ... it was a tour arranged by a museum in Frankfurt, and I caught up again with some of the actors, they came to my show and it was really nice.

Rosa wasn't quite sure how he was eventually going to finish the picture so a lot of it ended up on the cutting room floor. It don't matter. But a lot of the scenes I took wound up on the cutting room floor. But I got paid to do it so it don't matter.

Yeah, it was rather a schizophrenic film ...

Well, eventually it turned out to be, eighty percent of it was this video he shot of this lady trying to make up for her sexual escapades, that she didn't do earlier in her life. That he did completely after all this other footage, and it was like DUMPED in ... but that happens, you know ... I knew that probably might happen — that's okay. But I had a good time, goin' around Germany, like I say. And the pay was very good. To me it was sorta like a vacation.

He always mentions being inspired by the Kuchar brothers' films.

That's nice, it was nice he wanted me to come in and shoot, so it was fine.

Was there a mutiny against Rosa on the set of that film or something?

Oh yeah ... (laughs) well ... the thing was it wasn't turning out and then he called George to do the film, and George hates traveling and didn't want to do it. But he also had a job and I didn't. So he said, "What about Mike?" and I said I would, and that was great.

But ... ah ... it wasn't a happy set. He was nice to me because everything was turning out fine, but, ah ... he really was kind of groping, he really didn't know what he was looking — I don't know if I should tell you — you gonna WRITE all this?! (laughs)

We did a pretty big interview with him in our last issue, I know him pretty good so I'm not gonna try to create any big upheaval or anything.

(laughs) Yeah, there was gonna be a big mutiny, the main actors were gonna walk right out, yeah, sure, there was a big fight right in the middle of everything, yeah. And then, ah, well ... he had a way of ...

L to R: George, Mike and George's painting on the wall. George actually saw this woman pass by later in life, under some el tracks in the Bronx. Photo by Camille J. Cook.

"Two-headed monster" ... George on right (probably) and Mike in the VERY early years.

Mister Robot (Bob Cowan) considers love "a million years in the future" in Mike Kuchar's *Sins of the Fleshapoids*. →

Janis Jones (left) and Donna Kerness (right) in *Born of the Wind*.

whenever he was there on the set they would forget their lines because I presume there was beginning to be an animosity growing. Well, I mean it wasn't a set, if I — it wasn't a set (laughs) ... that I would have if I was making a film — it would definitely not be that kind of a set. (laughs) But that's between him and them.

The leading lady said, "Look, I'll stay on the set if he (meaning me) continues to be assistant director and photographer, and lighting man." So it got to that point. But that was nice, I was sort of like a glue to hold the production together. (laughs)

Who is the evil twin, you or George?

... "Evil" ... I don't know.

That question just popped into my head, I don't know what it means.

Yeah ... ah — he has a life of his own and I have mine ... though sometimes we live together, we each go our own way. This way then you can live together. You know what I mean? We have things to talk about, but otherwise we do have our own lives ... keep a certain distance ... makes it easier and okay.

Do you have any projects coming up?

Ah ... no ... I have nothing that I'm itching to make at the moment. So, really, ah ... no. I THINK I'll make another film, I'm not really sure. (laughs) I'm not thinking about it.

You've financed all your films yourself, right?

I financed them all myself, it always winds up ...

But you made a little money on *Sins of the Fleshapoids* ... do you still get any residuals?

Not too much now, but it certainly paid its way back then, many, many times over. And I still have shows, and the artist fee they give me, it's nice, and ... I never expected any money anyway when I started making films, so this is kind of like a slap on the back.

So you could never see yourself makin' a big budget Hollywood movie?

Well ...? No — not to go out, like, and push for it. If somebody ever contacted me and said they'd finance me, then fine — I'm all for it. But I'm not ... I don't have the ... I don't care about going out and pushing for it. Whatever I really wanted to make, I went ahead and made it. With whatever I had to work with. So I don't feel stifled, I don't feel like I haven't made a mark anywhere — I made some mark SOMEWHERE I guess, I don't know. And I do have a kind of a following that did come up, ah ... so it's like whatever I needed to do I somehow managed to do it.

You have a following out there ... does that surprise you?

It's nice ... that, ah ... every once in a while I get asked to play films, and that's nice. Sometimes I have a show in front of five people, that's kind of nice. (laughs) I feel good about it. It's intimate and I rather enjoy those shows. Sometimes it's even better than a full house. Then at times you GET full houses. Even if sometimes I'm asked to give a show in a place that only fits eight people — that's fine with me. (laughs) I like showing, actually, at ripped-up little joints, joints with ripped-up sofas ... the films feel at home there. (laughs) I feel at home in places like that. It's not like intimidating or ...

Did you meet a lot of the other New York filmmakers back in the '60s? Like Warhol or Jack Smith?

Yeah, sure. I met Warhol a few times ... "Hello, how are ya?" and I used to see him coming out of my shows. I would go see his shows, and sometimes he would bring the films in, 'cause sometimes you have to give directions to the projectionist who ... and at that time some of their projectionists were my friends.

Mike in a recent photo

★★★★★
FINAL

DAILY NEWS
NEW YORK'S PICTURE NEWSPAPER ®

8¢

10¢ OUTSIDE L.I. AND SUBURBS

Vol. 49. No. 296 Copr 1968 News Syndicate Co. Inc. New York, N.Y. 10017, Tuesday, June 4, 1968★ WEATHER: Sunny and warm.

ACTRESS SHOOTS ANDY WARHOL

Cries 'He Controlled My Life'

'Flower Child' Surrenders. Detective and policewoman (r.) escort actress Valerie Solanas, 28, into E. 21st St. station to be booked in shooting of pop art movie man Andy Warhol at his 33 Union Square West office yesterday. Last night, Valerie surrendered to a cop in Times Square, allegedly admitting shooting, and saying: "I am a flower child." Warhol is in critical condition. His associate, Mario Amaya of London, also was shot. —*Stories p. 3; other pics. centerfold*

NEWS photo by Frank Russo

And I met Kenneth Anger, met him a couple of times. That was, ah, we say, "Oh — we finally meet!" 'cause I'd heard of him and he'd heard of us.

An interesting thing about Warhol was that one evening I was walking home late at night and I had a vision in front of my eyes, and I saw a woman with no face ... in other words there was a woman but there were no features, and she was shooting him. And it was a "vision," like late at night, you know, and the thing was I felt the PASSION that she had. It was like I was suddenly possessed by this, like, vision.

And then it left, it was just like a few seconds — it was very disturbing so I got it completely out of my mind because I wanted to forget about it ... this whole scene that I saw in front of me.

And then the next day, an uneventful day, but then my brother came in and said, "Did you hear Andy Warhol got shot?!" I said, "Oh no — this is incredible ... 'cause I had this terrible vision the night before, and I saw this woman with no face and she was shooting him," and I felt the thrill like, of pulling the trigger. But I saw it in front of me, this vision — just grabbed me right by the throat. It was like supernatural ... it was really scary. I was really shaken.

But here's the thing — then the next day I heard the news that it was a woman, and then they mention the name, and then I said the NAME is so familiar. Then I realized that about a month before I had the vision we had both received a script in the mail. Somebody had mailed us a script and it was HER. She had mailed us a script wanting to know if we were interested in doing this film of her script. I wasn't — I was working on a film, my brother was working on a film, and I never MET her. I didn't know what she looked like. But I remembered the name — I put it back in another envelope, re-addressed it and said, sorry, I'm not interested in doing it.

Obviously she was sending the script around to have filmmakers work on it, and she probably sent him the script and he said, "Well, let's get together and meet," and somehow he would up with her, and ... she shot him.

But the vision I had of her was accompanied with this ... I FELT her complete hatred and thrill of pulling the trigger. I remember, it was late at night, I was walkin' home through a park.

But I never liked to talk about it 'cause it was — I felt like I was "in" on it, or something, you know what I mean? I not only saw it but I felt it.

And everything changed after the shooting, Warhol became more reclusive and Paul Morrissey took over the filmmaking, still in Warhol's name. In a 1980 interview Morrissey described it as "an ill-wind that blew somebody some good."

I always liked *The Chelsea Girls,* that's a real good one. That's Warhol's, completely. And Warhol would come up at his shows and just give the projectionist little key notes on how they should project that movie, which was a double-screen thing. But he was never saying like you HAD to be here or there — he was very open, so the projectionists could actually interject their own creative impulses on when to turn up the sound or whatever. In other words, there was a lot of elbow room, which was kinda nice.

I guess those days are over, though. I mean, it seems there were a lot of good things happening in those days. Those WERE the days of "Underground Films" and in fact, when I talk to John Waters today he speaks of it as a specific period that is over, most definitely.

Yeah, now it's like a lot of, ah, art schools and colleges, now they've incorporated film as part of the art department. And now there's a lot of students making films and it's sort of gone into that. A lot of films are being made, and students are making them in film classes. And I guess some of those underground filmmakers become film instructors at some of the fine arts schools. They sort of filtered in there. Most institutions and museums now have an understanding of independent film production.

An awareness of underground or independent films has been incorporated into the mainstream of film exhibition and whatever, you know, and it's carried on into the classrooms, too. It depends on the school, some focus on the academic or industry side, others on the more fine arts side. Depends on the school.

But back in those days the people who were making films WEREN'T students, like you guys, John Waters, Andy Warhol, Jack Smith, Kenneth Anger ...

That's right, just people who just made films, just all of a sudden took it upon themselves, you know, dropped either the paint brush or writing and went into film, yeah.

And I think that "movement," so-called, opened up independent films, like today with David Lynch or David Cronenberg, where it's not just industry films. It opened it up — it wasn't all just Hollywood films after that.

Yeah.

You teach film courses you said.

Every once in a while I do, I don't do it often.

Do you think film CAN be "taught"? How do you approach ...

Well, to me the most important thing is to be inspirational. I think inspiration is what it all comes down to. If I can be inspirational ... and also, not to have the students feel intimidated that they have a big obstacle as far as technicalities, 'cause it really isn't. It's just imagination, really, and a kind of a spirit that one should go about one's work and — that's really the most important thing in one's work: the spirit.

I mean, if I could be inspiring to somebody — not that I want them to make films like mine, you know, God forbid (laughs) — but if I can show that you can make a film if you got an idea and you like working with the camera, and don't worry, just go about it any way you can. Because it is the spirit that is most important in the film. And try to capture that spirit so other people feel it. That's all. And not to be intimidated by technology, because it's all an illusion, really — you can get something to look very, very good using very little.

And you can spend vast amounts of money and get nothing.

Yeah, because it can be completely empty and lacking in spirit, and it's a complete waste of money, so money's not the thing. You get an idea, there's many ways to do it and you can cut a lot of corners. Gear it to what you can afford. There are little tricks, and you can do it. I mean you can buy a light meter for five hundred dollars — you can also buy one for fifty dollars — you can get stuck in a big budget racket. It's all just a racket. You can do the same kind of films for like ten times cheaper also. If you're resourceful and you see a way.

Kenneth Anger says his whole life has been devised as a means of avoiding a regular job. Did you ever work a nine-to-five job?

Yeah, I've done it. The longest I ever did it was six years. I was in the commercial art field. That was right after school. That's what I made *Sins of the Fleshapoids* on. It didn't cost much anyway.

Then I left it after six years, thinking that I'd probably have to go look for another job in a week or so. Then the films started bringing me some money so that kept holding me off getting work, then I actually retired for six years on my films, because museums bought them and whatever — that was kind of nice.

Now, every once in a while, I do have to support myself. Temporary jobs or whatever, teaching or illustration jobs. Or also sometimes just a real schlop job, but I know I'm gonna get out of it, just have to weather it out until something else breaks, or save up enough money to take a vacation. (laughs)

But a filmmaker, a painter and a writer — they need time to daydream. Plus with daydreamin' you need a lot of time, free time, you know. So it's very important (chuckles) to incorporate that in one's life. 'Cause that's the only thing you're really interested in: your own visions, your own thoughts. Your own work. The other stuff is just there for a paycheck.

Did you ever get any grants?

I got a grant once — 1985. I got three thousand dollars. I did a poem series, I did these kinds of meditative landscape picture poems. I did one on the forest, one on the sea and one on the mountains. So I went to Asia and I photographed the Himalayas. **END**

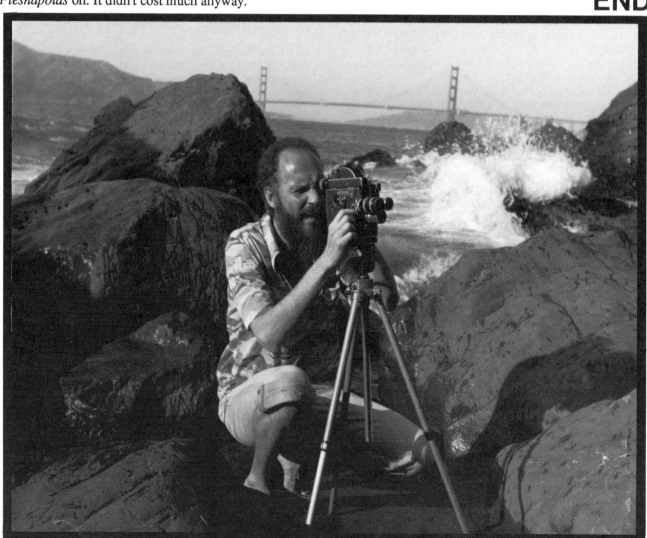

Mike Kuchar backdropped by the Golden Gate Bridge. 111

THE FILMS OF MIKE KUCHAR

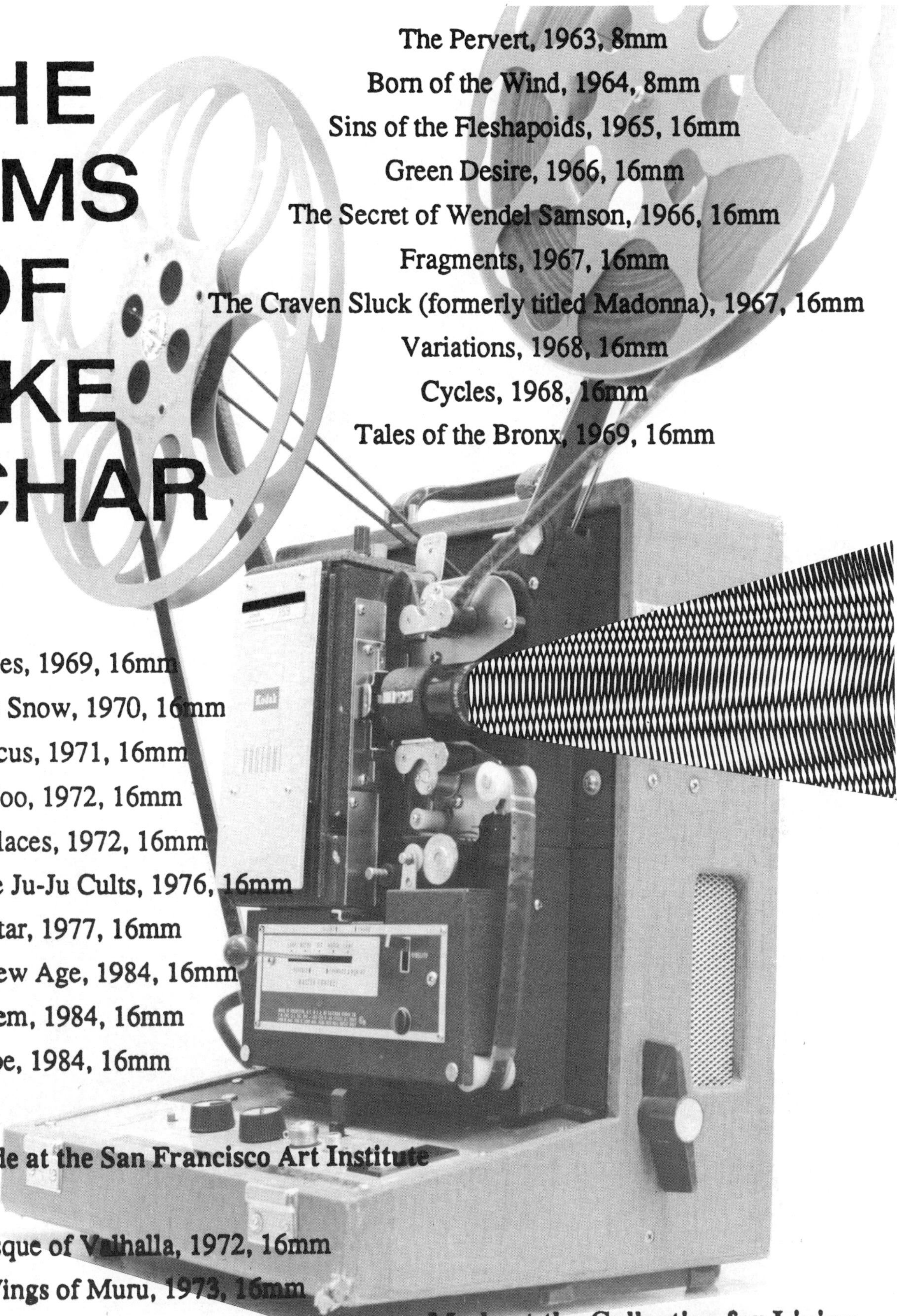

The Pervert, 1963, 8mm
Born of the Wind, 1964, 8mm
Sins of the Fleshapoids, 1965, 16mm
Green Desire, 1966, 16mm
The Secret of Wendel Samson, 1966, 16mm
Fragments, 1967, 16mm
The Craven Sluck (formerly titled Madonna), 1967, 16mm
Variations, 1968, 16mm
Cycles, 1968, 16mm
Tales of the Bronx, 1969, 16mm

Chronicles, 1969, 16mm
Abode of the Snow, 1970, 16mm
Aqua Circus, 1971, 16mm
Didgeridoo, 1972, 16mm
Faraway Places, 1972, 16mm
Death Quest of the Ju-Ju Cults, 1976, 16mm
Dwarf Star, 1977, 16mm
Fable for a New Age, 1984, 16mm
Tone Poem, 1984, 16mm
Seascape, 1984, 16mm

Class Films Made at the San Francisco Art Institute

The Masque of Valhalla, 1972, 16mm
The Wings of Muru, 1973, 16mm
Blood Sucker, 1975, 16mm
The Passions: a psycho-drama, 1977, 16mm
Isle of the Sleeping Souls, 1979, 16mm
Circe, 1984, 16mm

Made at the Collective for Living Cinema's Dramatic Narrative Class

Scream of the Damned, 1987, 16mm

Ondine (left) and Roger Jacoby in Minneapolis, 1983

Ondine

Ondine and Andy

the papal interview

by P. Hollis

In March of 1983, Ondine arrived in Minneapolis to introduce three infrequently shown Andy Warhol films: *Chelsea Girls*, *Vinyl* and *Loves of Ondine*, all three of which feature Ondine. Most people are more familiar with the later Warhol films for which Warhol acted as producer and Paul Morrissey directed, such as *Trash*, *Heat*, *Flesh*, *Dracula*, and *Frankenstein*. The films actually directed by Warhol were more experimental, testing the styles and conventions of filmmaking. Ondine was interested in pornography and the interaction of the first "Factory," of which he was a prominent member.

After his involvement in *Chelsea Girls*, Ondine left Warhol's Factory and appeared in a couple of films by Theodore Gershuny: *Sugar Cookies* and *Silent Night, Bloody Night. Sugar Cookies* is a classic sexploitation mystery that stars Mary Woronov, Lynn Lowery and a hilarious character played by Ondine. It also features a supporting cast of trash regulars and X-rated stars. This film, the superior of the two by Gershuny, is elegantly shot and coolly acted.

Since then, Ondine has gone on to a number of different projects, including starring roles in a number of Roger Jacoby films. He also returned to his first love — theater. In addition to teaching courses in drama, he starred in *Glamour and the Glory of Gold*, a 1987-88 Theater of the Ridiculous production authored by the late Jackie Curtis.

Ondine was given prints of the three Warhol films by Andy himself who long ago withdrew his [Warhol-directed] films from commercial distribution. The Whitney Museum of New York has recently screened a number of these "long lost" films, such as *Blow Job*, *Couch*, *My Hustler*, and *Lonesome Cowboys*, as part of its 1989 Andy Warhol Retrospective. The museum also staged a one night invasion of Boston (3/23/89). But the prospects of viewing the three specific films that Ondine possesses rest almost entirely with his capacity and desire to tour. During his 1983 tour, Ondine announced that these films were screening for the last time in the western world. There have since, however, been infrequent screenings and Ondine remains open to the possibility of future shows.

Ondine lives today with his mother in Queens, New York. Interviewing him in 1983, I found him to be charming, gregarious and still possessing the wit and magnetism that resulted in his "superstar" status within the Factory.

Ondine Interview

Tell me how you initially met Warhol.

Well, we were at a party, and there was somebody in the back of the party who wasn't joining in, and I just told the host, "I don't know who the hell that guy is, if he's gonna join, he's gonna join, if he's not, we'll kick him out." So of course he was thrown out of the party, and he approached me later and said to me, "I've never been thrown out of a party before." He said, "You know who I am?" And I said, "No, I don't know who you are." He said, "I'm Andy Warhol." I said, "Yeah, big deal. What the hell does that mean?" He said, "Would you like to make movies?" I said, "Sure, why not?" So, that's how we got that going.

What year was that?

1962.

The first movie that you're noted as being in is *Couch*.

Mmhhmmm.

Was that the first one that you did with Warhol?

Yeah, it was the part of a collection called *Three*, I mean, we made a little film called *Three*, and that film, if I was going to make films with Warhol, I was going to make pornographic films, that's the way I felt that it was going, so we made this little pornographic segment called *Three*. I didn't know it was going to be included in a film called *Couch* later, but it became, in fact, included in it. It's just a little five-minute segment, but we saw it on the screen and it was really powerful and people were just, you know, leaving in handfuls screaming, "Oh, this is awful! Oh my God, this is terrible. Oh, how horrible, how embarrassing. Oh ..." You know, and they left. And I said, "It's pretty good, you know." So, then I thought, why not? You can reach — if you can do that to a group of people, do it. So, that's when I really started to think seriously about making films with him. And *Vinyl* came out of that and then the thirteen or fourteen other films I made with him and then finally it culminated in the *Chelsea Girls*, which, you know, was the apex of that kind of filmmaking. And then, as a kind of homage, they did *Loves of Ondine*, which is not a really good movie, but which is witty in certain ways, and from that point on, Warhol and I were ... we had ... we no longer worked together. I no longer fit into the Factory and it was just fine with me, too, you know, because he went his way and I went mine.

To get back to *Chelsea Girls* a little bit, when did the Pope, how did that character come about?

It was a New Year's Eve party, and this girl told me I have a great religious presence. She went down on

Ondine in New York City in the 1960s

115

Chelsea Girls, Ondine and Ingrid Superstar

her knees and said, "Would you please hear my confession?" And, we said, "Oh, we have a new Pope." So I was crowned the Pope, and I said, "I will only hear your confession in the shower." So she went into the shower. She called herself Dale the Instant Jew. She was hysterical. So, she confessed to me and I turned the cold water on her and then the hot water on her, and I said, "You're absolved my child ... blah ... blah ... blah." Then I went back to Andy and I said, 'We have a fabulous new character." I said, "You know, I'm the Pope." He said, "Oh, we've got to do it in front of the camera." I said, "Sure, I'd love to." He said, "Well, let's set up a series of confessions." So, we set up a series of confessions and that's how that character was born.

And two ended up in *Chelsea Girls*.

Two. There was originally three, and when the *Chelsea Girls* was eight hours long, the third was included, but it's fun, it's charming. And I'm wearing all kinds of outfits, but it's really not very good. I mean, it's good, but it's not, you know, of that quality because all of the stuff in the *Chelsea Girls* is of a special quality.

That's how it appeared to me when I saw *Chelsea Girls*. I think I mentioned that to you, even though they're all separate reels, there's no cutting, and they're played out, it was just so powerful.

It's powerful. It's a very powerful film because all of the reels of the film themselves have that particular power, and over a period of eight months as well, the film originally started and it was an eight hour film, and you know, we showed it to audiences and packed every night. I mean, it was just packed. The people at the co-op couldn't believe it, every time we showed the film, thousands, not thousands, but hundreds of people came. So, it was a little too long, you know, I mean, we knew it was too long, so then we began to strike out certain sections and then we played it. We used a graph to see how it would work out structurally, and it had to be 1, 2, 3, 4, 5, 6, 7, 8 so that in every possible way you were assaulted by this cross-current. When the sound's off here, you look there, when this was going ... it's all A & B, but it works very well. In that film it worked splendidly. I don't know very many films that work like that ...

It surprised me that it worked.

It still does. It still packs them in. They get freaked out.

To move on and talk a little about *Loves of Ondine*, in Steven Koch's book you mention that it started out well, but it fell apart into a Mack Sennett type of comedy, almost, later on.

Well, I finally have remedied that. I've taken scissors to the goddam thing, and made a film out of it. There was a good film there, there's a lot of other footage lying around the Factory that should have been included in *Loves of Ondine*, but wasn't. And, in the

116

middle of the film, I mean they had to put that film into the Bleecker Street Cinema because the Bleecker Street Cinema was opening and that was listed as the first film. Well, in fact, it wasn't done. There was no cutting. So the stuff that Morrissey filmed was just tacked on the end of it and put in like reel one and reel two. I mean, the hell with my reputation, the hell with everything, and it didn't matter. So I got lambasted in all of the magazines. They said this was the worst movie we ever saw. There just is no excuse, blah, blah, blah ... it's terrible ... it's terrible. And when I saw the film myself, I said, "This is a fucking atrocity. It's just terrible." So finally, like two years ago, I said to myself, if Morrissey can add, I can take it off. So I took it off and rearranged the reels and fixed a couple of things here, here, and there. Now at least you can sit through it. It's not the greatest movie. It is not, at least, funny, It wasn't funny then, though. I mean, you laughed a couple of times, but then the jokes started to get stale. I mean, really stale. It's not the garbage scene that makes it

Paul Morrissey today

stale, that's fine in its own thing. It was the business of the fact that Warhol was not behind the camera. So, what was happening behind the camera is what's happening in front of the camera and is essential to what you see. And Morrissey who did just a straight imitation of Warhol at the time — Morrissey has since developed his own style and become quite a filmmaker, but at that point he wasn't and the *Loves of Ondine* became a vehicle for Joe Dallesandro and I just thought that was terribly unfair because why should it carry my name. So that's the way I felt about it. So, now, I've made it into a nice film. You know, it's a good little film. It's not that great, but it's good.

And then after that period of time, Warhol got shot, Morrissey kind of took over, and then there seemed to be the gradual weeding out of some of the old people in the Factory with a new group, then you went on to do ...

I went on to Woodstock to cure my drug problem which was really heavy. I mean, I was so paranoid, I couldn't go out. I spent the whole day looking through the crack in the floor, expecting people to break in. I mean, I had overdone it, you know. And it just became the end of a way of life. So I went up to Woodstock and got clean and was still in touch with the Factory and still worked with Andy looking for property up in Woodstock for him to buy and mailing him tapes of interviews with Philip Gusten and people like that which were all very charming and very, very good, and part of a new book we were going to do because we had done a novel that is 24 hours of conversation with me and Andy. But it started at the funeral of Judy Garland and never quite got off the ground and we ended it right there. It was five hours of tape. They weren't very good. So we moved out of each other's realm. It was just as simple as that. The weeding out was essential for, I think, Warhol's protection because he was — I don't think that the people who were involved in the Factory were necessarily going to hurt him ... it was that you needed somebody at the door or somebody behind the door who was going to be able to tell the true psychotic from just the speed freak. And he was surrounded more and more by demented people. Just demented people. Totally demented. I mean, we were crazy, but after awhile we just went away. It was like the real crazies got very heavy, you know ... it was very heavy.

THE END

Chelsea Girls

Billy Name cutting Edie's hair on the Factory fire escape, with Ondine tape-recording

KENNETH ANGER

Introduction
by Dale Ashmun

I first met Kenneth Anger in 1980 at a swell little East Village joint called "Club 57." Located in the basement of a Polish Catholic Church at 57 St. Mark's Place, the club was managed by Ann Magnuson, who specialized in booking a highly eclectic schedule of parties, concerts and mixed media events. With help from Bill Landis of *Sleazoid Express*, Club 57 scheduled an evening with Anger, in which all of his films were screened complete with commentary by Anger between each film. The place was packed and Anger seemed flattered by the East Village punk/art crowd's interest in his work.

Jump up to 1985 and the publication of *Hollywood Babylon II*, Anger's sequel to his legendary Tinseltown gossip bible. I was visiting a friend up at *Oui* magazine the week the book came out and pitched a feature on Anger to editor Barry Janoff. He was interested in the piece, so after contacting Ken's publicist at Dutton, I was invited to the Anger abode a few days later to get the dirt on the King of Dirt himself.

At that time, Anger was living in a spacious railroad flat in the East 90s. As you can well imagine, Anger's pad housed an amazing collection of movie memorabilia. Most of the pieces were circa 1930s and '40s and he especially coveted items connected with Mickey Mouse and Rudolf Valentino.

Anger was generous with his time, and after taping an hour of his easy flowing conversation, I asked him about the photo on page 285 of *Hollywood Babylon II*. In his chapter titled "Indiscreet," a photo of Marlon Brando flashing an especially wicked shit-eating grin is cryptically captioned, "Why is he laughing? He knows I can't print the indiscreet photo of HIM."

"I'll show you the photo," Ken announced. Then he cautiously checked the lock on his front door and asked me to wait in his kitchen for a moment. A minute passed before he called me back into his den where he had extracted a large portfolio from some sacred hiding place.

As I sat down, Ken showed me a large black and white print of someone who certainly was a dead ringer for the young "Bud" Brando, with his lips encircling the head of an erect cock. It looked as though he were puffing on a cigar, while only the penis and torso of his sex partner were in view.

Ken refused to speculate on the identity of the other figure nor would he give the slightest hint as to the source of this curious momento. However, this final bit of "show and tell" capped a fascinating discussion with him. It also stamped a strong forbidden photo image onto my brain cells that never fails to materialize whenever I see a Marlon Brando movie.

[Editor's note: This interview was printed in the March 1985 issue of *Oui* magazine in a severely edited and condensed version. *Oui* focused, predictably, on certain scandalous passages, snapping up the sex and lawsuit related gristle that Anger threw out to them, material very much in the *Hollywood Babylon* vein. Conversely, they ignored the more personal, if less inflammatory passages where Kenneth talks about his past, about his family and his early years.

These are subjects that rarely surface in Kenneth's books and interviews, and with all respect to Kenneth, whom we consider to be perhaps the most original independent filmmaker of the century, we are happy to be able to focus, if ever so briefly, on the "unseen" Anger ... on the man himself.

What follows are the unpublished passages from the *Oui* magazine interview.]

Interview with ■■■■■ ■■■■■Kenneth Anger

[Looking around Ken's apartment.] I want to ask you right off — those metal masks, where are they from?

They are aluminum molds for Halloween masks. I found them in a metal scrapyard. They looked like old ROCKS — they were completely black and I had them polished up. Each one weighs about 75 pounds, 'cause they're from a stamp mold — a stamp machine. They'd be a lethal weapon if any of them ever FELL. (chuckles) But I've got them up there pretty securely.

And you've got Snoopy up there ...

Uh-huh, and Peter Pan, and this one up here ...

[Discussing Kenneth's trip to Paris, France in 1950 to show his films at the Cinematheque at the invitation of Henri Langlois.]

Now, I want to ask you ... did you literally steal silver from your family and sell that to get the money to take the boat over to France?

Well, it wasn't like I broke into a NEIGHBOR'S house, it was ... they were kept in the attic, they weren't used hardly at all except maybe at a christening or something like that. They didn't miss them for several years.

In other words, you put the silver to a better use, it sounds like.

No, I mean it isn't like I broke into a neighbor's house.

Now did your family know that you were going to France or did you just kind of have to run away from home to do this?

They certainly had heard for quite some time that I WANTED to go — I was graduated from high school. Beverly Hills High. And, they refused to help me financially and I said ... I wasn't like a MINOR — I was old enough to legally do it without being a runaway child! (chuckles) You know what I mean, a runaway kid.

My grandmother was sympathetic to the idea, but, you know, Paris was like the Sodom and Gomorrah or something in their imaginations. Particularly that, my family was what people hardly believed existed: a family of Hollywood Puritans.

You see, Loretta Young is not the only Hollywood Puritan. My family was Scottish Presbyterian, and that meant no smoking, no drinking, no games or picture shows on Sunday — which was like to me the kiss of death. Because, I mean, a Sunday matinee was the one time I could go to the movies without school [interfering], so I went to movies ALL DAY Saturday. In other words, I went to a matinee where we had a serial, several cowboy films and a feature — a thriller, something like that. And then I went to ANOTHER movie and saw another show, so Saturday was all day long. But I snuck away on Sunday a few times too where I said I was going to a friend's house and actually went to the movies.

But Hollywood Puritans — they do exist even to this day. Dale Evans and Roy Rogers — they're Hollywood Puritans.

When you got to France and met Henri Langlois and he showed your films at the Cinematheque, did you get a job with him soon after that?

Immediately. And I was living in a maid's room in what they call "Seventh Heaven," the seventh floor of a walk-up of an old, old house overlooking the Seine, with a view out the window of the back of Notre Dame Cathedral, and you can't get more romantic than that. And my neighbor, who used to walk his dog all the time just down the street, all the time — of course he had a big luxurious apartment, was Bresson, the famous French director.

And you stayed in Paris for 10 years?

Yeah, I travelled — I went to Egypt, I went to Italy. I went behind the iron curtain ... I travelled extensively but I used Paris as a base.

• • •

In East Germany, in Czechoslovakia, they have FABULOUS film collections, equal to the Museum of Modern Art or the Cinematheque, with money from the State. The same goes for Moscow, they have a fabulous film collection, and they're very interested in preserving ... and also Moscow is very

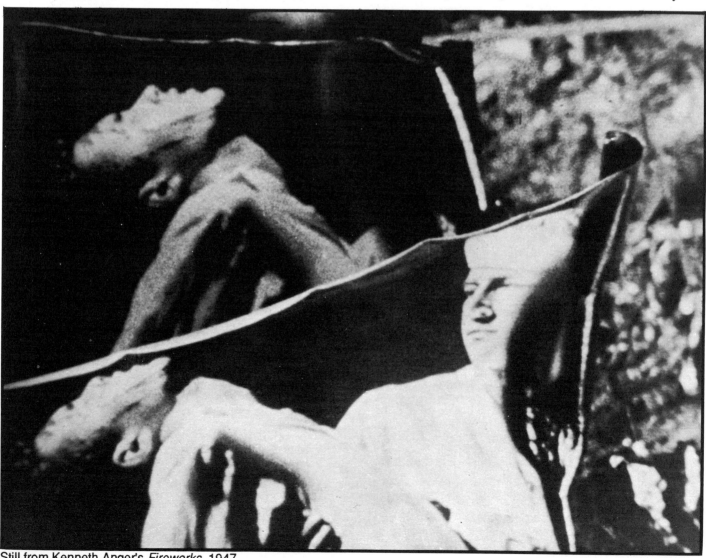

Still from Kenneth Anger's *Fireworks*, 1947

Kenneth Anger

Inauguration of the Pleasure Dome, 1954-1966.

Above: The Five Star Library Edition of William Shakespeare's *A Midsummer Night's Dream*, adapted from the Warner Bros. picture starring Mickey Rooney as Puck and featuring an infant Kenneth Anger as the changeling prince. Published in 1935 by Engel-van Wiseman Book Corporation, New York.

Left: Cameron Parsons and Peter Loome in *Inauguration of the Pleasure Dome*.

much concerned with the problem of preserving COLOR, which of course is fading all over the world. Color movies are like written in sand: they're totally fugitive. A film as recent as *Giant* has faded. Even a film as recent as the first *Jaws*, the blue is disappearing. If you can imagine, the blue of the water is going! But Moscow has been experimenting with deep-freezing films, sub-zero temperatures where the master-negatives are plunged into quick-dry freeze, and ... unfreezing them to print them again, takes something like two and a half weeks of gradually increasing the temperature with vacuums sucking off any moisture during that time.

At least they're working on SLOWING down the process of fading, that doesn't mean it has eliminated it. Because unless there's some way of a future video technology that will do dot-by-dot reproduction on video tape, that possibly is going to come along in the next century, I hope before such classics as *Gone With the Wind* turn to toast colors.

• • •

There's a reference in Hollywood Babylon to Hugh Hefner BUYING a star on Hollywood Boulevard. How could that happen?

Well, ANY millionaire can approach the Hollywood Chamber of Commerce and buy a star. Adnan Khashoggi could buy a star if he wished, because he's produced — put money into several films. So could Menachem Riklis with Pia Zadora. She will have her star bought and paid for by Menachem Riklis, her old boyfriend. And she DESERVES one: she's a pop figure like Jayne Mansfield. But it's really stretching a point to call HUGH HEFNER as being involved in the movie industry ... but you know he did produce Polanski's *Macbeth*.

• • •

Who is Samson DeBrier?

Samson DeBrier is a Hollywood legend. His claims to fame are two film parts: he was the slave who committed suicide in the silent version of *Salome*, and he's the star of Kenneth Anger's *Inauguration of the Pleasure Dome*, playing Lord Shiva, and a dozen other roles ... before Alec Guinness did multiple parts in Kind Hearts and Coronets. And Sasha Guitry did some films where he played three or four parts.

It's been said that many people thought Samson was a witch. Do you think he was a witch or an all-American boy?

He's not an ALL-AMERICAN BOY — he's the bastard son of the King of Romania. So his roots are in Europe.

I mean, he tongue-in-cheek referred to himself as an "All-American Boy."

Well, he's from Atlantic City, so in one way he's very American. But his background is sort of the "Yellowbook." In other words, the way I'm nostalgic for the 1920s, he's nostalgic for the yellow '90s. Which was before HE was born. (chuckles)

Do you know Samson pretty well?

I've known him since the '40s. In other words, I hate to say how many years that is ... I've known him 40 years. He moved from Atlantic City to Hollywood.

• • •

Working in the Hollywood studios as a child (*Midsummer Night's Dream*) must have been like fantasy land.

It was. Except at the same time I knew perfectly well that it wasn't just like Disneyland or something, it was a place where magic was made like a factory.

And the things that fascinated me were all the cameras and the lights and what was actually behind the cameras — that's what fascinated me. And that's when I decided that I wanted to be a movie director.

So you must have been very intelligent at that young age, "precocious," to use a word.

Well, I was a child prodigy that never got smarter. In other words, I think I was as smart then as ... (chuckles) ... and in a way I have sort of "coasted" off my precociousness. For instance, as a child I played the piano quite well, but I've never studied it enough to be good at playing the piano. I wish I had — I look with ENVY at other people playing the piano.

And your grandmother must have been very supportive toward you.

She was the only member of the family that was. But even then she wouldn't give me the money to go to Paris.

Was your family involved in movies at all?

My maternal grandmother worked as a costume designer. She worked on Rudolph Valentino's film, *The*

Lucifer Rising, Part I, 1974

Kenneth Anger's Latest Major Acquisition

The "lost" 24 sheet billboard poster for Erich von Stroheim's GREED (1924)

See elements of Kenneth Anger's Motion Picture History Collection on tour with the Smithsonian Institution's travelling exhibition, HOLLYWOOD: LEGEND AND REALITY: appearing coast to coast in major cities in 1986.

KENNETH ANGER
COLLECTION

Eagle, and also on his last picture, *The Son of the Sheik.*

Were your parents involved in movies at all?

Not at all. My father was head of the electronics department at Douglas Aircraft. He was totally unsympathetic to show business. My brother went into aviation and I was expected to also. And, quite young, I told him, "The only thing I'll be good at flying a plane, I'll be very good at crashing."

My brother graduated from Berkeley, in Science. Masters degree and all that. And then of course he went into the military, and was what I call, technically, a war criminal. He taught bombing in Korea AND Vietnam. I would have had my way paid through Cal Tech if I had gone into aeronautics instead of show biz, or being a ... "bohemian," I suppose.

Now, the story about Eunice Pringle and the Pantages Scandal. You mentioned a line that she did confess on her death bed.

She did.

How many years after the case was that, approximately? Twenty, thirty years later?

Oh quite a bit. She died, like, fifteen years ago.

She's GORGEOUS in this one shot [from *Hollywood Babylon II*] where she's doing the weight lifting.

Well, she was a very strong, acrobatic girl, that's why I have that photograph. And Mr. Pantages was smaller than she was, and was like, pushing sixty, you know?

Did he have a reputation as a ...

Well, they called him "the Great God Pan" ... he was, certainly a WOMANIZER, in the way Greeks can be even though they're married and everything. But in this case I doubt if he would have used a broom closet for his affairs. And girls are a dime a dozen in Hollywood. The most beautiful girls are AVAILABLE, particularly if you have a chain of movie theaters or if you're head of a studio. You know he wouldn't be so hard up that a dancer comes into his office, hoping to dance in his stage show — that was part of the movies — half the thing was live stage show and half was movies. That was called the "deluxe policy," the Deluxe Theater where you had the stage show and the movies, the live organ, live orchestra and all of that. So it was highly improbable that he was so hard up that he would have tried to attack this teenager.

Now ... [flipping through *Hollywood Babylon II*] this story, when you're talking about "Rose Bud" — which is just about my favorite story in here — you refer to it "Duris Genatillia?"

No, the real name of Marion Davies — that's her stage name — her real name is Marion DOURIS. And in Hollywood Cemetery the tomb where she and her sister are buried, it's just marked "Douris," it's by the artificial lake in the center of Hollywood Cemetery, behind what used to be RKO Studios then became Desilu Studios, and I think it's been taken over by Columbia or another studio now. It's off Santa Monica Boulevard.

At the main office of the mortuary — the cemetery office — they will provide you with a free map! Where it's marked on the map. Valentino and Harry Cohn and ... Marion Davies ... Douglas Fairbanks also. There's very famous people. And, ah ... Charlie Chaplin's abortion! Well, I mean "miscarriage." His first wife, Mildred Davies, had a miscarriage, and the thing that was born, he called it when he saw it dead — stillborn fetus — he called it "The Monkey."

• • •

[Discussing the difficulties Orson Welles faced from Hollywood's unspoken boycott of *Citizen Kane* upon its release.]

It was very hard to find any theater that would play *Citizen Kane*. It played in Hollywood at the Hawaii Theater, which was a brand new theater, just built, on upper Hollywood Boulevard, way above Vine Street, which is now the tabernacle of some cult religion. It's still there, the auditorium's still there but they've taken down the sign that said "Hawaii." And that's where *Citizen* played for several months IN STEREO.

Was that movie even a critical hit when it was first released?

Life magazine raved about it, as well they should.

Was it a commercial success?

It lost money on its release across the country. It was a huge critical success in New York, Chicago, San Francisco, Los Angeles — big cities. It bombed in the small towns — people were very confused about the flashbacks and the story technique. And people like my brother's wife, she came out of seeing it and demanded her money back because the movie was ALL BLACK, she couldn't see a thing! Like there was so much in shadows that she couldn't see it, she was used to having bright pictures, and it has the most brilliant photography, by Gregg Toland, of practically any movie ever made. What she was saying when she said it was "all black" — her name was Natalie — a real BITCH, a right wing bitch. Well, anyone that would marry my brother is ... that's the Republican side of my family. My sister, too — "Re-elect Ronald Reagan Committee."

Are they settled in California?

Very settled. He's settled in San Diego County, which is farther right than ORANGE County. And she, my sister, lives in Pacific Palisades, a neighbor — used to be — of Ronald Reagan. That's when he had his house there before he went to the White House.

Do you feel any "hot breath" from Ronald Reagan as a result of *Hollywood Babylon II*?

I already got it! I call it "Ronnie's Revenge." The day after the official publication date [10/30/84] I received a letter in the mail from the I.R.S. saying you are being audited for 1983. I call it "Ronnie's Revenge" 'cause the idea of auditing Kenneth Anger — this is the second time I've been audited in five years — and I call it harassment from Washington, D.C., and it doesn't mean I'm paranoid because they DO have a list of people they dislike.

• • •

[Ken discusses his ... general attitude.]

I do not work for anyone else, I have what I call an "independent lifestyle," which means I'm unmarried, I'm without ties. I don't have to report to any office for a 9-5 job, and I hope to God that I never will have to, because my whole life has been devised as a way to avoid that ... working for someone else, having to say "yes boss" to someone else. And I've had times where I've lived in an unheated maid's room in Paris, where I had to go to sleep with gloves and overcoat on, it was so cold in the winter. I think it was good for me. In other words, I don't think things like that damaged me. I'm living now in a walk-up in what is officially called a tenement — they either want to tear it down or renovate it. But I've made it my own inside — once the door's closed it could be anywhere, you're not aware you're in New York here. And I'm surrounded with things, some things I've had since I was a child. That was my Mickey Mouse from the time I was a baby. And it's in good condition; I treated my dolls very carefully when I was — I didn't chew off the NOSE. Many babies will, like, pull it apart, pull off an arm or chew off the nose or something. Or suck on the FEET! (chuckles) [looking around the apartment] There's several things I've had since I was a child. That little Shirley Temple book, I've had since [goes and gets it] ...

So maybe you will do a third *Hollywood Babylon* book?

I'll probably have to do something, I seem to run out of money on a regular basis every ... Of course the first *Hollywood Babylon* was the most shoplifted book in America in the 1970s, I was told. Many copies were ripped off from the stores, particularly in college towns. It ducked into purses and under coats ... you know I'm not getting a penny of royalties from a stolen copy ... I disapprove of that. It's outrageous. But I still get royalties from the first book.

Did you know Jayne Mansfield?

Yes I did — I adored her. She was the greatest P.R. creation of all time.

And she was her own P.R. person.

Absolutely. She lived for P.R. She got her orgasms over these little triumphs like opening a supermarket, or having her name once again on the cover of a magazine, and her picture on the cover of a magazine with her boobs sticking out in 3-D. She was an

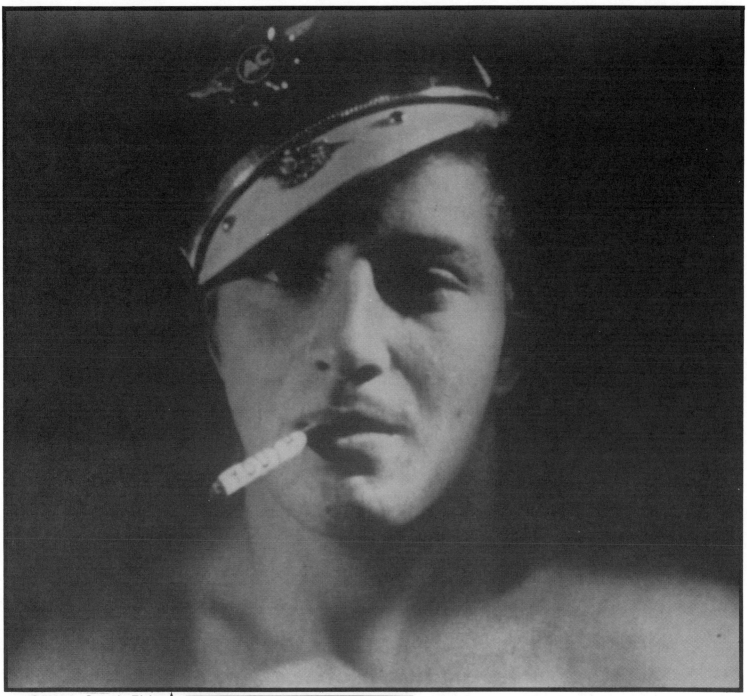

Still from *Scorpio Rising* ↑

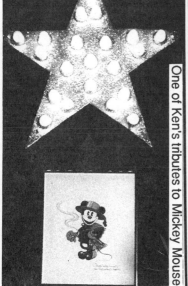

One of Ken's tributes to Mickey Mouse

Bruce Byron as the Dean-Brando look-alike star of Kenneth Anger's *Scorpio Rising*

INCREDIBLE manipulator of the press and the media.

She would appear in ANYTHING, including some of the worst things ever made, because she wouldn't say no to anything. She was in something called *The Wild, Wild World of Jayne Mansfield*, which is revived once a year at the Thalia. Don't miss it if it turns up again! It's fabulous. It's in Cinemascope and it was taken during her last tour of Europe. She visits a gay bar, she visits a French nudist colony ...

THE END

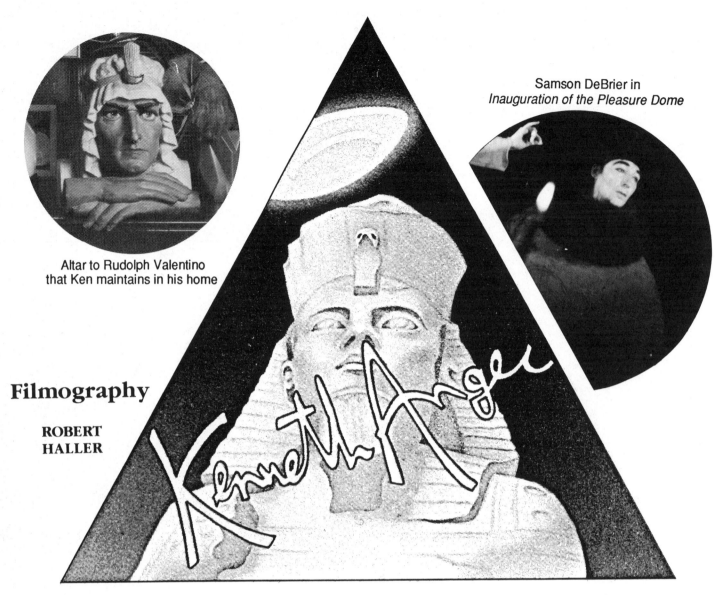

Altar to Rudolph Valentino
that Ken maintains in his home

Samson DeBrier in
Inauguration of the Pleasure Dome

Filmography

**ROBERT
HALLER**

*Unless otherwise noted, the films were conceived, directed
and edited by Kenneth Anger. Films denoted by an asterisk
are no longer extant.*

A MIDSUMMER NIGHT'S DREAM.
1935, by Max Reinhardt and William Dieterle.
Anger played the changeling prince.

✱ **FERDINAND THE BULL.** *1937.*

✱ **WHO HAS BEEN ROCKING MY DREAM BOAT.**
1941, 7 minutes, silent.

✱ **TINSEL TREE.** *1942, 3 minutes, silent.*

✱ **PRISONER OF MARS.** *1942, 11 minutes, silent.*

✱ **THE NEST.** *1943, 20 minutes, silent.*

✱ **ESCAPE EPISODE.** *1944, 35 minutes, silent.*
Remade in 1946 with sound in a 27 minute version.

✱ **DRASTIC DEMISE.** *1945, 5 minutes, silent.*

FIREWORKS. *1947, 14 minutes, tinted b/w, sound.*
Camera assistant: Chester Kessler. Music by Respighi.
Filmed in Hollywood. Cast: Kenneth Anger (Dreamer),
Gordon Gray (First Sailor), Bill Seltzer (Second Sailor).
Festival Prizes: Brussels, Cannes, Biarritz and Paris.

PUCE MOMENT. *1949, 6 minutes, color, sound.*
Music by Jonathan Halper. Filmed in Hollywood. Cast:
Yvonne Marquis (Star).
A fragment of the never-completed *Puce Women.*

✱ **THE LOVE THAT WHIRLS.** *1949.*
Filmed in Mexico, destroyed by laboratory.

RABBIT'S MOON (LA LUNE DES LAPINS).
1950, 7 minutes, tinted b/w, sound.
Camera assistant: Tourjansky. Filmed in Paris. Cast: Andre
Soubeyran (Pierrot), Claude Revenant (Harlequin), Nadine
Valence (Columbine).
Not released until 1972, then in a 16 minutes version with
a pop soundtrack. In 1979 the shorter 7 minute version
with a soundtrack by Andy Arthur replaced the 1973
version.

✱ **LE JEUNE HOMME ET LA MORT.** *1951.*
Study film of the Cocteau ballet, intended to be used by
Anger in subsequent filming of ballet in 35mm, color; this
second filming, the movie, never took place.

✱ **LES CHANTS DE MALDOROR.** *1952.*
Only tests and rehearsals conducted.

EAUX D'ARTIFICE. *1953, 13 minutes, color.*
Camera assistant: Thad Lovett. Music by Vivaldi. Filmed in
Tivoli (Italy). Cast: Marmilla Salvatorelli (Lady).

INAUGURATION OF THE PLEASURE DOME.
1954, 38 minutes, color, sound.
Camera assistant: Robert Straede. "Sacred Mushroom
Edition" has music by Janacek (*Glagolithic Mass*). Filmed
in Hollywood. Cast: Samson DeBrier (Lord Shiva, Osiris,
The Great Beast), Cameron (The Scarlet Woman, Kali),
Katy Kadell (Isis), Renata Loome (Lilith), Anais Nin

(Astarte), Paul Mathison (Pan), Curtis Harrington (Cesare the Somnambulist), Kenneth Anger (Hecate), Peter Loome (Ganymede).

Other versions had music by Harry Partch (41 minutes, 1954–56), and the Electric Light Orchestra (38 minutes, 1978). A 41 minutes 1958 version was presented at Brussels on three screens.

Festival prizes: "L'Age d'or Award," Brussels International Experimental Film Festival.

"Dedicated to the few; and to Aleister Crowley; and the crowned and conquering child."—K.A.

✱ THELEMA ABBEY. *1955.*

Sound documentary on the ruins of Aleister Crowley's temple in Cefalu, Sicily.

THE DEAD. *1960, 11 minutes, silent.*

By Stan Brakhage.

ARABESQUE FOR KENNETH ANGER.
1961, 4 minutes, sound.

By Marie Menken. Although Anger does not appear in the work, physically, he is present as an idea, as well as the subject of the film's dedication.

✱ STORY OF O. *1961.*

Filmed in France.

✱ SCORPIO RISING. *1963, 29 minutes, color, sound.*

Camera: Kenneth Anger. Music by Little Peggy March, The Angels, Bobby Vinton, Elvis Presley, Ray Charles, The Crystals, The Ran-Dells, Kris Jensen, Claudine Clark, Gene McDaniels, The Surfaris. Filmed in Brooklyn and Manhattan. Cast: Bruce Byron (Scorpio), Johnny Sapienza (Taurus), Frank Carifi (Leo), John Palone (Pinstripe), Ernie Allo (Joker), Barry Rubin (Fall Guy), Steve Crandell (Blondie), Bill Dorfmann (Back), Johnny Dodds (Kid).

Festival Awards: First Prize, Evian, France, 1966. Golden Cup, 11th Festival of Rapallo, Italy, 1965. First Prize, Third Annual Independent Film-Makers' Festival, Foothill College, CA. First Prize, Documentary, Poretta Terme Festival of Free Cinema, Italy, 1964.

"Dedicated to Jack Parsons, Victor Childe, Jim Powers, James Dean, T. E. Lawrence, Hart Crane, Kurt Mann, The Society of Spartans, The Hell's Angels, and all overgrown boys who will ever follow the whistle of Love's brother."—K.A.

KUSTOM KAR KOMMANDOS.
1965, 3 minutes, color, sound.

Camera assistant: Arnold Baskin. Music by The Parris Sisters. Filmed in San Bernadino. Cast: Sandy Trent (Car Customiser). A fragment of a larger, never completed project.

✱ LUCIFER RISING. *1966.*

Central footage of this first version stolen.

INVOCATION OF MY DEMON BROTHER (ARRANGEMENT IN BLACK AND GOLD).
1969, 11 minutes, color, sound.

Camera: Kenneth Anger. Music by Mick Jagger (Moog synthesizer). Filmed in San Francisco at the Straight Theatre and the Russian Embassy. Cast: Speed Hacker (Wand-bearer), Lenore Kandel (Deaconess), William Beutel (Deacon), Kenneth Anger (Magus), Van Leuven (Acolyte), Harvey Bialy (Brother), Timotha (Sister), Anton Szandor LaVey (Satan), Bobby Beausoleil (Lucifer). Made from remains of the 1966 *Lucifer Rising* project.

Awards: Tenth Independent Film Award (for the year 1969) by *Film Culture*.

LUCIFER RISING. *1970–1980, 30 minutes, color, sound.*

A presentation of Anita Pallenberg. Camera assistant: Michael Cooper. Music by Bobby Beausoleil and the Freedom Orchestra (Tracy Prison). Thelemic consultant:

Gerald J. Yorke. Filmed in Luxor, Karnak, Gizeh, Externsteine, London, Avebury. Cast: Miriam Gibril (Isis), Donald Cammell (Osiris), Haydn Couts (Adept), Kenneth Anger (Magus), Sir Francis Rose (Chaos), Marianne Faithfull (Lilith), Leslie Huggins (Lucifer). An earlier version carried a soundtrack by Jimmy Page.

Omissions:
Senators in Bondage, (1976), Color/Sound
Denunciation of Stan Brakhage, (1979), B&W/Sound, 15 min.

130

Hubert Selby, recent photo

Hubert Selby Jr.

The facts about anything, and especially about a man's writings, are usually so much dust in the eye. What is important to know about a writer is given in his writing. No amount of information about a writer will clear up the controversy which his work arouses, if he is a controversial writer. The discerning ones will read between the lines; the patient, plodding researcher will only grow more confused.

HENRY MILLER

MAY 1988

I wouldn't be the first person to suggest that Hubert Selby is one of the more important American writers of the twentieth century. But, for some reason, he's never achieved the recognition of writers he is occasionally compared to, for example, William Burroughs and Charles Bukowski. He certainly never developed the public persona that surrounds both these writers and, in fact, keeps a public profile that is low to the point of invisibility. Until recently, few people even knew that he was still alive.

A film adaptation of Selby's most famous work, *Last Exit to Brooklyn*, is in post-production at the moment, scheduled for a fall release. It is a German-American project, a lot of the footage was shot in Brooklyn. The film is produced by Bernd Eichinger and directed by Uli Edel. Selby lent his enthusiastic support to the project in an advisory capacity.

Although Hubert Selby is best known for his book *Last Exit to Brooklyn*, his other works certainly deserve attention: *The Room*, *Demon*, *Requiem for a Dream* and *Song of the Silent Snow*.

I wonder if you would tell us a little of your past prior to *Last Exit*.

Well, briefly, I left school when I was about fifteen and started working in the harbor on dredges and tug boats and when I was sixteen, I went to Europe on a liberty ship. I had been a big kid, a healthy kid, and just never went to school and I never bothered using my head a hell of a lot, so when I got sick, it really screwed me around because when I was eighteen, I was taken off the ship in Germany with TB, and they said I wouldn't live more than a couple of months.

What year was that?

That was 1946, and I came back to this country in October of 1946, and they used Streptomycin to keep me alive and eventually they cut out ten ribs and collapsed a lung, cut a piece out of the other lung and I spent three and one-half years in the hospital.

Is this back when they had TB sanitariums?

Right. So it really turned my life around. I started to read books, shoot-em-up and things to pass the time, and then I eventually got out of the hospital. I was in and out for awhile and for awhile I hung out with some friends of mine down around the army base in Brooklyn where *Last Exit* takes place. Then I started hanging out in a bar with some friends from the neighborhood in Brooklyn where I lived and one of them was Gil Sorrentino, the writer, who was really my mentor. They were going to college, I guess, at the time or something, I don't know. Anyway, I used to sit and listen to them and they would talk about people like Ezra Pound, William Caulder, Williams, etc., and I would listen and try to remember as many names as I could. Then the next day I would sneak over to the library, making sure nobody saw me.

Didn't want to ruin your reputation?

Yeah. And I'd get out whatever books I could. I started reading and——reading everybody at once, which is really kind of nice because I didn't have to work out of any influence. I remember when Gil was moving, we were helping him move, and he had this big box of papers, manuscripts and stuff, and naturally we sat around and he started reading it. He'd read something, and you could tell who he was reading at the time. That's the stuff he wrote when he was a teenager. You could tell he was reading Williams or Eliot or Pound, you know, because that's what the poems sounded like. So I didn't have to work out of any influence like that because I never concentrated on one writer or one country or period of writing. I might be reading Hemingway one day, Anatole [France] the next day, or Rabelais or Homer, whatever I could get at the library.

Self-education.

I suppose that's what it would be called.

So, then what prompted you to begin writing *Last Exit*?

Well, a couple of times they said I wouldn't live, and then I finally got out of the hospital. I was married and we had a daughter a couple of years old, and I was back in the hospital with asthma, and this one doctor, a so-called specialist, told me, "You know, you just don't have any lungs, and you can't live. Nothing we can do for you, just go home, sit in a chair, and don't move." He walked away and sent me a bill. You know, consultation fee. He never even came into my room. I remember him so clearly, just sitting in the hallway and he talked to me for about two minutes.

I work in the medical profession in my regular job.

Oh, really. Then you know, man, they're just unscrupulous, unbelievable. Eventually I was back in the hospital again. This time an allergist started treating me, and I was on disability; my wife was working at Macy's, if I remember correctly. And I had an experience, what I realize today was a spiritual experience, although at the time I never thought of it as such. Just something that happened. But, as you know, with spiritual experiences, they are more real than any experience we have on this level of living. It was very intense and I experienced it in all of my dreams.

•••

When you finished writing your stories for *Last Exit*, did you have any problems publishing that?

Well, by that time I was hanging out with poets, writers, and painters and musicians, and every weekend just about, we were over at Roi's house, Le

Roi Jones, now Amiri Baraka. He always had a big apartment, and we always just kind of slept out there, hung out there, and people would read my stuff and they liked it. And Seymour Kren, a commercial publisher, had me send the stuff up there, and they asked me to come up for lunch to talk about it. What they wanted me to do was sign a contract with them to write a novel, and after they published the novel, then they would publish this book. They said no, a book like this never sells, and so on. It's never successful, so you write a novel first.

I went into the bar that night, Cedar Street Bar, where we all hung out, and I was talking with Roi. We were feeling good. I was telling him what had happened that day at the publishers, and he asked, "Why don't you get an agent?" I said I don't know anything about agents, I don't know anything about publishing. As I said, I was just trying to write the best story I could. He said, "Well, Sterling Lord is Jack Kerouac's agent, why don't you try him?"

So I did. I called him, and he said to bring the manuscript up. A few days later he called me and said, "I read it and I think we can make money together." So he submitted it to Grove, Grove accepted it, and by that time, Gil Sorrentino was working as an editor at Grove or as an assistant editor, and he had written a really thorough detailed critique of *Last Exit*, one of the things that Grove did to help sell the book. They sent out a copy of Gil's critique along with all the review copies.

I didn't think of *Last Exit* as being unusual or anything else, but evidently it was. It's not a very common kind of book, so these people who make a living reviewing books, etc., are usually rather academic people and have no idea what the hell is going on in the world. Coming across something of this nature, I realize today from what I've been told, would dumbfound them. They wouldn't know what the hell to do, they would be afraid to say they like it, and they were afraid to put it down because they

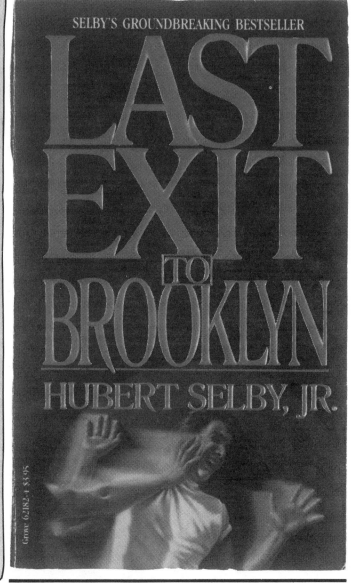

133

didn't want to look like fools. Having this triumph, so to speak, helped them, and it got some wonderful reviews and then another thing that really helped was *Time* magazine reviewed it almost immediately and attacked it. They called it "Grove's dirty book of the month." That gave everybody ammunition to attack *Time*, and *Newsweek* gave me a big spread with a picture and an interview and a review and all that sort of thing, and then Grove took out a big full-page ad in *The New York Times* and the thing just went on from there.

How was your life following publication? I believe it went on to sell quite a few thousand copies.

Yeah, it did very well. It went through a couple of printings in hardback and then paperback, and it was translated into quite a few different languages. So it did rather well, and I just went on from there.

You had no problem with censorship?

Well, in England they had a debate in the House of Commons for two weeks and they had a big court trial that ended with them forming an organization of people like Anthony Burgess and Sam Beckett and

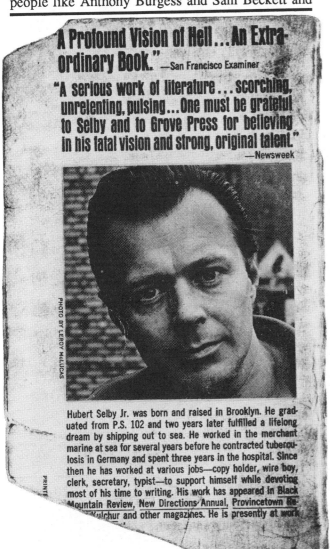

"A Profound Vision of Hell...An Extraordinary Book." —San Francisco Examiner

"A serious work of literature...scorching, unrelenting, pulsing...One must be grateful to Selby and to Grove Press for believing in his fatal vision and strong, original talent." —Newsweek

PHOTO BY LEROY McLUCAS

Hubert Selby Jr. was born and raised in Brooklyn. He graduated from P.S. 102 and two years later fulfilled a lifelong dream by shipping out to sea. He worked in the merchant marine at sea for several years before he contracted tuberculosis in Germany and spent three years in the hospital. Since then he has worked at various jobs—copy holder, wire boy, clerk, secretary, typist—to support himself while devoting most of his time to writing. His work has appeared in Black Mountain Review, New Directions Annual, Provincetown Review, Kulchur and other magazines. He is presently at work

Back cover of original Grove Press edition of *Last Exit to Brooklyn*.

so forth, to defend the article. That organization is still in existence.

A similar thing happened to Henry Miller's stuff when they tried to print it here. To switch topics, when did you start writing *Demon*?

Demon. When in the hell did I write *Demon*? Oh, 1975, I think.

Why the long time period between books?

Well, *The Room* was written before *Demon*. I wrote *The Room* in 1970. After *Last Exit* was published, some money started coming in. I found it very easy to sit around and do nothing but stay drunk.

Were you a success at that?

Well, I think so. I drank myself to death and haven't had a drink in nineteen years, so I guess I was a success.

Certainly you went as far with it as you could.

Yeah, I couldn't go any further without drowning. I mean, when something kills you, that's about as far as you can go with it.

Can't take it much further than that. When you started to write *The Room*, was it prior to your decision to stop drinking?

No, that happened after. I was sober when I wrote *The Room*. That book is a good example of a lot of things for me. I didn't read that book for twelve years and I just reread it a year or two ago, and my initial impression was right. It's the most disturbing book I've ever read in my life. It's horrifying, but at the same time, I think it's a masterpiece. It's really a great book, and I can see in the last stage, it took me six years because I had to learn how to write. *The Room* is a great book, but there are parts of that book when it came out and suddenly I saw it on the typewriter, I couldn't believe it. My initial reaction was no, I'm not going to write this, you now. But, as I say, I don't have the right to do that, it's up to me to understand the story that has been given to me and to meet the needs and demands of that story, so the stuff was there coming out. I just put it on paper and when the book was finished, it all worked. So I don't have the right to not write that stuff just because I don't want people to think that there's something wrong with me.

What was going on at that time in your life that you were writing that stuff, other than you'd stopped drinking?

My life was wonderful at that time. That particular period of my life was wonderful. I had been sober and I was living with a young lady I eventually married. She had a little girl, and my life was just terrific.

It was interesting to me, reading that book. Part of my job is to deal with people who are having similar problems, and *The Room* has a certain screaming to it of realizing the lack of control in your life or that feeling of lack of control.

You've hit it.

It's very common, and when I talk to people who are saying those things, they're thinking those things, no matter how logical or illogical.

You're right.

The cage may be bars or the cage may be addiction or the cage may be your marriage.

We create it ourselves, but we don't see it, the guilt that we feel. That's absolutely right. Lack of power is of the limit. You look at the best seller list, I guess as far back as they had the best seller list, in the non-fiction category, and you'll always see at least half the books have to do with power. How to exert power over other people. How to be a success. How to have more power, in one way or another, they're all talking about power.

Or powerful people explaining to you how they became powerful.

Right. In one way or another, that's right.

How was _The Room_ accepted once it was published?

Well, it got the greatest reviews I've ever read. I mean I wouldn't have the nerve to write a review like that of my own book. You know. Like Walt Whitman did, I wouldn't. I mean, they were great reviews. In _The Saturday Review_ and _The New York Times_, just outstanding reviews. Not only were they very complimentary, but they understood the book.

I notice the French tend to label it existential.

I don't exactly know what that means, to be perfectly honest with you.

I don't either. _The Room_ just seemed to be a picture of one man who's caged and doesn't know how to get out.

At the end of the book they open the door, but he stays in the cage. Yeah, I want to explain something. When I talk about understanding that story, I don't necessarily mean a psychological understanding, moral or ethical. For instance, _The Room_, the basis of it, the thing that I understand and work from was variations on a theme. That's right, it is a musical concept in _The Room_ and it's more a jazz concept than a classical concept, in some sense, simply because it's contemporary. But it's also the simple baroque kind of variation or trio sonata, so to speak, and it has to do with whatever the facts may be. It has to do with memory, it has to do with fantasy. It's all variations on the same thing, almost like a Rosh Hashanah in a way. Which story is true in Rosh Hashanah and which story is true in this guy's head. We know, I think you know, by the time you finish the book, you know which is true and which isn't. But the point is, it doesn't make any difference because he's already found himself guilty. And it's the same thing, I had to understand, like with _TraLaLa_.

Now _TraLaLa_ is only about twenty pages long, and it took me two and a half years to write. Of course, I was working at a job during the day, and I'd come home at night and work. That's how _Last Exit_ was written, you know, at night, a couple of hours every night.

Were you able to devote all your time to writing when you were doing _The Room_?

Yeah.

And then after _The Room_, when did _Demon_ come out?

Demon came out in 1972, I think.

How long did it take you to write that?

Oh, wait a second. I guess _The Room_ didn't come out until 1972, and then _Demon_ came out in 1976.

Four years. How much of that time was spent writing?

Well, let's see, as I wrote _The Room_, I spent a year working in a gas station, pumping gas, and I spent a year as a stockboy and was unable to do any writing at all.

Was your health posing you any problems with working?

Yeah. That is an ongoing problem. I want to finish this thing about _TraLaLa_ because I think it is important to understand the story, and I'm not capable of just sitting down and thinking. I don't know how many people really are, I guess there are a few people like Einstein who are, but very few. I have to think out loud either talking or on paper and so I kept trying to write this thing and throwing it away. Finally, after a couple of years, I realized what the demands of this story were, what I had to do, and very simply, what I had to do in _TraLaLa_ was to reflect the psychodynamics of an individual through the tension and rhythms of a prose line. Once I realized that, then the story just went. I mean there was no problem. So whatever they say, it's not necessarily a psychological, moral or ethical understanding that has to come. The basis of it can be anything else, like in _The Room_ or _TraLaLa_. However, usually because it's my experience and my personality that all this is being filtered through, there will be a sense of morality.

I think Terry Southern said that you are one of the moral writers of our time.

I can't get away from that. But there doesn't seem to be judgment in it. You know, the word moral is like the word God. It's a tough word, man. It's got bad press. A real bad press. But it doesn't have to be judgment in the sense of morality. In other words, it doesn't have to be that way. I believe true morality is totally lacking in judgment and that's one of the things people respond to in a lot of my work.

If they dare to.

Yeah. Ha, ha.

As opposed to Josephine Hendon who did an article in _Harper's_. The title of the article was _Angry S&M As a Literary Style_. She said about you, "There are writers who hate people, who thrive on the rage that bristles in every city. They know the crowd craves blood because they crave it themselves to feel thoroughly alive."

That's what she said about me?

That's what she said.

That's funny, that's not what she said when she reviewed *The Room*.

This is where she lumped you and William Burroughs and Barthelme and Hunter Thompson, which I think is a kind of an odd grouping of people anyway, but that is what she said. She also went on to say that "from human dregs, from the unremittingly tormented, Selby extracts the very odor of rage or essence of that free-floating danger that lies like a pall over all of us." That seems somewhat accurate to me.

Yeah, she reviewed *The Room* for *The Saturday Review* and it was an absolutely great review. I think she called me the poet of our decline.

Although it is interesting, in this article, she said that "in Selby's rare heterosexual love scenes, most of his characters hate women so totally and do not want to get close to them, even to destroy them." I don't necessarily have that sense of your writing.

I don't know, but I can certainly understand how she might react that way, especially as a contemporary woman. I don't know if I would totally disagree. You know what I mean, I can see where that could be a valid interpretation.

I guess what I look at is that the alienation and fear aren't necessarily directed at women. It just so happens a lot of relationships involve women.

That's true. If you look at the work, I think you'll see that alienation between everyone. For instance, in *Demon*, the only real relationship that Harry has is with his wife, and he has, to the best of his ability, a loving relationship with her occasionally.

A friend of mine, after he read *Demon*, said that he thought it was a religious book, but not necessarily in the sense of Catholicism or a formal religion. It is a view of a person's looking for an answer, and whether you want to label him a sexual psychopath, a sexual addict, or whatever, it's that striving to find an answer to things that are going on.

I think the Epigraph really tells you the whole thing. A man obsessed is a man possessed by a demon and it doesn't make any difference what the obsession is.

You can feel obsessed with gambling, with eating, with drinking, drugs, women, with money, you know, power. You just can't satisfy an obsession.

That seems to be a recurring theme in your writing.

Yeah. Just like that lack of power. It was very interesting that you noticed that loss of control because one of the things I did after I had written a couple of little things was to reread them and see what was in the work that hadn't been deliberately and consciously put there. The thing I noticed, what really leaped out at me, was that they all failed because they lost control, not because they were immoral or anything, but they lost control.

I guess I have a lot of empathy for Harry.

Which Harry?

They're all Harrys. Harry White.

Harry White. Yes.

Because even though his acts could be viewed as immoral, you had sympathy for him, not necessarily because he chose not to do it, but as you said, once you get started and feed it, it doesn't stop. There is no time you can just say okay. It's kind of like getting a little bit pregnant or having one drink or just going to play a friendly game of cards. Once you start, the ball starts rolling and it just doesn't stop.

That's right, man. Try and get a little bit pregnant. Man may one day accomplish this, but hasn't done so yet.

That's right. In dealing with people with addictions, there is no in-between. It's not a "Well, I can drink as long as I don't shoot junk." And the same thing in today's world is true of sexual addicts. It's like, well, I can just cruise the streets and look at 'em as long as I don't touch 'em.

Yeah. Lot's of luck, Charlie. I'm gonna buy *Playboy* for the literature in it. I've heard so many people say that as if they're going to convince someone they are buying *Playboy* for the literature.

In a sense, I agree that guilt was the first step of an obsession, because of the self-consciousness.

Yes, guilt is the first step of human existence, right. What I mean by human existence is human life as we are experiencing it now. If it wasn't for guilt, we would realize the truth about our nature, wouldn't we? But when we feel guilty we are afraid to look and see that we really are God.

Catholicism has done a good job of implanting that in most people.

Mea fuckin' culpa, man.

Yes, I remember being an altar boy. Having them tell me every day, you even think you're going to think that thought — that's it.

I remember, of course, it's much different today, but when I was a kid, I was in a predominantly Irish-Catholic neighborhood and I was a "Black Protestant," and in those days, we used to have what they called Brooklyn Days, in May, which was really like the anniversary of the Methodist Sunday School.

There was a big parade in our area. It was terrific, with ice cream and cake, and all that, and I remember my friends. How old were we? Ten years old, eight, twelve, around that age. I remember them being told by the nuns, my friends who went to Catholic school, or the ones who went to public school, had to go to religious instructions one day a week after school for what they called confraternity classes, and they were told that if they even looked at that Protestant parade, they'd go blind. Jesus Christ.

I remember in the Catholic church, they said, "You're not allowed to enter another church, that's a sin."

That's right.

After *Demon*, how long was it before *Requiem*?

It wasn't too long, *Requiem* was probably from 1978.

I noticed similar remarks about it. That is, people thought you were Black after you wrote that book. First they thought you were a professional inmate after *The Room*, and a sex addict after *Demon*, and then you wrote *Requiem* and everybody thought you were Black. But a lot of it is the same story and your morality of talking about all those different situations and people. It seems there are similar themes of getting trapped and sometimes being afraid of getting out of the trap because it's more familiar than taking a chance on something you don't know.

Same self-delusion.

Were you able to support yourself with your writing up through *Requiem*?

Through *Requiem*? Yes, I was. I was doing a couple of little movie things and so forth. I was doing very well for a while, and then I got sick. Physically sick. Oh, shit, for five or six years I was unable to do any work, and everything just fell apart. I went back East for five years and eventually my wife left me.

Your first wife?

No, this was my third wife. I met her in January of 1968, actually, I was still married, as a matter of fact.

I wrote a thing for Stanley Kramer, *Remember the Sabbath Day and Keep It Holy*. Back in 1974, ABC Television was going to do a special on the Ten Commandments, a two-hour movie, on each of the commandments, but not with a religious or historical theme. Just a contemporary story and it's very funny because ABC took five of the commandments with an option on five.

That's typical.

I can just see them do all ten and they get this great rating, so they send Moses out for another five, right?

Either that or they go, "Gee, we got good ratings on seven, but eight really isn't making it, should we drop it and go to nine?"

I tell you, it's just marvelous. So I wrote that and I just lived it. Then the whole thing got cancelled, but I guess it might not have been done because Kramer said to me, "You know, this is the most beautiful and wonderful script I have ever read that will not be done on television." He said, "You wrote literature."

Have any of your adaptations or original screenplays made it up there yet?

One in Europe.

What was the name of the film?

Oh *Day and Night*, I think. Or *Night and Day*.

Who did it?

I think it was *Day and Night*. I was on welfare at the time, my son and I. When my wife left, my son de-

cided to stay with me. He was twelve at the time and we came back out here. A friend gave us a place to stay with him for a while until we got on welfare, which is not a fun thing to do. But anyway, he and I got a place of our own finally, and I got this letter from a guy in Switzerland. He said he had been in the movies, a young fellow, a cameraman for Jean-Luc Godard, and he always wanted to do a movie, based on Dostoevsky's *Notes From the Underground*, but he had never been able to come up with a good script, and he had read my book, *Demon*, in French. He said he knew I was the only one to do it. He asked me if I would, and I said yes right away because I've tried to get more open to things, because when good things are presented to me, it's usually a case of saying yes to it. And also, if I think about it, I would say no. I mean, this guy's in Switzerland, I'm in L.A.; he doesn't speak English, I don't speak French — and he wants something — a contemporary story that has to take place in Geneva, and this is going to be based, or more or less loosely based, on *Notes From the Underground*. Now you know, all of this is impossible. Totally impossible.

It does sound that way.

So, I said yes, and I wrote this thing, and it came out right. Got off welfare, anyway.

That's where you got your money and the movie did get made.

Yeah. That's the only one that I wrote that was made.

I noticed in one of the old articles that Robert DeNiro and Stanley Kubrick were also interested in doing some stuff. Did you see *Taxi Driver*? And what did you feel about that film?

Yeah, I enjoyed it. I enjoy anything with DeNiro. That guy is just marvelous. If I had been writing, I would have written it differently. I thought Harvey Keitel was good. I enjoyed it.

And you liked Scorsese as a director?

Well, I saw *Mean Streets* and I enjoyed that very much. I liked *Taxi Driver*. I think that's all I've seen actually, I've missed the others that are supposed to be so good, like *Raging Bull*.

Do you have a TV at home?

No.

If you're going to see a movie, you'd rather see it in a theater?

Yeah.

Are there any films in particular now that you like, or filmmakers?

Well, let me see. Unfortunately, with my memory, I forget, but I go each week to the Writers Guild with my son, and I see some like *The Unbearable Lightness of Being*. I enjoyed it very much except it was forty-five minutes too long and tough on the bottom. Otherwise, it was a good movie. One of the funniest things I've seen in a long time was *Blue Velvet*. Did you see that?

Selby on the set of *Last Exit to Brooklyn*

Yes, I did.

That was fantastic. I got such a big kick out of that.

A lot of people didn't see some of the humor in it though.

Well, but it was almost like a take-off. He was just taking off on the whole genre. I mean, the whole thing. I don't know how you could miss it. It was very blatant. Anyway, I got a big kick out of it, but I've seen some English movies I thought were terrific.

You know, I don't get to see many foreign films, but *Au Revoir Les Enfants* was marvelous, I thought. *My Life As a Dog* I enjoyed thoroughly. I liked *Dark Eyes*. That was good.

I saw *Broadcast News*, which was fun, a lot of laughs. Most of the American movies today are just hopeless, you know. They're unbelievably hopeless. They're made by young kids, I mean the people at the studios and all that, who have, I guess, MBAs or something, and who've been raised on television and have no idea what life is — they have no life experience. They just have TV experience and they're re-making old movies according to their interpretation of life as viewed from *Father Knows Best* or something. I don't know what, but it's really amazing what they do with the money. I mean, they spend 20, 30 or 40 million dollars on a movie and it's dreadful. It's

not like the old movies where they were hopeless but they were a lot of fun. These are not a lot of fun.

I hear there are now a couple of your books that have been optioned again.

Yeah.

Are you going to be involved in those in any way?

Well, the option of *Demon* I'll have nothing to do with. He does this thing by himself and he's in France, so I have no idea what's happening to that. The option is up next month so I suppose I'll find out by then what's going on. I've heard nothing about it. But the *Last Exit to Brooklyn*, I'm involved in. They ask me about everything that comes along. They want my input in everything.

Who is going to do the screenplay?

Well, that's been done by a guy named Desmond Nakano

Have you read it?

Yes. It's very good. It should be a marvelous movie.

Have you written in any style other than fiction? Poetry? Critiques? Non-fiction?

Not really. I've written a couple of dozen psalms and I have a thing on El Salvador that's non-fiction.

Is that recent?

No, I actually wrote that for a benefit we had back in May 1980 or 1982, or whenever the heck it was.

You've also been doing some readings in California.

Yes, there were a few I did lately with Henry Rollins, three with Henry and Lydia Lunch. Then I did one with Henry and some other people up at the Roxy.

How did those go?

Oh, it's wonderful, just really wonderful. One of the great things about it is that the young people, like people in their 20s, really respond to my work. I didn't notice, but there is evidently a whole following out there of young people. It was a big audience.

There are a lot of people, including filmmakers and other people who have been close to your work who have been praising it and sending it to other people to introduce them to it.

Oh, really? I'm not aware of any of it. As far as I'm aware, I'm dead. You know, I have never been acknowledged as existing in this country by more than a couple of people.

It's somewhat surprising when you look at earlier copies of your books with all the reviews that are quite laudatory, but somehow ...

Reviews, but you notice there has never been, other than Gil and Mike Stevens, a word written about me, not even by other writers. You read interviews with writers, and they say who their favorite writer is. You never see them mention me.

• • •

Some of my books will get back in print again.

I think in the *LA Times* interview you sent me you mentioned that, I think, four out of the five are going back into print. *Songs* is already in print and *Last Exit* is still in print.

Well, *Last Exit* will be out pretty soon.

I can still find that in the stores here occasionally.

Next month *Requiem For a Dream* will be reissued.

Great, that's the only one I have a problem finding.

Song of the Silent Snow is still available. So it's *The Room* and *Demon* that I'm hoping somebody will pick up.

As a matter of fact, when I go to the library, they don't even have those. I had to literally scour used book stores for about a month to find a copy of *The Room* and *Demon* to reread them since I sent my copies away. I went to the library and they said they no longer carry them.

I know a guy out here who just bought a copy of *The Room* and paid $75.00 for it.

It's too bad you don't get a cut of that. And now you're wondering why didn't I keep all those copies at home.

• • •

I noticed that after rereading *Silent Snow* and your other works, it was interesting to look at the comparisons of Harry in *Strike*, and Harry in *Penny for Your Thoughts*. There are some similarities, but I look at Harry in *Silent Snow* and he is still obsessed and still has some of the fantasies but he makes some choices. Although there is some resignation after he had made the choice, he had made a choice.

Yeah. Well, *Penny for Your Thoughts* was written around the same time as *Strike*, before *Strike*, I believe. Yeah, it was written before *Strike*.

Why did you wait so long to publish it?

What, the story? Nobody wanted to publish it. I think it was actually published in a little anthology that Roi put out once.

Is it true that many of the stories in *Silent Snow* were older stories that had not been published?

Right.

So it's not relatively new material?

No, I had put the dates on the manuscript, but it never got into the book. I should have made certain that it did, but unfortunately it didn't.

Do you feel any kinship or do you communicate at all with some of the writers who are your contemporaries, such as Burroughs or any of those? I know he is a big fan.

No, I don't get to see anybody. William Kennedy, I love. I wrote a little note to him, but there is just really no communication.

Ironically, I see a certain kinship with Bukowski, even in terms of what's happened in your lives.

Oh, really.

Well, he writes about similar people, and it's fairly nonjudgmental, although he tends to be a little more experiential, which you choose not to be, and he asserts himself more. For years, people weren't interested in him, and now, of course, he is gaining a resurgence.

Yeah, well that's been going on for quite awhile, as I understand. For quite a few years now he has been making a lot of money, reading in Europe and all that kind of thing.

He has been doing more appearances and stuff.

I remember seeing a little article in some magazine, oh, I don't know, it must have been at least four years ago, or more, where he had just bought a $250,000 house and all that kind of stuff.

I guess that would make it a little bit more difficult for him to write about the hotels he lived in. Are you familiar with his work?

No, not really.

What authors are you reading now that you appreciate who are your contemporaries?

Well, I just finished reading a thing by Milan Kundera that I really liked very, very much. Like I said, I love Kennedy. God, he's marvelous. Just fuckin' marvelous. Michael Stevens and Gil. I love Gil's stuff. I read a thing by this guy, I forget names sometimes. One of my problems. But I don't read as much as I like because I teach one night a week at USC, so I spend a lot of my reading time going over the students' stuff.

Do you enjoy that?

Yeah.

How did you fall into that job?

Well, in a roundabout way. Somebody I knew was taking a course at the UCLA Extension, and one of the books, I believe, the teacher had them read was *Last Exit*, or he recommended it or something, and she mentioned to the guy that she knew me, and so he asked her to ask whether I would talk to the class. So, one night I went over to his house and he had, I think, he said twenty, thirty or forty of his students there, and I talked to them for a couple of hours. It was a really nice night, and one of the people there was involved with the USC program they have called Master of Professional Writing. She was also involved with the *Southern California Anthology* and asked me if she could do an interview and then invited me to an open house at USC, where most of the people involved in that program, the MPW program, read a little bit or talked. I went there and met the head of the department, John Richards. He teaches there now. They invited me to join them, and I did about two years ago this month. I do that one night a week, it's really very enjoyable.

Are you working or doing anything besides writing and teaching?

No. I had a job for a couple of years, but that ended the end of November, so now I've just been home trying to finish this new book.

Are you close?

No, I have about 160 pages done, and I have no idea if that's half the book, or a third of it, or what it is.

You're not quite sure where everybody is going yet?

No, this is a whole new kind of thing for me. It's a first person book and it's just a whole different approach.

Can you tell me just a little about where you are headed with it?

Well, there is a man who is, I think, in the book he is fifty years old, and looking back at his childhood, trying to understand the child. In that process he tries to understand his father, and through that, he understands his relationship with God. How this all started is really kind of fun. Like I say, I try to say yes to life. Whatever is put in front of me, I believe, is an opportunity for love and service, so I just try to say yes to life. I was reading a story by one of my students and one line didn't make any sense. I read it about three times, four times, and it just didn't make any sense and I couldn't figure out what the hell was

wrong with this line. Then, I noticed I was misreading it. So many people have told me how they read what they experienced in life. The line was, "Eyes filled before the tears came," and I kept reading, "He remembered how his father felt before the tears came." And I said, "Ho, ho, Mr. Freud. What do we have here? Ha, ha, ha, isn't this an interesting thing." So I wrote down the line as I had misread it, and shortly after that I typed it, and I have been going ever since. ■■■

Bernd Eichinger presents
a **Neue Constantin Film Production**
an **Uli Edel Film**

Stephen Lang, Jennifer Jason Leigh
Burt Young, Peter Dobson, and **Jerry Orbach**
Co-Producer **Herman Weigel**
Edited by **Peter Przygodda**
Costumes Designed by **Carol Oditz**
Production Designed by **David Chapman**
Director of Photography **Stefan Czapsky**
Based on the Novel by **Hubert Selby, Jr.**
Screenplay by **Desmond Nakano**
Produced by **Bernd Eichinger**
Directed by **Uli Edel**

Credits not contractual

PSALM III

How long the night of my pain Lord,

And short the days of my joy?

Why does darkness shroud my soul at noon

And the light stop at my doorway?

Is it my knees You want me to bend?

Is it my will You would have me surrender?

I bow to no man so how can I surrender to You?!

You talk of mercy,

But I dispense judgements.

You talk of Love,

But I must live in strength.

You talk of forgiveness

Yet must I be ready to defend.

I deal with my tormentors as they would me!

Better I should not hear Your voice

When all You say drives me mad,

And all I can do is scream at the darkened sun

Shine!   SHINE!

And thaw the frozen marrow in my bones....

O Lord

                                          O Lord

How short the days of my joy?

How long the nights of my despair?

Frederick Wiseman

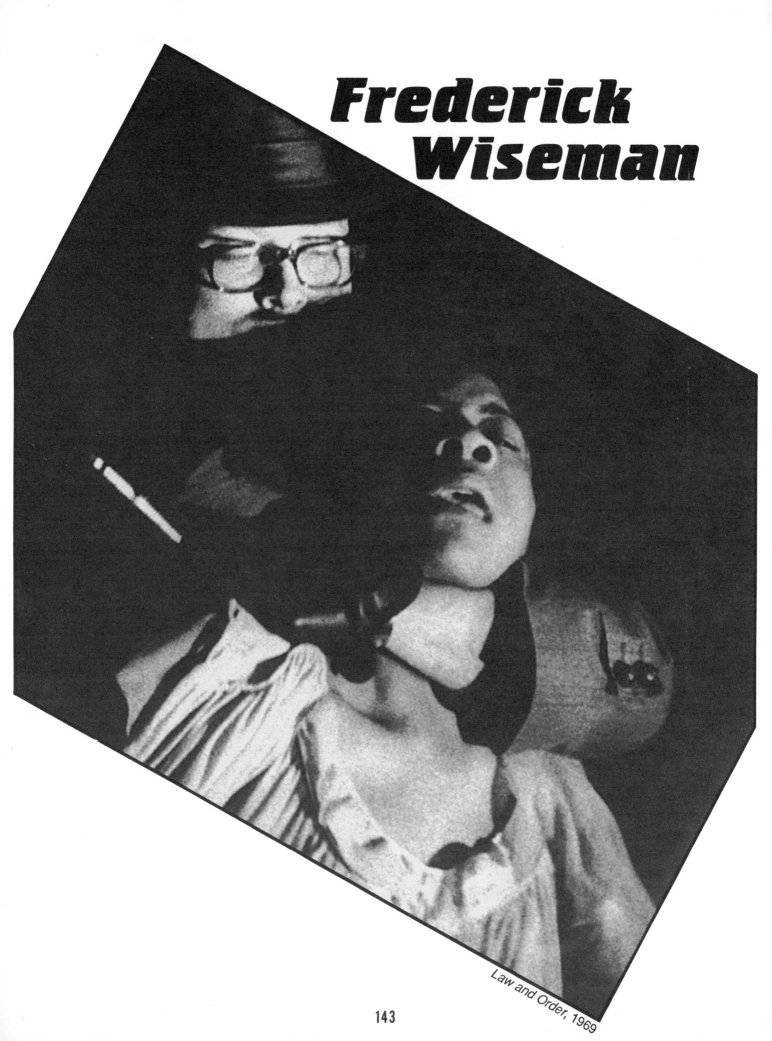

Law and Order, 1969

Titicut Follies

The Film That's Banned in Bridgewater

(and the rest of the world)

by Gary Miller, 1987

Frederick Wiseman is considered to be one of America's pre-eminent documentary filmmakers. His work, which includes such films as *Meat*, *Racetrack*, and *Juvenile Court*, have garnered both critical acclaim and popular following. His first film, however, was reviewed by a quite unusual critic. It was banned by the Massachusetts Superior Court.

In the early 1960s, Wiseman was making a transition from teaching law to filmmaking. He often took his Boston University students on field trips to prisons and other institutions to give them a feel for the legal issues of incarceration. Bridgewater State Hospital for the Criminally Insane was one of Wiseman's stops. Conditions there presented prime material for a documentary.

Although not the worst in the U.S., the facility was far from a center for rehabilitation. It was overcrowded and dirty, short-staffed and ill-maintained. Patients were confined to squalid cells, sometimes without proper bedding and even clothing. Bridgewater did, however, have a superintendent, Charles Gaughan, who was committed to change. He was anxious to bring Wiseman to his facility. A film, he felt, could publicize conditions there and bring in needed funding.

Wiseman was also anxious to begin filming, but a political obstacle stood in the way. He applied to the Department of Corrections for permission to film inside the facility, but his request was denied.

Fortunately, Lieutenant Governor Elliot Richardson intervened on Wiseman's behalf. He telephoned the Commissioner of Corrections and persuaded him to reverse his ruling. Wiseman began shooting *Titicut Follies* in the spring of 1966.

A year later the film was released, and its initial screenings elicited wide critical acclaim. It took top honors at the Mannheim film festival in West Germany and was featured at New York's Lincoln Center Film Festival.

It was panned, however, by the Commonwealth of Massachusetts, despite the fact that Gaughan and Richardson had welcomed an airing of Bridgewater's dirty laundry. And no wonder. Spliced between footage of a bizarre inmate amateur hour for which it is named, it succeeded in capturing the true essence of Bridgewater.

In one scene, a callous, cigarette smoking doctor interrogates a young man imprisoned for child molestation. He focuses infinitely more attention on his smoke than on his patient. His questions, totally devoid of concern, are eerily mechanical. "How often do you masturbate?" he asks. "Why do you do this when you have a good wife?"

Later, a thin man in his twenties delivers an eloquent plea for transfer to another facility, claiming that "I get worse. Obviously, it's the treatment I'm getting. I want to go back to prison. At the other places, I have the facilities I need to improve myself." A faceless committee denies the request. He is, they decide, becoming more paranoid. An increased dosage of medication is prescribed.

In another scene several attendants hold a frail looking man down while a doctor performs nasal feeding. Needing lubrication for the tube, he asks repeatedly, "You got any butter?" Later the man's corpse is

---

Titicut Follies
Frederick Wiseman,
USA, 1967 (F)
Prisons and mental institutions, where recalcitrant or ill-fitting citizens are put out of sight, are the dirty secrets of civilized society. As they are owned and controlled by precisely those who wish to keep them secret, and are also confined to specific, enclosed spaces, filmmakers are easily kept out. Wiseman's achievement in creating this unique film document is therefore all the more impressive: it is a major work of subversive cinema and a searing indictment — without editorializing narration — of the 'system'. Wiseman (and his extraordinary cameraman-anthropologist John Marshall) officially gained entrance to a state prison hospital for the criminally insane, where the film was shot, and obtained the co-operation of its psychiatrists, guards, and social workers. Massachusetts, however, subsequently obtained an injunction preventing the film's exhibition, thereby keeping the secret.

This is a gallery of horrors, a reflection of man's infinite capacity to dehumanize his fellow-beings. Broken men, retarded, catatonic, schizophrenic, toothless — many incarcerated for life — vegetate in empty cells, bare of furniture, utensils, toilets, or beds. They are incontinent, they masturbate, babble, put on a horrifying annual variety show (the Titicut Follies'), beat against the bars in rage, and scream. They stand on their heads for minutes on end while chanting self-invented hymns, or are force-fed through the nose while a Dr Strangelove psychiatrist himself (!) pours liquid down the stomach tube. They are taunted or patronized, drink their own dirty bathwater while in the tub (smilingly calling it champagne), and die, ignominiously, their bodies shaved before burial and cotton-wool stuffed into their eyes. The camera flinches from nothing; here it is, it says, and since you are not doing anything about eliminating this, at least have the courage to watch.

Excerpt from *Film as a Subversive Art* by Amos Vogel, 1974.

seen being shaven in preparation for burial in a desolate plot on the grounds of the hospital.

It was owing to the graphic nature of this footage that Frederick Wiseman found himself in Massachusetts Superior Court fighting for the right to show his film. Following initial screenings, the state moved legally against Wiseman, seeking a ban. Surprisingly, it was former ally Richardson who spearheaded the move.

Speaking from his office at Zipporah Films in Cambridge [Mass.], Wiseman explained, "When the film was released, Richardson was attorney general, and I guess his political advisors told him that he might get into trouble because he helped me get permission for the filming. That was one of the reasons he moved against the film."

In court, the Commonwealth listed two complaints against Wiseman: first, that he had breached an oral contract giving the state the right to censor the film; second, that the film represented an invasion of privacy of one of the inmates, who was shown naked in his cell (he was, according to Wiseman, naked in his cell for seventeen years) and that all receipts should be held in a trust for the patients.

Wiseman feels that the state had an altogether different motive for seeking the ban. The real reason, he said, was that "the state was embarrassed at the kind of place they were running at Bridgewater. Instead of coming out and saying, 'Look, if you think this is bad, you should see what's going on in other states. We allowed him to make the film because we wanted to do something about these conditions ...' That was their other choice. As is characteristic of Richardson, he made the weak choice."

Wiseman found himself on the losing end of a ruling handed down on June 24, 1969. The court denied Wiseman and anyone connected with *Titicut Follies* from showing it, other than to a select group specified within the ruling.

Since then, according to court mandate, the film has been shown only to "legislators, judges, lawyers, social workers, doctors, psychiatrists, students in these or related fields, and organizations dealing the the problems of custodial care and mental infirmity." Two documents must also be signed by those screening the film. One states intent to show the film only to qualified viewers. Another states that this was, in fact, done.

The ruling also included a clause that effectively protected those responsible for conditions at Bridgewater from even the probing of a limited, state-defined audience. The court ordered that "at any such showing, a brief explanation shall be included in the film that changes and improvements have been made at Massachusetts Correctional Institute Bridgewater since 1966."

Wiseman was forced to include the disclaimer, despite the fact that he had "no idea" that any changes had actually been made. "It's possible that there were various new treatment procedures, but I did not

know of them of my own knowledge. I was no longer welcome at Bridgewater."

And so it has been for nearly two decades. *Titicut Follies* has been distributed according to court order by Wiseman's Zipporah Films. Except for mental health professionals and students, it has been largely forgotten. But Frederick Wiseman still feels strongly that an injustice was done. "It's an issue not just for my film but for documents of any sort. Whether it's my film or somebody else's newspaper article, the fact is that I don't believe in censorship, which is what it is. If people can't see it, they can't make up their minds."

————END

In-person interview (by Stevenson) with Frederick Wiseman conducted 10/11/88 in Wiseman's Cambridge studio.

What's the status of your appeal to open up distribution on *Titicut Follies*?

Well, the Massachusetts superior court has appointed a guardian, and the guardian is investigating whether it's in the best interests of the surviving inmates to have the film shown, and he will issue a report sometime in the next couple of months. And we'll see what happens from there.

So you've taken out ads in newspapers to attempt to locate surviving inmates of Bridgewater.

No, I didn't take out those ads — the attorney general's office did.

Is the film restricted only in Massachusetts?

It's restricted everywhere. The whole world. It can only be seen by limited audiences consisting of doctors, lawyers, judges, legislators, people interested in custodial care and students in these and related fields — but not to the merely curious general public — on condition that a week's notice be given of any screening, and then an affidavit has to be filed that everybody who saw it is within the class of people who are allowed to see it. So that means it can't be shown theatrically or on television. It can be shown under those conditions in schools and colleges to the class of people described above.

Do you feel the audience selection and setting of that film should ever be controlled even in the tiniest measure?

Not at all. It's the only movie/play document of any sort in American constitutional history, other than one involving obscenity or national security, that has a partial restraint on its use.

Would you find it at all troubling or at all the slightest bit distasteful if maybe some people might go to see it simply on the strength of its reputation as an "extreme" film, almost a horror movie in a sense?

I have no wish to control what people do.

So it's been suppressed ever since it was made in 1967 — had a limited release and then was suppressed?

That's right.

Is it at all "dated" in your opinion, or do you think it still stands?

Well, there were five people that died for unexplained reasons at Bridgewater in the spring of '87, so, presumably some of the same kinds of conditions still exist. Although I haven't been there in 22 years, so I have no idea, really.

The whole situation surrounding *Titicut Follies* is really an example, a method of censorship, wouldn't you say?

It IS. It IS an example of censorship.

Even though they tried to cloak it in the privacy issue?

You're right, they tried to cloak it in the privacy issue, but the argument that we made was that Bridgewater is a public institution and what goes on there is news, and therefore protected by the First Amendment.

Prior to the film, the department of correction was not very concerned about the privacy of the inmates. There were 10,000 visitors a year who saw the same thing that people see in the film. Among the visitors were a group from St. Colletta's School for Exceptional Children, which means retarded children ... and I also have on film a group from a high school, I think it was Norwood High School, who were being taken through Bridgewater by their football coach to teach them the folly of a life of crime.

So prior to the film, Bridgewater was run as an open institution. If the State was really concerned about the privacy of the inmates, they wouldn't have kept them in the conditions shown in the film.

I think that the privacy issue was just an excuse. At least from my point of view it was an excuse. Because there's no such thing as an "ABSOLUTE right of privacy," and in fact in Massachusetts, at the time the film was made, and at the time it was released, there was no right of privacy. So putting aside the issue of whether there should have been the right of privacy — the right of privacy only exists by virtue of common law tradition or by virtue of STATUTE — there was not a common law tradition in Massachusetts nor was there any statutory right of privacy. So it simply didn't exist. Even in those jurisdictions where it does exist, it's not an absolute right. The courts always have to weigh competing interests: the right of privacy versus the public's right to know. And in any number of decisions the U.S. Supreme Court has found the right of privacy to be the lesser value when it comes up against the public's right to know.

What happened in this case is they cooked up a theory that I had contracted away my First Amendment rights by — because they asserted with no evidence whatsoever that I had agreed to give the Superintendent, the Commissioner of Corrections and the Attorney General the right of final cut, the right of censorship over the film. And therefore, by asserting that, and having that claim brought in the Massachusetts Superior Court, the court never dealt with the First Amendment issue because they said it was irrelevant since I had contracted it away. So the First Amendment issue was never dealt with squarely by the Massachusetts courts.

So does your appeal today confront that issue?

The state is at the point where they've appointed a guardian to look into whether it's in the best interests of the surviving inmates to have the film shown, but that is not, again, dealing with the First Amendment issue.

Where are the inmates today that were there when you shot the film in 1967?

Well, 30 are dead, 17 can't be found, and 15 are located.

Blind, 1986 ———————————

146

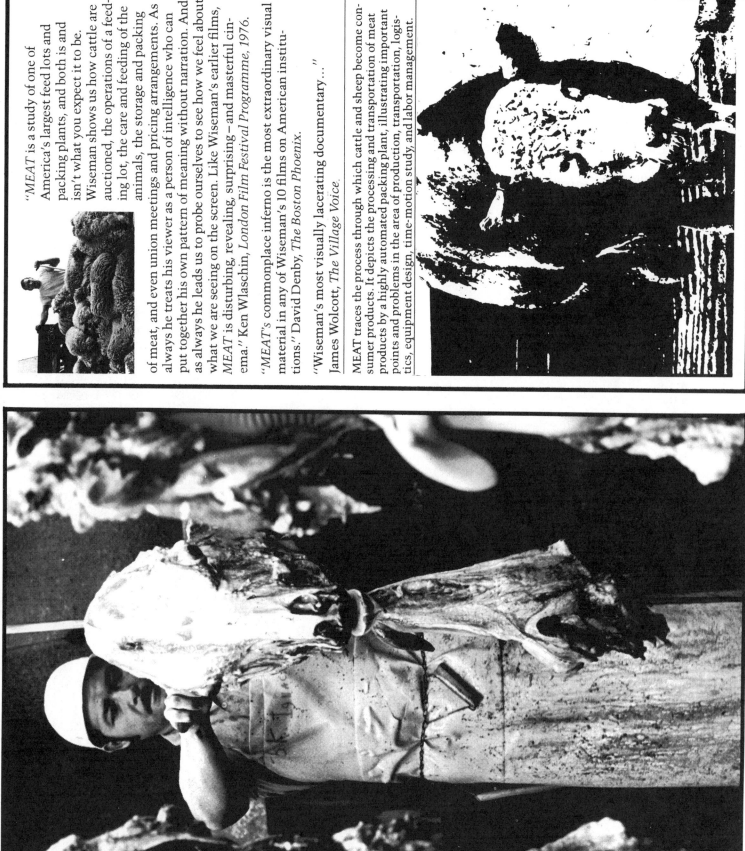

"*MEAT* is a study of one of America's largest feed lots and packing plants, and both is and isn't what you expect it to be. Wiseman shows us how cattle are auctioned, the operations of a feeding lot, the care and feeding of the animals, the storage and packing of meat, and even union meetings and pricing arrangements. As always he treats his viewer as a person of intelligence who can put together his own pattern of meaning without narration. And as always he leads us to probe ourselves to see how we feel about what we are seeing on the screen. Like Wiseman's earlier films, *MEAT* is disturbing, revealing, surprising – and masterful cinema." Ken Wlaschin, *London Film Festival Programme, 1976.*

"*MEAT*'s commonplace inferno is the most extraordinary visual material in any of Wiseman's 10 films on American institutions." David Denby, *The Boston Phoenix.*

"Wiseman's most visually lacerating documentary…" James Wolcott, *The Village Voice.*

MEAT traces the process through which cattle and sheep become consumer products. It depicts the processing and transportation of meat products by a highly automated packing plant, illustrating important points and problems in the area of production, transportation, logistics, equipment design, time-motion study, and labor management.

MEAT

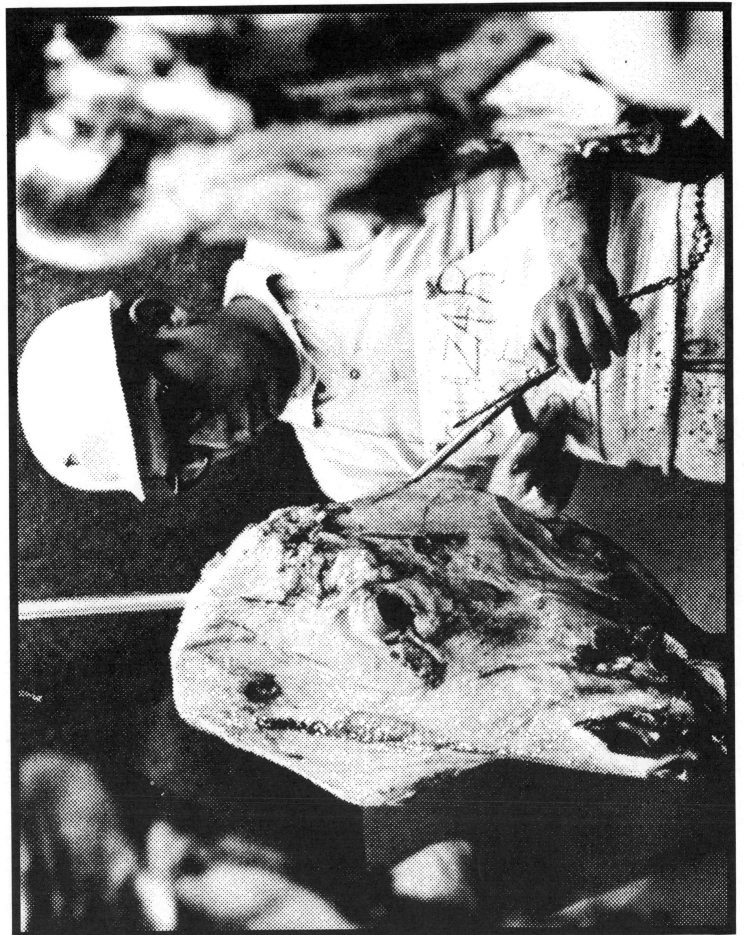

Meat, 1976

Bridgewater State Hospital. Photo: George Rizer

STATE
HOSPITAL
VISITORS
ENTRANCE
←

Law and Order

Missile, 1987

In documentary filmmaking politics always seems to intrude in one way or another, as with the repression of certain films. Have you ever run up against this with any other film of yours?

No. There have been slight flurries, but never any legal action.

Do personal politics ever intrude on objective documentary filmmaking?

Well, there's no such thing as objective documentary filmmaking. Because a basic thing about documentaries, or any films, is they involve CHOICE: subject matter, camera angles, what to include in the film, how long the film's going to be. Everything involves a choice.

I think it takes that personal orientation and conviction to give it strength and force.

Well of course. That's so obvious really, I can't believe anybody still thinks there's such a thing as "objectivity."

Do you do any video work these days?

No.

Do you think that TV as a medium is inferior to film in any sense?

Well, all my films get SHOWN on TV, but I much prefer working in film. I much prefer to have them shown in the theater because to get a bigger picture looks nicer.

Video, in a sense — like Camcorders and that, the new technology — seems almost tailor-made for shooting documentaries; it's unobtrusive, easy to handle ...

Well so is film. But it depends on what kind of volume you shoot. I usually have about sixty to seventy hours of film. I don't like editing video — film is "hands-on" editing and video is electronic editing. I haven't had much experience with video and the experience I've had I don't like. So I'm going to stick to film.

But you say most of your films are now shown on TV.

Yes, they're shown on public television. They're MADE on film and transferred to video. But at least in doing the transferring you can preserve the "film look." Video, I think, is too flat. I don't particularly like the look of video.

Unless you're filming people totally incapable of conscious acting, such as perhaps in *Titicut Follies*, isn't it impossible to get complete spontaneity from people once you point a movie camera at them?

Well, there's no way of knowing that for sure. My experience is the presence of the camera and tape recorder doesn't change people's behavior. If it did, there would be ... better acting in Hollywood and the theater. For reasons I don't seem to understand, people don't seem to mind and they go about their business, and act the way they ordinarily do. And the TEST for that is when you're making one of these movies — most of the time you're not shooting, so you're just observing the people when the camera's not on. Or maybe not even out of its case. This gives you a sense of what ordinary behavior is like in the particular situation.

And you're not always right about it, but you get very sensitive to the issue; if you think somebody's acting for the camera you stop shooting — if you don't realize until you get to the editing room, you don't use the sequence. Like in any other profession, you can make a mistake.

But you get sensitive to the issue of being conned. I mean, just as you, a journalist, if you think somebody is conning you when you do an interview, you adjust to it. you say, "hey, get off it," or you stop, or you don't use the interview. You're making the same kind of judgment when you make a documentary film — you think somebody's conning you, you stop.

Speaking of a recent documentary currently playing in Boston, have you seen *The Thin Blue Line*?

I'm a great fan of Errol Morris. He's a terrific film-maker. He made *Gates of Heaven* and *Vernon, Florida. Gates of Heaven* is the funniest movie I've ever seen in my life.

Do you ever watch much TV at all?

... the Celtics.

In the beginning, did you ever have problems financing your films?

I ALWAYS have problems with financing.

But now you've become more secure?

No. It's always a question of finding money for the next film — it's never easy. From 1971 to 1981 I had a contract with Channel 13 in New York to make one film a year for them. But that's been over for seven years.

You started out in law and changed to filmmaking. How did that come about?

I was TEACHING law, and I never liked law school, and I didn't like teaching — I figured I'd better do something I liked.

Was it a lot of work getting into filmmaking?

Well, it was a lot of work. It's always a lot of work. The first film I made (*Titicut Follies*)grew out of the law school teaching experience. Then it occurred to me what you could do with a prison for the criminally insane you could do elsewhere, like a high school.

Is it the kind of thing that makes money? Do you live on it?

I make a living out of a combination of things: trying to make one movie a year, giving talks on the movies — because you can make more money talking about a movie than making it, and I own the movies, so whatever comes in on the 16mm distri-bution, after expenses, I get to keep.

Do you tour with your films, at festivals and so forth?

Yes, I go to a lot of festivals in Europe.

Are your films shown much in the Boston area? I've never seen them.

At SCHOOLS, not at theaters. That's the market. It's very hard to get documentary booked into theaters. It's very rare.

Have you ever wanted to make a non-documentary film?

I have made one, *Seraphita's Diary*. And I'd like to make some others, I have some ideas for some others.

What are your future plans and projects? Do you have a film in the works right now?

Well, I've got a script for a fiction film I'd like to do, and I'm thinking about doing another documentary, but not until the spring.

THE END

[Further information on Frederick Wiseman's films can be obtained from: Zipporah Films, 1 Richdale Avenue, Unit 4, Cambridge, MA 02140.]

Titicut Follies, 1967
High School, 1968
Law and Order, 1969
Hospital, 1970
Basic Training, 1971
Essene, 1972
Juvenile Court, 1973
Primate, 1974
Welfare, 1975
Meat, 1976
Canal Zone, 1977

Sinai Field Mission, 1978
Manoeuvre, 1979
Model, 1980
Seraphita's Diary, 1982
The Store, 1983
Racetrack, 1985
Deaf, 1986
Blind, 1986
Multi-Handicapped, 1986
Adjustment & Work, 1986
Missile, 1987

Robert Whittington

Frederick Wiseman

Filmography

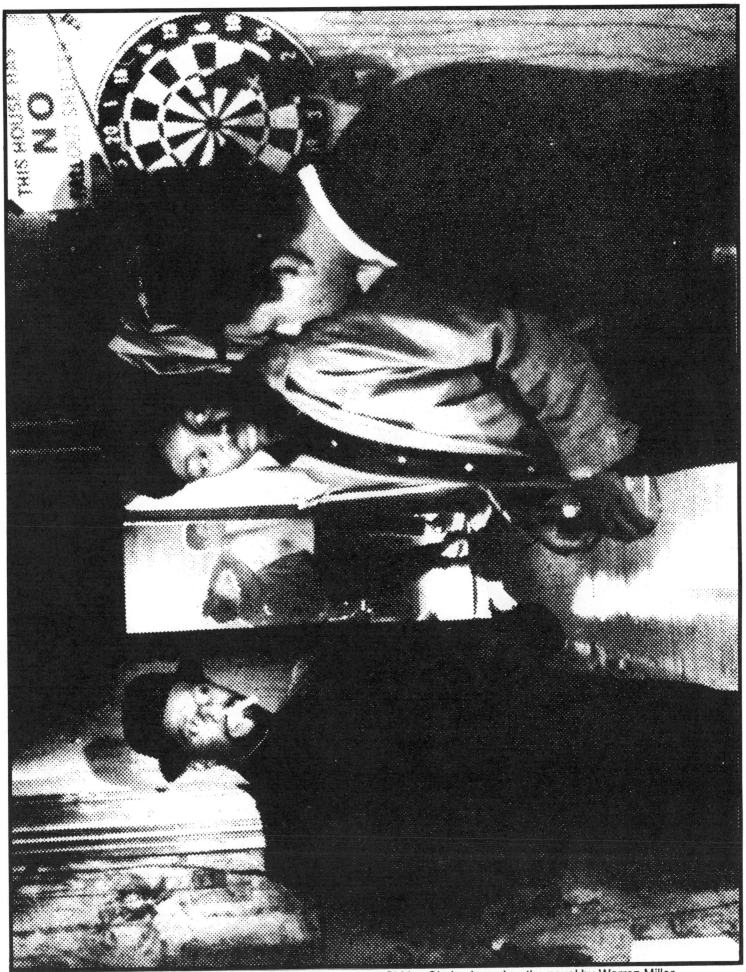

The Cool World, produced by Frederick Wiseman and directed by Shirley Clarke, based on the novel by Warren Miller.

JOHNNY ECK

"Step right up, folks! You are about to see a sight that will amaze you, thrill you ... possibly even shock you!!!"

This is the kind of barking carny spiel that would have assaulted your ears as you strolled the crowded dirt-and-sawdust midways of the American carnivals of the 1920s and '30s ... *and outside the biggest tent on the midway a mob scene develops as a large crowd waits to enter the next show. Pathways are cleared as the previous audience now begins to file out of the tent with looks of amazement on their faces, chattering to each other about the spectacle they've just witnessed: Johnny Eck — The Most Remarkable Boy Alive!*

Born on a stormy August night almost 80 years ago in a working class section of Baltimore, Johnny Eckhardt would have his name shortened to the more theatrical Johnny Eck by his first manager when he began public performances. Johnny was a natural performer, born into the era of showmanship when carnivals and circuses did a booming business and frantically sought to outdo each other with exhibitions of the incredible. Every midway boasted a "freak show" in which the handicapped or deformed people would make a living exhibiting themselves without the con- demnation that could be expected today. Eventually claiming the title of King of The Freaks, Johnny became one of the greatest stars of the midway.

Johnny saw himself as a versatile performer who could juggle, walk the tight wire, and perform magic and trick pictures. The charisma and charm of Johnny's personality, combined with his amazing physical appearance and agility, packed carnival tents all over the continent and eventu- ally attracted talent scouts from Hollywood which resulted in a starring role in the classic 1932 "horror" film *Freaks*. This film — which for many years he has refused to discuss — features Johnny at the peak of his career and survives as perhaps the last opportunity audiences will have to see him in action.

But there was much more to the life and career of Johnny Eck than his performance in *Freaks*. He began to paint at 8 years of age, designing his own circus promotion and later specializing in screen paintings. He became adept at woodworking and constructed miniature fully-functional circuses with his brother Rob. He incorporated diverse acts into his shows over the years, includ- ing animal training and feats of strength, as well as magic and acrobatics. He played in a combo — Johnny on alto sax and Rob on piano and organ — that toured roadhouse joints in 1927. He claims to have conducted an orchestra in Baltimore during the off-season. He even drove a midget race car at 60 m.p.h. in all the big southern state fairs at one point.

Johnny entranced and amazed audiences not so much because he was a deformed freak, but because he was the one and only Johnny Eck — daredevil, showman, optimist, and friend to thousands.

Johnny retired in 1940. He recalled in conversations of 1980 that "people wanted sex from then on ... now it's crime, dope and filth." Historians of American culture have described the demise of the great carnivals in slightly different terminology, but in any case, the era of classic carny showmanship has since come to a close. The public mentality, not to mention sense of style, seems to have changed irrevocably.

In 1980, two friends of Johnny's, Mark Feldman and Tom Fielding, formed Anaconda Press. Their goal was to publish a book about Johnny's life and they began the task of collecting documenta- tion, focusing on the words of Johnny himself. They received cooperation from Johnny in the form of a typed biographical introduction, a ninety-minute phone interview (featuring Johnny's hillbilly Baltimore accent), and prints of many of Johnny's personal never-before-seen pho- tographs. Cartoonist R. Crumb was commissioned to draw a cover illustration.

Due to the death of Mark Feldman in 1984, the project was shelved indefinitely. However, *Pandemonium* has been fortunate enough to acquire these materials from Tom Fielding and we owe deepest gratitude to both of them.

And so, without further ado, allow us to present Johnny Eck, the world's greatest freak!

Robert (left) and Johnny at age one.

On a hot summer night, some years ago during a violent thunder storm, in the second-floor bedroom of a red-brick row house there would occur an event that would shock the neighborhood. It was 10 o'clock and the first baby would emerge normal and weigh six pounds. Twenty minutes later in this dim room lit up only by the flashes of lightening and an open-jet gas burner , a second baby be gan to emerge; with more than half of it seemingly missing. This baby, with almost nothing below his rib cage- (a monster?) It weighed two pounds.

These were the years that children were born at home, attended by mid-wives with neighbors helping out, and so it was that the room had a number of "first viewers" on hand. Eager hands reached out and took up the normal baby; no one cared to touch the "monster" or rather dared to even come near it, lying on the bed. And then, an elderly devout and wise woman bent over and said, "My God, My God, this is a broken doll!" And that is what I appeared to be! I was less than eight inches in length. As my nurse stooped to pick me up and turned me toward the gas-jet, I was accidentally brushed against one of the neighbor women who let out a scream and fell in a faint to the floor.

It was as if God himself had chosen this family for me to be born in. There would be caring parents, and an ever loving sister, and she would be the twins first teacher. Her name was Caroline.

We were both taught to read and to write when not quite four years of age. When five, I was writing and receiving my own mail! All credit must go to our sister for this. She came into the house one day with a large package. "Come boys! I'm going to teach you two How To Play Post Office!" And she opened the box and put together a miniature building, complete with a walk-up window, and packs of white envelopes, sheets of tiny gummed red, green and blue stamps. We could write and mail our letters to each other!

Before the coming of radio, there was little if any entertainment in the home. Of course if one was well off, you might have a wind-up graphophone or player piano which was powered with one's two feet. We had neither. But I soon became a real home entertainer. My dear mother at our birth "promised me to God, should I, somehow, live." And so, when friends came to visit, I was called on to "preach". I would climb up atop of a small box and preach against drinking beer and damning sin and the devil. Our guests loved it. Then one night after my "sermon" (my mother intended me to be in the ministry) I decided to take up an offering. I passed around a saucer, and collected 65¢ My mother was hopelessly embarrassed. And that ended my ministry.

At seven years we enrolled in a public school. This created problems. Big boys would fight each other for the "honor" or "privilege" of lifting me up the stone steps, in my childs stroller. And the glass windows in the class room doors had to be blocked out. And Robert and I would always be let out ten minutes early to avoid being crushed by the curious.

One cold day in December, 1923, Robert and I were invited to see a big magic show to be held in the auditorium of a church. Any time church was mentioned, our dear mother would be over-joyed. She would go along with us this fateful day. I must add that the audience would be made up of poor and also crippled children, and of course I already passed that test. We were very poor, and of course, poorly but neatly dressed. Though in winter, brother Robert was wearing patched up knickers, long black stockings with holes in the knees and cheap tennis shoes. I had on a tiny pale-blue sweater with the elbows out and the bottom beginning to unravel. Our mother gave us a firm warning: "Keep under cover and don't let people see you two!" She also said she'd be watching our every move.

The first shock she received was when the Great Magician asked for a
volunteer assistant to come up on the stage. There was a great shuffle of feet
and a clatter of crutches, canes and sticks and braces from the audience. None
could leave their seats or attempt to climb the run-way steps to the stage.
One brave soul did however; my twin brother Bob. I thought I heard a steam
pipe burst. It was steam alright. It was our mother. There stood Bob on
stage under a spotlight looking like a scarecrow right out of a corn field.

But the show moves on quite smoothly until the magician tears a large
sheet of paper and it turns into a "lace table cloth." The magician invites
anyone to come to the stage and get it--free. Once more there was shuffling
of feet,rattling of crutches, canes and sticks. And suddenly a lone figure
darts out from the audience and swoops right up on the stage, standing on one
hand, and reaching up with the other; gratefully accepted the prize! The figure
sitting down to roll up the table cloth seemed to go right through the floor
of the stage, and then taking the paper in his teeth, returned to his seat.
The audience went wild; they applauded, they screamed; hadn't they just
witnessed and extra added attraction-- a monster?   Our poor mother fainted.

The magician became so unnerved at this time he hurriedly brought his show
to a close, and learning through my brother my idenity, immediately sent for
our mother to come back stage. All he could do was look at me and for a full
five minutes--gasp. Then he started to sweet-talk; I was a God-send to our
family. He would put me on the stage! That stage would turn out later to be
a six-inch pile of hay, covered over by an old worn green piece of carpet, in
a pit show on a rag-bag carnival. I would be paid a very high salary.
My parents signed a contract for one year, and the magician's business partner
changed the type to read ten years, simply by adding "O" after one, and "S"
after year. I was hooked. And we were threatened with law suits. I had to
live up to my contract. Or so I was made to believe. Well, I didn't believe
it. My new manager--(the magician) was raking in one, two hundred dollars
per day at county Fairs, and I was getting twenty dollars a week salary. I was
terribly saddened not only by the lies this manager was pulling off on me
but the pitiful wages I received each week (when we worked)and he never failed
to pay me in one dollar notes.   The year was 1924.

Toward the end of the "first" year of my ten-year year contract that
my parents had signed, I announced that I was ill, and would not continue
to work for nine more years for twenty dollars per week. My parents were
stunned and frightened. And rightly so, within weeks they were to receive
threatening letters about being sued for our tiny red-brick row house.
But I held fast; I would think about coming back to work-- when I was in
excellent health. I took one year to "recover." I was yet a child, and
my ex-manager adopted the Russian leaders "Time is on our side..." slogan.
I would put time "On my side."
Robert and I are now fourteen years of age, and having tasted the
nectar of traveling from one town to another and untold adventure, we both
knew our lives would never be the same again. We bought a show business
magazine called The billboard and checked the route section. Off went a
letter with a list of what we needed to put on our own side show. Three
days later we receive a wire: Johnny and Bob Eck, Baltimore, Md. "Join
us Plainfield New Jersey next week." Signed "Captain John M. Sheesley"

As time passed on, and there was no more threatening letters from
my ex-manager, our par ents were now more than happy to give us their
blessing and let us go. Captain Sheesley would have a crew at the station
with a big truck to greet us and take us back to the show grounds. There
we would find a brand new tent and a four-ton empty circus wagon, painted
Chinese-red trimmed in gold and with the biggest artillery-type wheels
I had ever seen. At times it would take double teams of heavy draft horses
to move off it the lot.

157

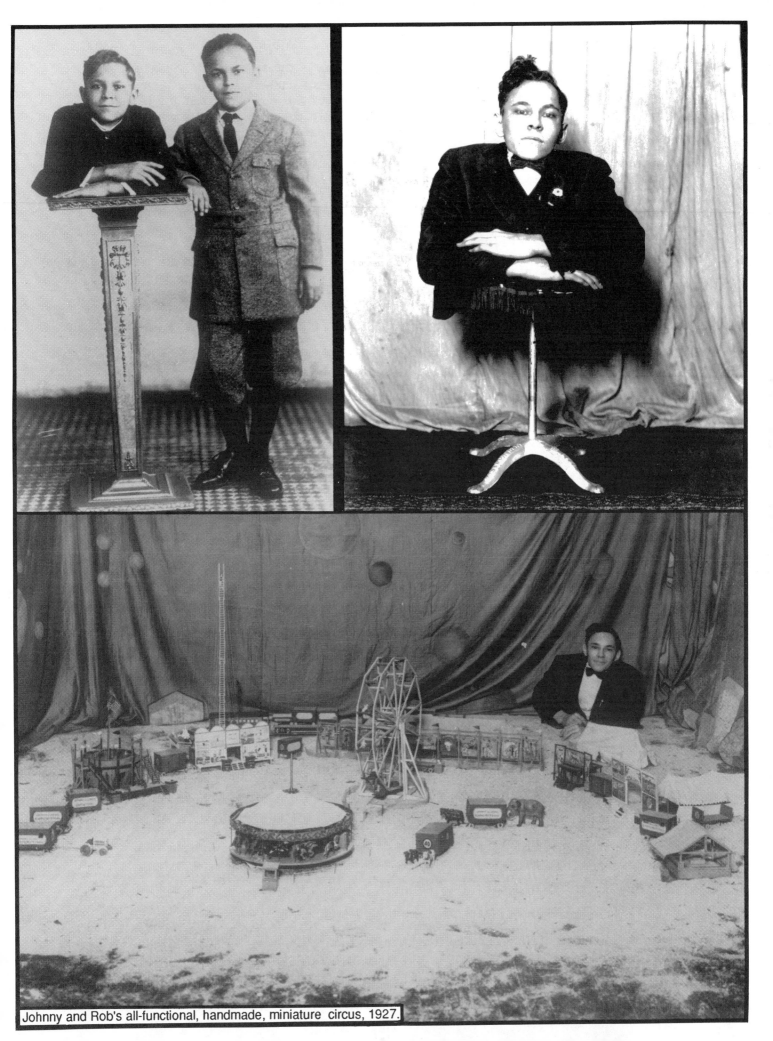

Johnny and Rob's all-functional, handmade, miniature circus, 1927.

This was a family-type and family run show. Captain John Sheesley would put up with no foolishness or drunkeness of any kind. He allowed no profanity on the midway. There were a number of children and of all things, when we first appeared on the lot in Plainfield, Captain Sheesley grabbed Bob and me and patting us each on the head looked at the crowd of show people gathered and said, "These are my boys! Take good care of them!" Later, our side show would permit us to send for our parents to be with us. It would be the first real train trip for my father.

Next would come the great depression and we had no money, nothing. We were about to lose our little red-brick house for un-paid taxes. And then I get a Special Delivery letter. Please phone me, it read. Let's let bygones begone. Signed by my ex-manager... I called him and he said he was managing a small park near Hagerstown, Maryland. And he would like to have me as a guest. I had nothing to lose, and accepted his invitation. I was a regal guest. I shall never forget how kind he was to me those weeks staying in a big log cabin with a wide clear stream gurgling by. It was Paradise to me. And I dined every day with him and oh, how he could cook! I should have been on my guard, as all this was just too good to be true, and I would find out soon enough.

It was now late summer and I get another letter from my ex- manager. I want you to be ready in two weeks, he writes; I have you booked for the Canadian National Exposition! Again I was elated! A bad sign. Brother Bob and I go to Canada and work in the Exposition as a "single O" which means I was considered such a strong attraction I would be the only feature in our big tent. I was truly happy. Now who would be in my audience at one performance but two talent scouts from Metro-Goldwyn-Mayer Studios in California. "Would I consent to having a film test?" I'd have jumped through a hoop of fire had they asked me. Bob and I made the film test out back of our tent, along with a giant rat which weighed 45 pounds. My day had at last arrived! Or so I thought.

Some four weeks later I was in Culver City, California, with my ex- manager, who had signed a contract unknowingly to me; I am under the impression we are still bound by the Canadian National Exhibition agreement which wasn't bad at all: a fifty-fifty partnership. My ex- agent had lied to me in Canada, telling me MGM's talent scouts weren't scouts at all but agents for Downey Brothers, a big circus in California. I believed him until I came on the lot-- and it was a back lot of Metro-Goldwyn-Mayer Studios! Our screen test had been successful. A few weeks later Tod Browning's immortal and famous classic film, "FREAKS" is well under way. And I would be in for a painful surprise.

It is a known fact that booking agents or managers are entitled to a certain percentage of the star or attraction's salary. This may vary from ten percent but never over fifty percent. To say I was hurt, deeply shocked would be putting it midly, when I found out that I was getting less than ten percent of my actual salary. My "manager" was getting the rest. It was then that I detested the man. I decided not to mention my finding out of his fraudulent scheme. I would, somehow, get my revenge. It turned out that it hurt me far more than it hurt him.

After returning to Baltimore I began getting letters from the camera crew and some of the stars that worked with me in "FREAKS" and in one of the letters was a news clipping on Director Tod Browning about another horror story in which he planned to film. Ironically, UNIVERSAL Studios in California had similar plans. They produced the classic "FRANKENSTEIN" film. Browning too, was planning and writing a story about experimenting with human bodies, to be molded into <u>monsters</u> and become criminals. Brother Bob and I would have the leading part. I passed out in shock.

Then the letters began to arrive; not from the M-G-M Studios, but from my ex-manager! <u>he</u> had been contacted directly by the studio! Having made one financial killing at my expence-- he was ready to do it again.

Unfortunately, we had no telephone in our home and I could only write letters. I know M-G-M Studios didn't care for that set-up, and they already were in contact by phone with my ex-manager. I also knew M-G-M would rather do business with an agent than me. Now I would get my revenge!

It would take me one week to become calm, cool and "forgiving"? I decided to write two letters, one to M-G-M in California, stating I was under contract to no one; I was acting as my own agent. I never received a reply. The second letter I sent to my ex-manager, here in Baltimore. "Dear Mr.*McCauley:" I wrote, "After my past unhappy business adventure with you in making the movie titled "FREAKS" out in California, I am not about to have you take financial advantage of me again. However I am ready to sign a legitimate contract with you for the term of not more than six months at a salary of $600.00 per week. The average film today can be shot in 12 weeks and I would have you put $ 7,200.00 in trust for me and Robert as a guarantee that I would not only get my rightful money but also recover that which you kept from me in your fraudulent scheme the last time we were together in California."

I only wish I could have been in his office the day my letter arrived. I understand he went into a rage and wrecked his office. And no small wonder; I learned later that McCauley had been in constant contact unbeknowns to me; it was confirmed I was to be (Robert and I) paid $ 600.00 per week <u>plus</u> <u>all</u> <u>expenses</u>; plus Pullman car drawing room transportation from Baltimore to Los Angeles and return! I also found out he had already lined up a group of people for this trip; his invalid wife, his girl friend, two valets (for himself) his lady friend's brother. At the bottom of the list would come Johnny and Bob-- the stars. And oh, how I wished my poor mother might have made the trip. It was not to be. I not only wrecked his chances of ever going back to California -- I wrecked mine too.

Time heals all wounds, and many nights I would cry, lying awake in the dark, thinking of how really wonderful and exciting to be working in front of the cameras on all the different giant sound stages. I got to know each member of the film crew; I was accepted not as a Monster Freak-- but as one of them-- not twenty inches tall, but a miniature super-man! Best of all, I was special to Director Tod Browning, and his assistant Director Earl Taagart. I would ride many times along side of these great men on a big camera dollie while they were shooting scenes. Now it was all over.

It is the month of April and things look very dark. The Great Depression is still on; no one working in our home; and we get two letters in the morning mail. First, I would open up the bad news; our small red-brick house is to be sold for non- payment of taxes. My poor dear mother read the notice of the pending eviction and began to cry. And then my eyes blurred and I said, "Oh no, God, please, don't let us lose our home!" I brushed away the tears; and could not believe what I was reading! <u>It</u> <u>had</u> <u>to be a dream!</u> But it was true. I would soon be with no other than Robert L. Ripley of "Believe It Or Not" fame and perform at Chicago, Cleveland and Dallas.

(AND OPENED THE SECOND LETTER)

* Not his veal name.

end

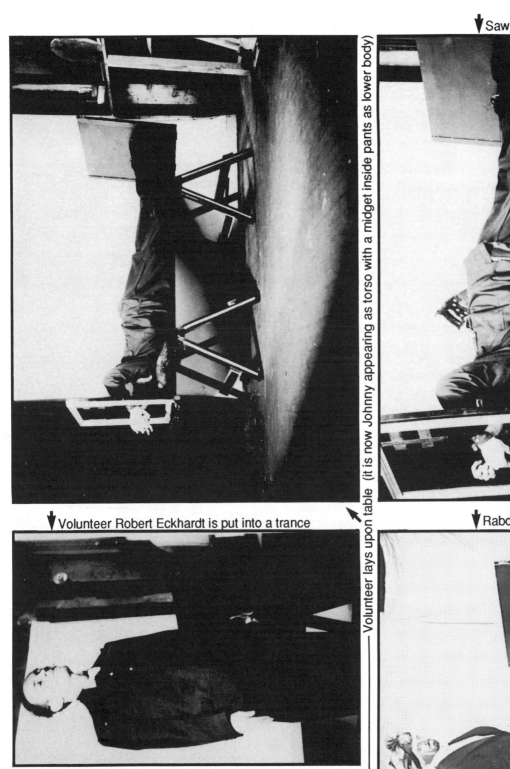

Saw half way through ...

(it is now Johnny appearing as torso with a midget inside pants as lower body)

Volunteer lays upon table

Volunteer Robert Eckhardt is put into a trance

Raboid begins to saw ...

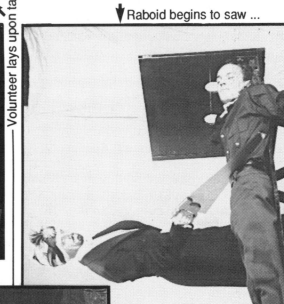

Raboid Rasha the Magician

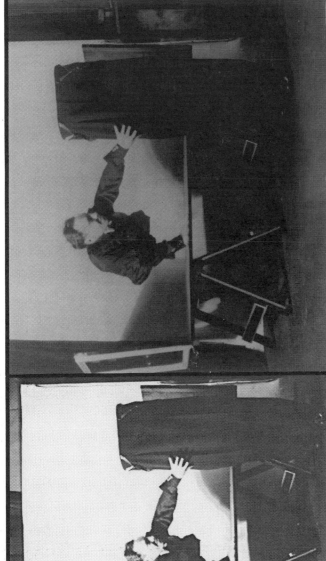

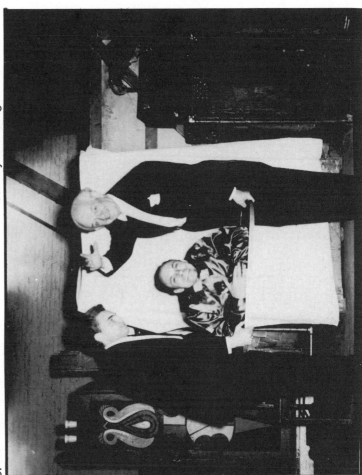

Johnny and midget

— Man sawed in half ... upper half rises and begins to chase its legs. —

Johnny with Blackstone the Magician years later ↑

Midget, magician and Johnny ↑

LIFE'S GREATEST PROBLEM SOLVED!

YOU HAVE NEVER SEEN HIS EQUAL JOHNNY ECK

THE MOST REMARKABLE MAN ALIVE!

RIPLEY

BELIEVE IT OR NOT . . . By Robert L. Ripley

On request, sent with stamped, addressed envelope, Mr. Ripley will furnish proof of anything depicted by him

The MOST REMARKABLE MAN ALIVE !

BELIEVE IT OR NOT
ODDITORIUM
Cleveland
Ohio

Johnny Eck

JOHNNY, ECK
Baltimore
BORN WITHOUT LEGS OR LOWER PORTION OF HIS BODY

M. J. MINTON'S HOME BURNED FEB. 1, 1917
HIS DAUGHTER'S HOME BURNED FEB. 1, 1927
AND HIS SON'S HOME BURNED FEB. 1, 1937

AMERICA'S LARGEST AIRPLANE TIRE
CONTAINS 45 MILES OF TIRE CORD
AND 4 MILES OF WIRE
Santa Monica, Calif

HUNCHBACK TURTLE
Owned by E. ROSS ALLEN
Silver Springs, Fla.

THE MOST REMARKABLE MAN ALIVE.

Johnny Eck was born in Baltimore, Md., Aug. 27, 1910. He is a twin, but his brother, Robert, is perfectly normal in every way. Johnny was born with no legs or lower portion of the abdomen whatever, yet he has gone to school the same as any other boy—walking upon the palms of his hands in regular stride. He graduated from high school at the age of 14, and has since become adept as an artist, musician, typist, acrobat, and entertainer. Always in perfect health, Johnny is possessed of an unusually sunny disposition. He has never had a sick day in his life, eats anything he wants, and he seems to enjoy life more than most normal folks.

The Largest Airplane Tire.

Johnny with Siamese twins — the Gibb sisters — at the Chicago World's Fair of 1933.

Bob and Johnny in later years.

Bob and Johnny. This photo was made into a postcard that was sold at the end of Johnny's act.

Johnny and armless girl at Ripley's show in Texas.

Excerpts from a phone conversation between Johnny Eck and Mark Feldman taped on April 20, 1980.

What did you think about during all this when you were a kid? Were you shy at all when you first started?

Well, the first performance I put on I was a little bit shy. And THEN, when I saw neighbors, people in the same block that came in to the tent, the exhibition, to see me, I felt like a fool! Jesus, I couldn't even look 'em in the face, I had to look at the ground. Then I thought — something told me — well why should I feel that way? I'm not gettin' their time — their company's gettin' it. So then I overcame my ... bashfulness.

And when we had the big tent ... I gotta give it to the man; he was good there. He did get a big tent and he was always boostin' me up. Now the banners that we had out front — like a circus sideshow? He got the biggest ones he could. They were ten feet high and twenty feet long, and colored. They were BEAUTIFUL. And of course they had me.

I like animals. He gave me two damn white cats, and a cage full of white mice and rats. He said, "Now here — you train 'em." And I DID. Man, I'd make them rats jump on little chairs and tables ... and the crowd, they loved it. Ha! And up on the banner out front I was called "THE GREAT JOHNNY ECK ... THE HALF-MAN, (or quarter man) WITH HIS UPSIDEDOWN TRAINED CATS AND RATS." (chuckles)

• • •

You must have loved the circus business, or carnival business ...

We did, we loved it.

Did you become friends with any of the other people in the carnivals over the years?

We made hundreds and THOUSANDS of friends. And the best of all what we liked about the carnival and circuses was campin' out under the big tent. And although we had first class — get a load of this — first class reservations on the show trains, we had

double state rooms and whatnot ... we didn't want to stay there. We decided to ride the flat cars, or cattle cars. Where the animals were. We loved to lay in that sweet smellin' straw and hay and watch the animals. We didn't care whether they were wild or whether they were crazy.

• • •

[Johnny talks about his show at the 1931 Canadian National Exhibition during which he made a screen test for the movie *Freaks*.]

He said, "Come on, step out the back of the tent," and I said, "What about the audience?!" Aw man — we were JAMMED, we musta had a thousand people in our show. In the tent. Remember — I'm by myself.

He said it'll only take a minute or two. So we went out back and we took some of my props with me.

What did your show consist of then?

Man, I was walkin' a tight-wire. I had a trapeze ... had my own trapeze. I had balancing pedestals ... I did magic. And trick pictures — cartoons. Man, I was — JUGGLING — man, I was doin' a real ACT.

So I went outside with the props that they could take. There's a guy with a portable film [camera], and he says to me, "Man, I know they're gonna want you!" I said, "Who's that?" He says, "Mr. Browning." But he never told me where he was from or who he was. I had no idea they were talent scouts.

So they filmed me on the pedestal ... and walkin' across the lawn, and walkin' up the rise and walkin' up and down the stair steps. Man, I had a beautiful pair of steps — painted white, trimmed in red and silver. And I would shake hands with Rob, and he would smile and shake hands with me. And that film went back to Tod Browning. In other words, these guys were lookin' for ... freaks, for possible use in the picture. And that's how I wound up in ... in the freak shows. 'Cause when that guy went back, instead of writing to me direct, the film company, they wrote to this guy on Baltimore Street, the first guy that got me when I was, what, twelve years old.

• • •

We went south. From up in Toronto we came to Buffalo. And I was in a pullman car, the diner, where one of the guys that was sittin' at a table got into an argument with another man, and what did he do, he stood up, pulled a gun out and shot the guy in the next booth where I was. ... Think that over ... And I said to the manager, Jack Burns, I said, "Let's get outta this car! Let's go back to our state room."

So we went back to our state room, and that was the only room in that particular car that had the door open, and the light was shining out in the hallway. So I went in there and I told the other crew what happened, our gang. I said, "Jesus, they just shot a man." They said, "Where?" I said, "Up in the diner." They said, "Oh my God — is he dead?!" I said, "I don't know, but, I'm afraid ..." Just at that time we hear some people talkin' and here they come up the

Johnny and the son of Prince Randian, The Living Torso.

hallway, and one man looks in our room and says, "We got a man here pretty bad, can we get him here and lay him on your bed?" I said, "Why CERTAINLY." ... So I got off the bed and they brought him in, and I took one look at him — they had taken his shirt off — and I looked at him and he was green.

Did you ever see a person dyin'? Well, he turned a pale green ... although he was still breathin'. There was a little bullet hole, a small hole right in his stomach. And instead of blood comin' out it was WATER. I said, "Oh Christ!" ... Remember, I was only twenty years old. And I looked at my manager at that time, I said, "Burns ..." and I shook my head. In the meantime, more people were comin' up and lookin' in, and, there was a — I'll tell you who brought him in, a half-man/half-woman. One of the freaks in the show. I said, "How come you brought him in here?" He said, "Well yours was the only room that had the door open, and I KNOW YOU and I know you wouldn't turn him down. Nobody would let us bring him in on their bed."

Then all of a sudden I looked out my window toward the back of the train — it's midnight, twelve o'clock, and I looked out my window and what do you think I see? A red light two cars above the caboose. We were the second section, 'cause the train was so long we traveled in two sections. I looked out and I see a red flare — one'a them railroad flares — goin' UP AND DOWN, UP AND DOWN.

Well, I knew, from bein' around a railroad track, that that was an emergency stop. And I said to Burns, I said, "Hold on, we're gonna come to a dead stop." And sure enough, the wheels come on and DAMN, the train stopped so dog-gone fast I slid across the floor and banged into the wall! (laughs)

And who boarded our car? Railroad men from the caboose. And they wanted to know what happened. So they came in and they looked, and I said "a man got shot." They said, "Oh my God!" So whatta you think they did? At that time there was no radio hook-up but they had portable phones. They both went out of the room, jumped down offa the train. I went with 'em of course. And it was at night — dark. And I watched to see what they'd do. One of 'em stood at the bottom of the telephone pole — telegraph pole? The other one climbed up and tapped these phones into the wire. And I knew exactly what he was doing — he was calling ahead for help. Because where we were parked was, oh, about twenty miles out of Buffalo, New York.

Johnny Eck show. Banners painted by Johnny and Rob.

So they come back on the train and they said you're gonna be boarded when we get into Buffalo. The train stopped in Buffalo. I looked out the window and again you could see red lights, and the minute our car stopped at a bridge the red lights started all wig-wagging and again the brakes come on the train. And who was the first one busted into our state room and grabbed ahold of me? State police.

I said, "Aaahhoooo! Wait a minute. What you want me for?"

They said, "You did it," I said, "I didn't do it!" And my manager said, "Leave him alone — he didn't shoot this man!"

They said, "Who did?" and we KNEW who did it, so we told 'em. So the police, they apologized. State troopers! Can you imagine that?

He was back in a private car, so they got him.

• • •

[Johnny returns to Baltimore, then travels to California to star in a circus — or so he is told.]

After the Canadian National Exhibition, we did a Southern tour. The last week that we were out on that show, I decided — I was crazy — I decided to buy a car! And I went out and DID. I bought a Chrysler limousine.

Brand new?

Oh of course not!!! They wanted $240.00. A CHRYSLER ... LIMOUSINE. In A-1 condition. Even had flowers, and a little brass ... vases in the back. Had window blinds. It was like they used in a funeral! I mean it was a BIG ... had BALLOON tires! Oh my gosh ... for $125.00.

What'd you do with the car?

Well nothin' lasts forever.

(laughs) I mean you didn't drive it, did you?

That's why I sent for this boy. He was around ... seventeen years old. I'm twenty, remember? But he could drive. Oh, he was smart. He didn't have a license. But I had already checked that out. Man, you're talkin' to a LAWYER. When I found out you didn't need a license, that's when I got him to come down. In North Carolina, that is — 'cause the car had North Carolina tags.

So, we got set into our car, and instead of getting a TRAIN to come home, I took all my baggage, my trapeze and all my riggin' and everything, and tied it on the back of this limousine. What didn't go on the back went inside.

And we come home to Baltimore.

We come back to Baltimore, I was only home here one week ... but unfortunately I was out with this damn big Cadillac — I mean Chrysler — when I come home my mother says, "Oh, Mr. McAslan was here and you're supposed to go to California and you're gonna work in a circus."

I said, "I'm gonna work in a circus? ... Oh my God, that's WONDERFUL," I said, "That's terrific." I called him up, he said, "Be ready!" By the end of the week I was on my way to California to work in a circus ... The Downey Brothers Circus. She said, "You'll spend, probably, the winter in sunshine."

So how'd you go out there?

Oh, FIRST CLASS! Train. Got a train here from Baltimore, went to Harrisburg ... well thank God McAslan wasn't cheap goin' out. He got a double ... super ... whatta they call 'em? Not a state room, a drawing room. It was BEAUTIFUL. It had three beds. It coulda really slept six people. And it was only we two. (chuckles) And that's how we went out — ALL the way. No changing trains.

And MGM studio sent a limousine to pick us up. And they had cameras, newspapers and everybody else waitin' for that special car, for that door to open for all the freaks to come out. GUESS who was the last one to come out?

[Silence.]

COME ON, Mark!

(laughs) Musta been you!

They always save the best acts for last! I was the last one. Man — I was DRESSED up. The only thing missin' was a top hat! I never wore a hat at that time.

• • •

I was put up in the Castle Apartments; there was a first floor and an upper deck level with all kinds of Spanish iron-grill work, tile roof ... stained glass windows ... you name it, it had it. And that's where I stayed.

We had three days to get acclimated. On the third we got a phone call, then after breakfast the limousine picked us up, and on to MGM. And when we went through that MGM gate that first time, I liked to DIED.

And I STILL thought that we were gonna work in the Downey Brother's circus tent, that the circus might be on MGM's back lot, the back lot. Because there was a big tent up. Did I get a shocker the first time I went in the tent ... it was made up for FILM work!

• • •

[The making of _Freaks_ — Johnny Eck meets Tod Browning.]

The chauffeur went over and he opened this big door and it was like going into a bank vault. He said, "Now we can go in." He said, "Now somebody's gonna take you and show you around."

Oh! This was like goin' into a cavern or an airplane hangar. You couldn't see hardly from one end of the building to the other. And naturally they had just certain lights on, and those lights had to be turned off whenever the camera come on.

JOHNNY IN CALIFORNIA

Fuzzy shot of Johnny and his manager taken by Angelo Rossito

Johnny on the porch of the hotel where the freaks stayed during the shooting of the movie

Betty Green (Stork Woman) and Johnny's manager 168

Johnny and Betty Green

Phroso	Wallace Ford
Venus	Leila Hyams
Cleopatra	Olga Baclanova
Roscoe	Rosco Ates
Hercules	Henry Victor
Hans	Harry Earles
Frieda	Daisy Earles
Madame Tetrallini	Rose Dione
Siamese Twins	Daisy and Violet Hilton
Rollo Brothers	Edward Brophy and Mat McHugh

THE CAST

So we go down front, toward the end, and the first person that stood up, that said, (majestic intonation) "Welcome to the family, welcome," ... was Mr. Tod Browning himself. And from that time on he never called me Johnny Eck, he called me "Mr. Johnny." He said, "I want you to stay as close to me as possible, and ALL the time. He said, "Whenever I have an empty seat or an empty chair, YOU are to sit alongside of me while we shoot."

HE was a prince! And by that he made a terrible mistake. The minute he said that he turned the rest of those freaks on me. They were jealous. Besides the Siamese twins and Harry and Daisy, I was the only one who had a private dressing room, "The Great Johnny Eck."

And that's how we got along beautifully.

Well, can you imagine me makin' up? Well, I didn't NEED any make-up to begin with. Of course I had to look in the mirror to see if I was ugly enough to ... (laughs) appear in front of the cameras. Ah, that was terrific.

• • •

There I met the assistant director. And his name was Earl Taagart. And he was at my side. I would go from one group of people to the other. The technicians, the sound men, the electricians, and the prop department, and EVERYBODY ... was my friend.

I had a letter — I'm sorry that I destroyed it, I was very foolish. It was from one of my co-actresses out there, and after the film was running down at the end, I mean in production, and I was let go, she wrote a letter and made me feel very bad. She said, (with formal, slightly lyrical emphasis) "THE SOUND STAGE NUMBER SIXTEEN WILL NEVER BE THE SAME WITHOUT YOU. NOTHING IS THE SAME SINCE YOU LEFT. AND EVERYBODY ... MISSES ... YOU."

Damn it, I shoulda saved that. That was from one of the co-stars, Margret Berts. She was one of the supporting cast. She was very cute. She was only about five feet tall. And she really adored me. Used to take me out to dinner ...

Well, this girl, she was about twenty-three years old. But me — I was crazy. I swear to God I was crazy. Now I remember ... I wasn't what you would call, interested in, what, girls? Sexual and all that stuff ... I don't know, I was more or less, ME, period. Although I really thought the world of her.

What was your agent making at the time *Freaks* was being filmed?

Well, at that time I assumed it was well over a thousand dollars ... a WEEK. Now, how 'bout that? How would you like to find that out?! I liked to died. I really did.

And who told me? That same girl. Because this one particular time we went out for dinner at night — you get it? And I smelled a rat because McAslan — don't use his name! — because he said, "I don't want

Daisy Doll in wedding dress from the feast scene in *Freaks*.
Photo taken by Johnny ● ● ● ● ● ● ● ● ● ● ● ● ● ●

Daisy Doll, star of *Freaks*, outside her home in early 1930s.

you seein' that girl anymore." I said, "Why?" He said, "Because she's a troublemaker." And I think he knew or smelled a rat that sooner or later I was gonna find it out. Remember, I was out there almost ... oh, dog-gone near four months. Think that over.

And you know, you get pretty familiar with people, and you learn a lot. So this one time, instead of takin' me out for dinner — she mostly picked me up on a Sunday. Remember, we worked Saturday, too, there was no day off except Sunday.

So anyway, he told me not to go with her, he said, "I don't want you to see her anymore." I said, "Well, I'm gonna see her." So she took me out, and when we'd had our dinner and she said, "I'm not takin' you home right away unless you want to go," I said, "Look, I'm with you ..."

  THE END

Hercules (Henry Victor) confronts Venus (Leila Hyams).

170   Commonly seen publicity shot from *Freaks* with director Tod Browning in center

"Normals" Phroso and Venus, friends of the freaks.

Hans and Cleopatra romancing

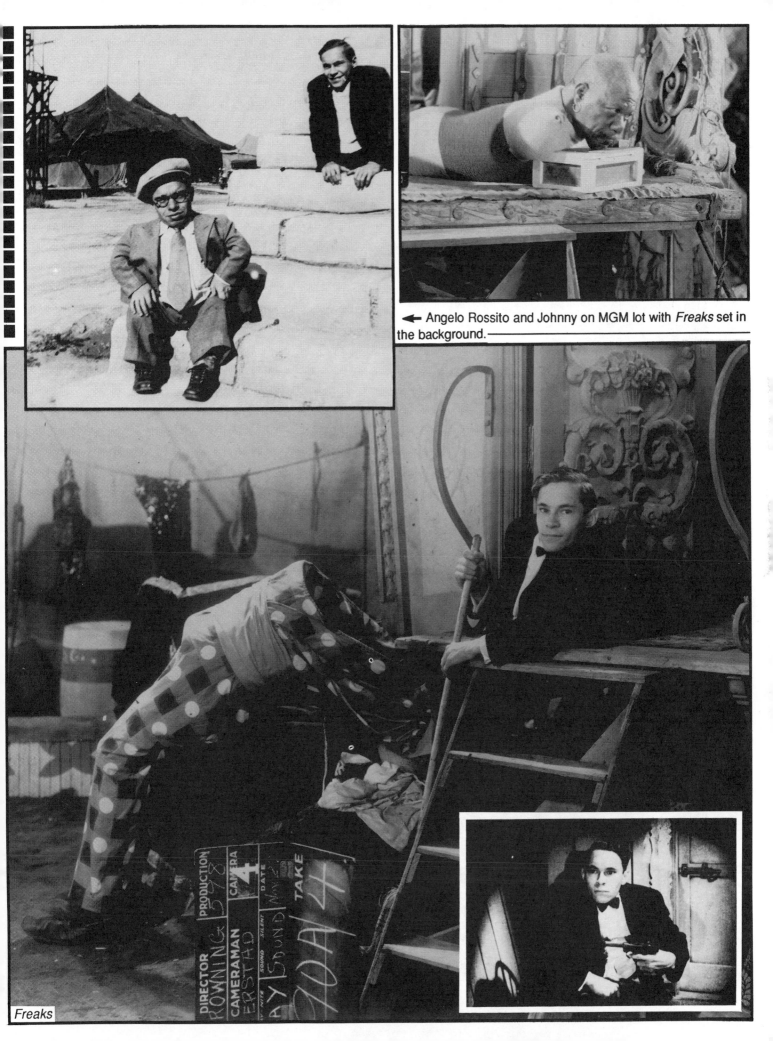

← Angelo Rossito and Johnny on MGM lot with *Freaks* set in the background.

DIRECTOR ROWNING PRODUCTION 578 CAMERA 4 DATE
CAMERAMAN ERSTAD
SOUND SILENT TAKE 44

Freaks

FREAKS the movie: a short history

By 1931, Tod Browning was acclaimed as one of Hollywood's leading horror film directors. When his boss at MGM assigned him to come up with the most horrifying film ever, he accepted the challenge. The result was his most personally felt and controversial film, *Freaks*.

Freaks had its genesis in the director's own past; at 16 years of age (1898) Browning ran away from home to join a traveling circus as a contortionist and clown. Stints as a vaudeville comedian and actor led to work as an assistant director on the 1916 film *Intolerance*.

Cut to 1925: Browning is among MGM's stable of directors with a string of routine adventure films and melodramas behind him. MGM production boss, Irving Thalberg, approves Browning's pet project, *The Unholy Three*, and his friendship and collaboration with German-born dwarf, Harry Earles, begins. The film, starring Lon Chaney, is a success.

At Earles suggestion, Browning explores the possibilities of adopting the Todd Robbins's short story, "Spurs," for the screen. "Spurs," essentially a comic sado-masochistic skit, involves a woman, Jeanne Marie, who marries Jacques Courbé, an egotistical and ill-tempered twenty-eight inch dwarf, for his inheritance. Instead, she finds herself dominated by the merciless miniature Caesar who uses spurs on her as she carries him about on her shoulders and employs a wolf-dog to protect himself.

Browning is given the green light by MGM to proceed on the project. The script expands and changes the story considerably (under the guidance of at least four scriptwriters), portraying the freaks in a sympathetic light more attuned to Browning's own sentiments. Harry and his sister, Daisy Doll, are to be the stars. Filming commences in the fall of 1931. Set in the context of a traveling circus, the remaining roles feature a number of real-life freaks whose deformities are directly confronted by the camera.

The result was a bizarre and superbly photographed, if occasionally stilted, tale of prejudice, betrayal, and revenge.

Freaks premiered in 1932 in San Diego.

The audience was shocked. A woman literally ran screaming from the theater.

On initial release, the film provoked an extreme response from critics, much of it damning. "Mr. Browning has always been an expert in pathological morbidity," praised the *Herald Tribune* in backhanded fashion, "but after seeing *Freaks*, his other films seem like whimsical nursery tales." "The difficulty," chimed in the *New York Times*, "is in telling whether it should be shown at the Rialto Theater — where it opened yesterday — or in, say, the Medical Center." To the critic at *Harrison's Reports* it was "so loathsome that [he was] nauseated thinking about it."

Many exhibitors found it so appalling that they refused to show it or insisted on heavy cuts. In England it was officially banned for thirty years. The film proved to be anything but the standard horror film audiences expected. They found it indigestible: too emotionally confusing, too graphic or simply too strange. MGM disowned the film and withdrew it from circulation. It sporadically reappeared under three other titles: *The Monster Show*, *Nature's Mistakes* and *Forbidden Love*. An apologetic prologue was tacked onto some prints. Several subsequent re-releases, including a 1948 attempt by Excelsior Films, fizzled as well.

Browning never outlived the stigma of this failure. His career ended four pictures later in 1939.

He retired to his home in San Diego where he died "in obscurity" in 1962, reportedly broke and alcoholic.

Ironically, the revival of *Freaks* began the year of Browning's death, at the 1962 Cannes Film Festival where *Freaks* was selected to represent the horror film category. Later that year it played for the first time in Britain and soon filtered back to America where it was championed by the underground film movement then underway in New York.

Today, *Freaks* is seen as something of a cult film and plays occasionally in Rep houses and on the Midnight Movie circuit where it continues to amaze filmgoers, many of whom have been fed on a steady diet of exploding heads and bubbling corpses from the Hollywood special effects labs and are normally considered shock-proof. Other modern-day critics praise the film for its boldness, originality, and compassion and consign it to a genre all its own.

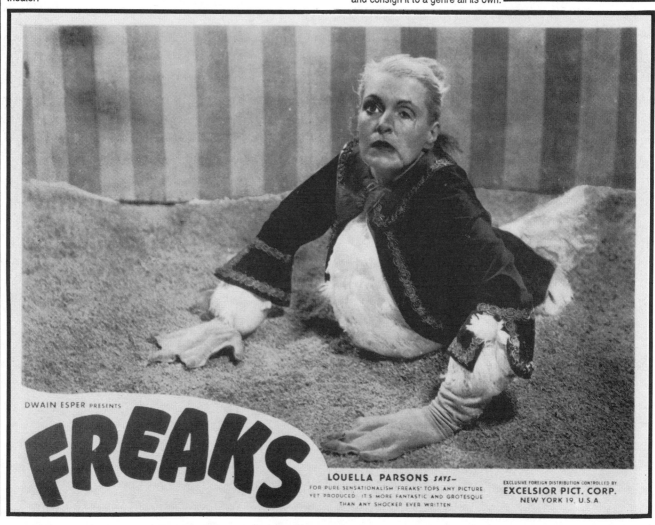

DWAIN ESPER PRESENTS

FREAKS

LOUELLA PARSONS *SAYS*—
FOR PURE SENSATIONALISM 'FREAKS' TOPS ANY PICTURE YET PRODUCED. IT'S MORE FANTASTIC AND GROTESQUE THAN ANY SHOCKER EVER WRITTEN

EXCLUSIVE FOREIGN DISTRIBUTION CONTROLLED BY
EXCELSIOR PICT. CORP.
NEW YORK 19, U.S.A.

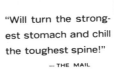
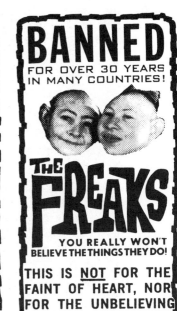

DWAIN ESPER PRESENTS

FREAKS

LOUELLA PARSONS *SAYS—*
FOR PURE SENSATIONALISM 'FREAKS' TOPS ANY PICTURE
YET PRODUCED. IT'S MORE FANTASTIC AND GROTESQUE
THAN ANY SHOCKER EVER WRITTEN

EXCLUSIVE FOREIGN DISTRIBUTION CONTROLLED BY
EXCELSIOR PICT. CORP.
NEW YORK 19, U.S.A.

DWAIN ESPER PRESENTS

FREAKS

LOUELLA PARSONS *SAYS—*
FOR PURE SENSATIONALISM 'FREAKS' TOPS ANY PICTURE
YET PRODUCED. IT'S MORE FANTASTIC AND GROTESQUE
THAN ANY SHOCKER EVER WRITTEN

EXCLUSIVE FOREIGN DISTRIBUTION CONTROLLED BY
EXCELSIOR PICT. CORP.
NEW YORK 19, U.S.A.

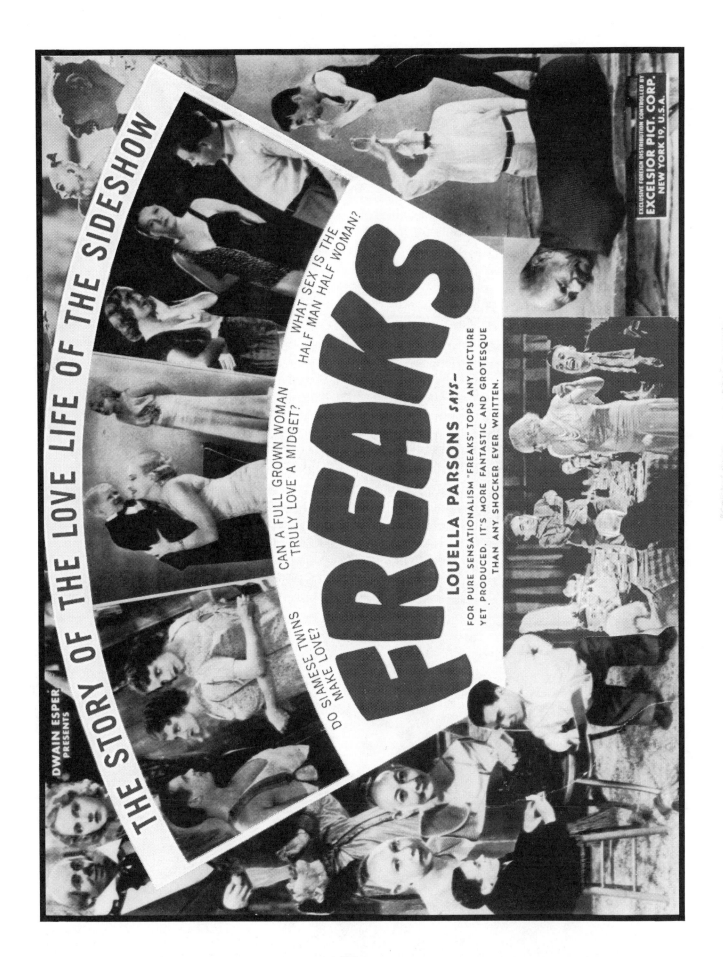

A MATCH FOR THE DEVIL HIMSELF

Directed by Tod Browning

Can a pinhead think?

What DIABOLICAL VENGEANCE

DID THESE HALF-HUMAN CREATURES INFLICT UPON THE BEAUTY AND THE STRONG MAN?

"THE FREAKS"

with

THE MOST AMAZING CAST EVER ASSEMBLED

Love-life and hate in a side show...

AFTER THE AUDIENCE HAS LEFT!

Olga Baclanova as Cleopatra—the trapeze artist, feigns horror at "menacing" freaks in a discarded publicity shot

This page: Theater posters for *Tarzan the Ape Man*, the first sound Tarzan movie, the first starring Weissmuller. Opposite page, top left: Johnny Eck played a bird creature in this film. Photos right: Johnny on Neil Hamilton's back in a staged photo. Lower left: Natives and white men alike take aim at Johnny's bird creature.

Johnny poses for photographers after a quick climb up the Washington Monument in 1937. The Monument is visible in the background ——————— [Johnny climbed up in 20 minutes ... down in 12.] ———

GAG PHOTO OF JOHNNY AND FRIEND IN CAR WRECK

Johnny posing with plane crew.

Johnny and carnival clean-up crew.

KING of the FREAKS

THE JOHNNY ECK STORY

ANACONDA PRESS

Johnny Eck, 1980

Johnny Eck and brother Rob at home, 1980
(print made from color Polaroid).

What a half-man in Highlandtown dreams of

The half-man has a dream.

The dream goes back more than 60 years, back to the days when Johnny Eck, the half-man, was known as Johnny the half-boy, back to the magic Sunday afternoons when Johnny's mother would carry her tiny, malformed son down from their two-story, red-brick row house on Milton avenue, out across Monument street, and up to the train tracks.

There, at the edge of the old Eager street tracks, as close as she dared take him, the mother would set her little bundle down, and Johnny, the half-boy, would spend the happiest days of his life.

Lying on the hot gravel, looking up at the sooty bellies of the freight cars as they sped through Highlandtown, Johnny imagined worlds too distant for an 8-year-old boy without legs, worlds a half-boy could only dream of.

Even today, more than 60 years later, Johnny remembers the bellies of the trains that roared past Eager street. And when he talks about the memory there is a faraway look in his warm brown eyes, a look that tells you this is the vision, the seed, the kernel that grew into the half-man's final dream.

"I'd spend the whole afternoon lying there watching those trains, and more than anything else in this world, I wanted to be an engineer, up there in the locomotive, going someplace," Johnny says. "Of course, it was physically impossible. But I was too young then to know what was possible and what was not possible."

Johnny Eck couldn't even walk. He was born—August 11, 1911, in the second-floor front bedroom of the Milton avenue row house—with almost nothing below his rib cage. Somehow, miraculously, Johnny survived. Rob, his twin

Matt Seiden

brother, emerged whole.

By the time he was 12, Johnny was being billed as "the half-boy," and "The Most Remarkable Boy Alive." He was about 1½ feet tall, as tall as he'd ever be. His parents wanted him to be a typist, but Johnny and his brother preferred the freak shows.

"When I saw those tents, that was the end of sitting at a desk for me. God, how I loved to get out under those big tents. I loved the animals, and I loved camping out. Rob and me, we'd go over to the horse barn and get the sweetest smelling hay for a bed, and we'd sit up late and shoot the breeze with some of the most wonderful people in the world. I met hundreds of thousands of people, and none finer than the midgets and the Siamese twins and the caterpillar man and the bearded woman and the human seal with the little flippers for hands. I never asked them any embarrassing questions and they never asked me, and God, it was a great adventure."

At the height of his career, the half-man starred in the Ringling Brothers Circus freak show, toured the country with a magician who specialized in sawing him in half (Johnny was the top

half), and was featured in a Hollywood extravaganza called Freaks, a movie which was showing here once again last week.

Then, in the 1950's, freak shows began going out of fashion. It was no longer considered polite to stare at freaks. It was no longer considered decent to make money displaying men who were half women, or women with beards, or 12-year-old boys born with nothing below the rib cage. Gradually, the word "freak" would be replaced by the word "handicapped"—a linguistic evolution that would mark the beginning of a new era for men like Johnny Eck.

But, ironically, the new, humane mentality put Johnny Eck and his brother out of business. They returned to Baltimore, broke after all their years on the freak-show circuit. "The managers got everything," Johnny says.

They moved back into the old red-brick row house on Milton avenue. Rob did odd jobs, and Johnny began lying on top of the marble front steps, balancing his handsome head precariously on his powerful arms, growing brown in the sun despite a sun-bleached straw hat, chatting with the neighbors, and watching the world go by.

To this day, the neighborhood children sit and chat with Johnny Eck for hours, and the half-man listens to them as few adults ever listen to children. Maybe it's because he's never had any children of his own; maybe it's because he has all the time in the world. Or maybe it's because he is their size, and, as he says, "I love all things small."

Sooner or later, Johnny tells his visitors about the trains. He tells how he always wanted to be an engineer, how "Brother Rob" once bought him an old

amusement park train, big enough for Johnny to ride in, strong enough to carry a dozen children around a miniature track. He tells how they tried for a while to run the train at church carnivals around the state. And he tells how they gave up on the idea when teen-age hoodlums jeered and stoned them.

Then the half-man tells you his dream.

His neighborhood is getting rough, he says. He's afraid to sit outside in the evening. He spends his days copying calendar pictures of a bucolic landscape where he dreams of spending his final days. In his dream, he and Rob run a small picnic and camping ground. "Brother Rob" is serving up home-made baked beans and barbecued franks and fresh lemonade.

There's a little corral with miniature animals, freaks that never get much bigger than Johnny. And then there's the old amusement park train, filled with giggling children, and there's Johnny, the half-man, perched in the locomotive, tooting the horn and speeding through the park, like a whole man, a man with legs, like the men who rode the old freight cars that once tore through Highlandtown.

"You get behind that locomotive," Johnny says, "and that engine purrs like a giant cat, and you move those levers, and boy, all of a sudden you're really rolling, and you turn around, and you see all your little passengers waving and having a great time, and you hit the curve and feel yourself careening around the corner, and you blow the horn and pull into the station and the kids clamor for more. . . ."

And that's what a half-man dreams of.

Column that appeared in a local Baltimore paper on July 20th, 1979.

Johnny and Mark Feldman at Johnny's house in Baltimore

1980

*To Mark
My Best to you!
Johnny Eck*

Original *Freaks* promotional button — a momento of the old days.

This material, collected in 1980-81 by Feldman and Fielding, as it turns out, may well be the last we ever hear from Johnny Eck.

In June of 1988, Johnny's home in Baltimore was burglarized and Johnny was badly assaulted. He has since recovered, but as a result he has closed off contact with many old acquaintances and lives today in self-imposed seclusion. He has given his permission for the publishing of this material but he asks that his fans respect his desire for privacy and not seek to contact or write him.

THE
END

By SYBIL WALKER

Cookie Mueller has acted in five John Waters movies: *Multiple Maniacs, Pink Flamingos, Female Trouble, Desperate Living* and *Polyester*. She also worked with Eric Mitchell in *Underground USA* and Amos Poe in the unreleased *Subway Riders*.

When someone asks me what "underground" is — usually I can't say — but obviously it's not accessible. That is — you have to "know" where the entrance is. Well most certainly it's not commercially successful. But not without artistic value, necessarily!

Perhaps it's a cult thing — an original idea that takes a while to catch on. John Waters' movies have survived on a cult following — obscurities often lead the public to find deviations — sexual and social — often relegated to the underground. John says he takes the money from each movie he makes and puts it into the next one.

While Cookie and I spoke, Richard Hell went out for cigarettes and beer.

S: If you could play any role in any movie, who would you play?
C: Let's see. Roles for women . . . they're getting more open now, I guess. There's a lot of roles I fantasize about playing There's always something wrong with the script. There's always something missing, in the scripts that I've been given that I could embellish upon but I don't want to, 'cause I don't want to deviate from what they've written. If they're directing, and I'm acting, then I want to do what I'm supposed to do.
S: Were you happy with your work in Eric Mitchell's movie? *(Underground USA)*
C: I could've done it differently, I could have done it a lot differently.
S: You were very intense.
C: I must say, that after being with John Waters for a long time, that he wants everybody to be bigger than they are, to be broader . . . really broad. The character has to be like, flat in John Waters' things. Certainly not three dimensional.
S: Looking at you, you're so great looking. Such an actress. I'm surprised you're as quiet as you are.
C: I'm not, usually. That's why it's real different to act. People look at me and they typecast me for my look. It has to go back to John Waters. He wanted a sluttish type of girl.
S: Does it carry over to your personal life?
C: Sure. I don't mind. I don't care. A lot of people think of me like that. It wouldn't matter. I'll be a slut. I'll be whatever anybody wants to think of me as. I know what I am. Sluts are great anyway. What's a slut?
S: All men want their women to be whores.
C: Everybody is a whore.
S: If they're not, they should be.
C: I was happy with my role in Eric's movie. I just wanted to do more. I was really gung-ho about doing it, and I said, "Is that all there is?" I said to Eric, "Give me some more to do! This is it?" I had no idea what the story was. I just came down from Provincetown to do it.
S: What were you doing in P-Town?
C: I was growing my nails.
S: Do you hang around mostly with women or with men?
C: Both. But I've been living with a woman for the past six years.
S: How does this jive with . . . uh, does this have anything to do with your role in the movies?
C: You mean, do you think that the reason that I'm living with a woman is because of the way people react to me?
S: Being bi-sexual is really common in New York, but it's different than in other parts of the country. There's only a few places.
C: I get real nervous around women who are exclusively lesbian. I walk in a women's bar and I'm a nervous wreck. I never go in 'em. So many lesbians hate men, because they think they're better than men, and it's only been since pre-Christian, Pre-Greece and Rome, and

Crete and Persia. Before Christianity and before Allah. This is really way back in history that there was a matriarchial society. Women were revered. It's been since the advent of Christianity that women have been bamboozled. They were forced into all this moralistic bullshit.
S: Men do as they please.
C: Well, women do as they like, too. Especially with Reagan. Do you believe it? No abortion? We should have a pagan as president. We need a pagan with religious advisors. That's what we need. Different advisors from every religion. Other advisors too — at least one atheist. I certainly don't hate men. That's for sure. I just don't feel like a lesbian. Those are only roles I get, lately. In Amos' movie *(Subway Riders)*, and in Rachid's movie and in John Waters last movie, I play lesbians.
S: In Rachid's last movie you played opposite Terry Toy, who in herself . . . she's a whole story to herself. She doesn't have too much to say about sex. Interesting, you would think she has a lot to say.
C: Yeah, you would think that she would. Yeah, I think that men are doing alright. I just think women are more equipped to handle . . .
S: Crisis?
C: Exactly. Emotional stuff. There's something to that. I really adore some aspects of men. Something unfathomable to me. I really don't understand men. I don't understand women either, I just don't understand men. I just think they do a real good job of separating their emotions from their intellect. Linear thinking as opposed to cyclical thinking.
S: Everything I find so frustrating in my world has to do with not being a boy.
C: I don't really see men as prize animals, but then I don't see women as prize animals either. I feel real easy about men and women. There's a difference and that's what's so wonderful. I don't think that women who hate men know what they're talking about, or why they do. I was reading this real funny book lately. It's called *The First Sex*. It's all about this woman called Elizabeth Gould Davis and it goes back completely into antiquity, before there was recorded history, to the present, about women. After she wrote the book she killed herself. She said . . . well it was really incredible. She said what men think of as love is just scrotal frenzy. I totally don't believe that. I just think it was real funny. It's funny that somebody could see men that one-dimensionally.
S: I don't think of people as people. I think of them as animals. I see myself as a monkey, some kind of weird chimp. You write, don't you?
C: I wrote a novel while I was pregnant, but I never finished it because I had my kid, Max. He's eight. You want to go back to Eric's movie?
S: Well I'm more interested in John Waters. In *Desperate Living* you played a one-armed go-go dancer and a lesbian in a bar.
C: Well in *Female Trouble*, which is my favorite role in my favorite film. I started off as a teen-age bad girl, a juvenile delinquent, so to speak. Then I went through Divine's life as her girlfriend in the progressing years. In *Pink Flamingos* I played a spy who tried to get information for Divine from the Marbles, about Divine.
S: Espionage. That's real cool.
C: Yeah I fucked this guy in chicken coop, with these chickens. Then in *Multiple Maniacs* I played the daughter of Divine. Just a little bad girl, you know? Interesting. But I really didn't know anything about acting. Still don't. I just rammed on through. Charged on through it.
S: You're successful at that, why not make it a whole style of acting? You're pioneering a whole style.
C: Style of acting? I don't think so.
S: Well John Waters pioneered. All his movies are very pioneering. Avant-garde isn't even the word.
C: No, that's bullshit. He's so American. He's the true spirit of the American pioneer. I always had these tattoos. I always thought I can't act because I have

COOKIE MUELLER

ALLEN BRAND

all these tattoos. Well I thought, I can't do any TV work. Actually I did do a TV movie this winter. It was called *P.I. Caprio*, and it was shot in New Jersey. It was non-union. I played a dominatrix. It was a small part and rather stupid. But we had a good time making it.
S: How do you go about supporting yourself?
C: Well, I used to make clothes, custom. People would order something and I would make it. You know, sell it to them. But I don't do that anymore. I do whatever I can.
S: Is it hard work being an underground actress?
C: Well, I don't get enough work. And I certainly don't get paid much. I didn't get paid for Amos' move . . . not for Eric's . . .
S: Do you ever do movie assistance?
C: Well, it's at some point I'm going to, but it's not a proven talent.
S: You've been in so many movies. You're a recognized talent.
C: I have never had a role big enough to show my talent. My biggest part ever was in Amos' movie.
S: Yeah, I just talked to Johanna and she said the editing was going along really well.
C: I think I did a really good job in that movie.
S: Have you always lived in New York?
C: No, I moved here four years ago, fror Baltimore and Provincetown.
S: Where did you meet John Waters?
C: In Baltimore. When I had gotten back from San Francisco I met John. I was born in Baltimore. I won a door prize to one of his movies and he did a little film of me and liked what he saw. And then he just

used me in *Multiple Maniacs*. John and I once shared a lover. That's how I got to know John really well. John was in love with this guy and I was in love with the same guy. We were very jealous of each other and that's how I really got to know him. John is really dogmatic. He certainly has a lot of strong feelings about things.
S: Have you thought of doing other film work?
C: I thought about doing sound, for some reason . . . lighting . . .
S: How old are you?
C: Thirty. I didn't really tell you much, did I?
S: What happened in your childhood that made you predisposed to acting?
C: I'd probably say it was because my mother really dug me as a kid. My brother died when I was seven. She wanted something really great. Ahh, she's put everything into me. I did ballets and stuff, and I started writing when I was in third grade. I used to make up cartoon magazines. She thinks I turned out totally, all wrong. She once said to me, "You got that bladder infection because you smoke marijuana. Now where is it? Smoke marijuana sitting on the ground with no underwear on." That makes a little more sense. Sitting on the ground with no underwear on, that isn't how you get bladder infections. Well, maybe it is.
S: We talked a lot about a lot of things. How'd you get your name?
C: My brother gave it to me. My real name's Dorothy Karen Mueller. It's funny about being an actor, how in your childhood you're treated like little dolls and dollettes. You get used to the attention and you seek it out. Not very mature, really.

Marilyn Chambers Goes 'Legit'

by Bill Mooney

A classic '70's success story: porn star goes legit, stars in "real" movies, makes the crossover and wins the hearts of middle-class American movie-goers everywhere. The lady lives down her past and conservative morality has won another convert.

"Behind The Green Door" heroine Marilyn Chambers would be the prime catch in the above scenario if she would just be a little more repentant about her x-rated beginnings. But the well-traveled 23-year-old is proud of her celebrity origins, knowing she wouldn't be where she is today without her exposure in the altogether.

And where the lady is today is starring in her first non-sex-oriented film, handling bayonet-sharp questions at press shindigs and — she hopes — cementing a solid financial future.

Her press luncheon was just the latest in a series of cross-country jousts with the fifth estate, billed as promo stints for her horror flick, "Rabid," but which eventually turn into round-robin sessions on sex, orgasms, sexual habits, fantasies, morality, public image and more sex.

ALL THIS AND MORE from the lady that a women's lib jury would love to convict, a woman who proudly confesses her dependence on males and openly acknowledges her debt to the hard-core arena.

"I depend on men for everything. I'm a submissive woman and women's libbers hate me for this," Chambers says, explaining that her business associates are mostly male. "I really admire Princess Grace. I remember in an interview she said the woman is the strongest because she holds the family together. Being considered a sex object is a compliment to me. I know women my own age are sometimes jealous of me, because my career is taking off. I always did what I wanted to" and that includes a little bit of everything: singing, dancing, modeling (you remember her Ivory Soap pose?) and acting.

Concerning acting, here's what you need to know about the New World Pictures Inc. production of "Rabid": for 90 minutes and $3.50, you can watch a woman's finger get cut off by scissors, a berserk construction worker attach a helpless chauffeur with a pneumatic drill, countless maniacs foaming green liquid at the mouth and biting others in the neck and all caused by Chambers' portrayal of a cross between a female vampire and a rabid dog.

"If a reviewer prints it (the movie) is repulsive (which it is) the people rush to go see it." The horror of the film is centered around graphic violence that would make Sam Peckinpah blush, but Chambers contemplates a return to the Hitchcock scare tactics of the '50's where the terror "is in the anticipation, it's off screen and

suggested. Things that go bump in the night are more scary than direct things. You go to the movies to escape for two hours.

"I see 'Rabid' as a stepping stone. There are higher points. Probably what'll happen — is they'll bust 'Rabid' for being too violent," Chambers says.

"I LIKE TO BE SCARED. I like a little bit of sex in movies," she admits, so for the Chambers' fans there are a couple meaningless scenes of topless Marilyn during "Rabid."

"Since I've met Chuck (Traynor, her manager and Linda Lovelace's ex) I've only done two X-rated films. Hard core films are on the decline," she feels.

She probes a possible high-class film career like a teenager anticipating a first date. "I would like to do a film with Clint Eastwood. . .I like romantic films like 'Dr. Zhivago,'. . .I would like to do a romantic film, done all by women. . .'" All this will have to wait, for her next film, also horror-bent, is titled "Pick-Axe," which she promises will be more in the subtle vein of a Hitchcock piece, with less of the outright bludgeoning of the senses as in "Rabid."

"It bothers me that women say there are no roles for women. It's not so. I will be the lead in 'Stuntman', a film about a stunt-woman." Confused about the title? So is she. Anyway, maybe one reason women can't find decent roles is because they aren't interested in spending a couple years on the porno circuit first.

SHE HANDLES THE ROUTINE questions on her sex life, her fantasies, her experiences, smoothly, but draws the line at what she considers would amount to being used.

"I don't think sex and politics mix. I wouldn't like to be a political advocate. If people just realized it was there, it'd be better for everyone." It would also make it easier for Chambers to get decent parts, then, too.

But she's not struggling, either. On the road about ten months a year, with investments in cattle out west, a nightclub act and an AM record behind her, a regular column in **Genesis** and a couple books on the Market, she won't take a back seat to anyone. She's been considered for a TV movie role. "That's a big step, they're straight." Yes, they are, Marilyn, yes, they are. She still has a long way to go. She has a lot of people to win over.

"If you can set up a way to live out your fantasies in the privacy of your own home, then fine. I think a lot of women don't admit their fantasies," she says.

The lady's goal, or fantasy, is respectability, acceptance. Porn star goes legit. She's not there yet. "Rabid" is one step forward, two backward.

The jury is still out.

THE DRUMMER   JULY 11 - JULY 18, 1977   NUMBER 461 Tuesday, July 11 through Tuesday, July 18

March 5, 1964
AN INTERVIEW WITH KUCHAR BROTHERS
by Jonas Mekas

Two weeks ago I wrote about a new kind of star cinema that is coming from the underground. Hollywood keeps complaining that there are no new faces. They are searching in the wrong places, that's their trouble. The underground is full of new faces and bodies. There is the Kuchar brothers' movie festival going on at the New Bowery Theatre. See the amazing gallery of the most fantastic creatures gathered in the Bronx, the lushest and sexiest cast of new faces. The Kuchar brothers have arrived on the movie scene. Here is the most macabre sense of humor at work. . . . Here is the Pop Cinema at its best pop. . . . Here are banality and corniness transposed into their grotesque opposites. . . . Here is the new entertainment cinema that even Ivan Karp says is great. . . . And all in 8 mm.! I had the following conversation with the brothers Kuchar:

Question: Why are you wasting celluloid, why are you making movies? Anybody can make a movie!

Mike Kuchar: I love to make movies because it's the bread and butter of my life. But if I was to lose my arms and legs or go blind I'd throw myself on a bread slicer. There's more to life than just movies. . . . There's still radio.

Question: Have you anything to say about your fantastic cast?

Mike Kuchar: Some film-makers are afraid to work with a big cast because they think that the group will get out of hand. But we love working with a lot of people. You can round them up like cattle and make them stampede to moments of cinematic glory. Animal instincts are unleashed and watching a film with a large cast is like going to the zoo.

Question: How did your film career really start?

George Kuchar: We're twenty-one now, but for many years our films have been scorned. At the age of twelve I made a transvestite movie on the roof and was brutally beaten by my mother for having disgraced her and also for soiling her nightgown. She didn't realize how hard it is for a twelve-year-old director to get real girls for his movie. But that unfortunate incident did not end our big costume epics. One month later Mike and I filmed an Egyptian spectacle on the same roof with all of the television antennas resembling a cast of skinny thousands. Our career in films had begun.

Mike Kuchar: At a special showing we prepared in high school for the Newman Club (a Catholic organization), our work was screened and labeled "Violent—Devilish!" The teacher was very nice, but she couldn't tolerate all the bludgeoning, stabbings, and climactic hatchet slayings that punctuated the program at frequent intervals.

Question: How is your work received now?

George Kuchar: Last week *A Woman Distressed* was played at the New York 8 mm. Club and mistakenly labeled a tear-jerker on their program sheet. The only one that shed a tear after the movie went off was me when it was criticized viciously as "sex-loaded" and "in bad taste." It wasn't sexy, but it was in bad taste, like they said. Their words rang with truth. I must have been depressed when I made that film. Coming home from the showing I prayed and began making plans for a film all about goodness. A film that will mirror the godliness of man and woman. I came across the idea of a beautiful ballerina who dances not for fame but only to please God. Suddenly the story began to change and I pictured her doing a leap and accidentally falling out the window. With both legs paralyzed she marries another dancer who loves her terribly. He becomes famous and she gets jealous. One night her mind snaps, and she saws his legs off after chloroforming him. To my horror the story had transformed itself from a mirror of God to a cesspool of human hatred and insanity. I walked down the subway steps and as I entered the train the ending of the film came to me: The ballerina's invalid husband kills her by ramming his wheelchair into her while she's cooking pot roast and her hair catches fire.

After discussing that screenplay with the two actors I chose for the parts, we unanimously decided to ditch it since it got way off the theme of God and love. So we arrived at a story that hit closer to home. One about a nun who's addicted to show biz and becomes a rock and roll sensation, leaving the church and God only to return with renewed faith after a series of incidents. It will touch on the theme: Does God punish the hurt?

Question: Your latest movie, *Lust for Ecstasy*, is being premiered at the New Bowery Theatre. Tell the people something about it.

George Kuchar: In my new film, *Lust for Ecstasy*, Donna Kerness overflows with passion and flesh in this, her most mature performance since *A Tub Named Desire*. Bob Cowan plays a part he is best suited for: a twisted and demented fiend wracked between the border of normalcy and moral decay. Also in the film is Cynthia Mailman, and her portrayal of a girl with deep religious yearnings will make you long for the early years when we were pure and good and everything that we did was honest. But now the devil has smashed us with his crowbar of evil. I find it very stimulating to film smashed people trying to cope with each other.

Lust for Ecstasy is my most ambitious attempt since my last film, *A Town Called Tempest*. I began filming *Ecstasy* during Indian summer and from then until now I have undergone emotional upheavals. So has the script. The actors didn't know what was going on. I wrote many of the pungent scenes on the D train, and then when I arrived on the set I ripped them up and let my emotional whims make chopped meat out of the performances and story. It's more fun that way, and then the story advances without any control until you've created a Frankenstein that destroys any subconscious barriers you've erected to protect yourself and your dimestore integrity. Yes, *Lust for Ecstasy* is my subconscious, my own naked lusts that sweep across the screen in 8 mm. and color with full fidelity sound.

FRIDAY-MAY 5-1989

AP photos

George W. Jorgensen as a GI in an undated photo (left); as Christine Jorgensen in 1953 (center), a year after undergoing the first sex change operation, and in 1977, 25 years after the surgery.

Christine Jorgensen, 62; was first to undergo sex change operation

Associated Press

SAN CLEMENTE, Calif. - Christine Jorgensen, who in 1952 underwent the first sex change operation to be transformed into a woman, died of cancer Wednesday in San Clemente Hospital. She was 62.

"She was a wonderful, understanding woman who loved everyone," said actress Dorothy Lamour. "She gave out so much love and was a God-loving woman, one of the finest women I have ever met."

Miss Jorgensen was born George Jorgensen Jr. in New York City to parents of Danish descent.

In her 1967 book, "Christine Jorgensen: A Personal Biography," Miss Jorgensen said she had a normal, happy childhood but on growing up became frustrated by feelings that she was a woman trapped in a man's body.

The ex-GI shocked the world in 1952 for undergoing surgery in Denmark to become a woman. The woman who left the Copenhagen operating room was an instant celebrity.

Her notoriety took her on the lecture and nightclub circuit. She met royalty and celebrities and ended up with enough money to live a comfortable life.

She never married and lived for the last few years in this seaside community about 50 miles south of downtown Los Angeles.

In a 1985 interview, she described herself as a homebody who loved to entertain but stayed away from crowds.

In a 1988 interview, Miss Jorgensen said that on the day she learned she had the same disease that killed her mother in 1967, she went home and took a long look at herself in her bathroom mirror.

"I said to myself, 'Look, you've coped with a lot already. You can handle this, too. So you might as well get on with it.'"

She also said that she had no regrets about the operation and is proud to have been part of the sexual revolution. And she acknowledged time had taken its toll. "Getting myself together takes a little more effort these days." But it also had its advantages, she said. "I'm not that recognizable any more. I can actually go into a supermarket and people don't know who I am, which is just wonderful and suits me just fine."

She leaves a sister and two nieces.

Even Dwarfs Started Small

ARTHUR ROSS

Laughter. Always laughter. It reverberates harshly throughout Werner Herzog's *Even Dwarfs Started Small*, showing June 7 at the Egg and the Eye. Mocking, malicious, grotesque, the pinched little faces congeal into a wall, an insistent motif of laughter that engulfs the audience in Herzog's horrifying vision of humanity.

However, this is the underbelly of humanity, the humanity we rarely see. Thirty years ago this film could not have been made — or at least would have remained unseen. In 1932 Tod Browning made *Freaks*, certainly a milestone in cinematic horror, but it was an unrecognized milestone because the majority of people never saw it. It was banned in England and had its first showing there last year to critical acclaim. What was the fuss about? Aside from the truly nightmarish climax, Browning attempted to show the daily lives of genetic outcasts in the milieu of a circus. The confined atmosphere of the circus served two purposes: it showed how we relegated "different" people into ghetto roles as objects of spectator sport, and it showed these ultra-sensitive people — *real* pinheads, armless-legless men, rubber men, Siamese twins — as objects of scorn and ridicule from "normal" society. In other words, we looked at ourselves through a distorting prism — and recoiled.

Freaks was an anomaly at the time and most people predicted that it could never be duplicated, but Herzog went further. He removed the "normies" and placed in the center of his universe. There are no references that we ck clutch except those in our imagination: no story, no psychology, no social parallels, and last but not least, no fancy. Yet *even Dwarfs Started Small* is the product of a rigorous imagination. of his universe. There are no references that we can clutch

except those in our imagination: no story, no psychology, no social parallels, and last but not least, no fancy. Yet *Even Dwarfs Started Small* is the product of a rigorous imagination.

The locale of the film is an institute for dwarfs controlled by normal people. At the opening, the dwarfs are in revolt. Conditions have reached a point beyond endurance. The usually docile dwarfs have imprisoned the man left in charge — also a dwarf — within his office, although he has taken a dwarf as hostage. The normal people have left the institution to the increasing menace of the disgruntled little people.

Herzog's allegory is clear, if labored. The little people (i.e. the Third World) no longer accept the handouts from the rich and powerful, those in control. At the first opportunity, they will strike. Even the divide and conquer tactics of the rich don't help them. A dwarf is left in charge but at this point the other dwarfs are not going to be pacified by one of their own representing them. They have nothing but mockery for one who accepts the "privileges" of normal society. The administrative dwarf's remonstrances to his hostage that he can do nothing are met with a smile. The hostage says nothing; he doesn't have to because time is on his side.

However, Herzog's satire takes a grim turn. The close-knit society of the dwarfs begins to break down. At first they ridicule their masters — such as the scene where the dwarfs prod two of their members into making love on an administrator's overlarge bed and the man can't climb up on it — but bitterness and chaos take over when the dwarfs begin to feel that they are essentially powerless. First they taunt two blind dwarfs. A sow nursing her piglets is murdered for no reason except to show defiance. A cock fight is started to vent the dwarfs' frustration, and chickens have their necks wrung mercilessly only because they belong to the dwarfs' captors. At the end, a monkey — no doubt symbolizing the treatment of the dwarfs as animal-men — is crucified.

Herzog's vision is merciless (so merciless, in fact, that I found myself getting angry and couldn't watch). Again and again he returns to scenes of relentless cruelty and the camera lingers on the scenes of carnage. And over all is the laughter and the repeated shot of the dwarf who stands back and laughs unnervingly as the holocaust continues beyond the edge. ■

June 2, 1972
Los Angeles Free Press

1/27/1967
Antonioni

In London, filming Blow-Up, *Michelangelo Antonioni talked with Nadine Liber of* LIFE's *Paris Bureau. Here are some of his remarks.*

When I was doing my first films it would take me 45 minutes of complete silence and solitude to prepare for the next scene. Now I can isolate myself very easily. What I still cannot do is concentrate when I feel the eyes of a complete stranger on me, because a stranger always interests me. I want to ask him questions.

An actor must arrive on the set in a state of virginity. I, too, must come to the set in a state of mental virginity. I force myself not to overintellectualize. I force myself never to think of the night before, the scene I'll be shooting the next morning. I always spend a half hour alone to let the mood of the set, the light prevail. Then the actors arrive. I look at them. How are they? How do they seem to feel? I ask for rehearsals—a couple, no more—and shooting starts.

I have never felt salvation in nature. I love cities above all. A landscape with its crowds of trees, flowers and grass that repeats itself indefinitely—the repetition makes me dizzy. It takes away all of the meaning of nature. It's like a word you repeat too often. The static immobility of nature is what really scares me. Take a tree. Nothing weighs heavier on me than an old tree. Look at it: it goes on aging for centuries without having ever lived, without ever changing. The Empire State Building doesn't change either, but people around it are changing all the time. An urban landscape is in a state of perpetual transformation.

I am so fascinated by space research that for many years I've wanted to do a film on the first man to land on the moon. Four years ago I wrote to President Kennedy asking for authorization to film the astronauts preparing for the conquest of the moon. I received an answer in which the President invited me to spend five days discussing the project. Then he was killed.

I could have tried maybe to do *Blow-Up* in America, but I have another project for the United States. I hope to do a film in New York this winter. It will be on violence.

● ● ● ● ● ● ● ●

The first time I put an eye behind a camera, it was in a lunatic asylum. We had decided with a group of friends to do a documentary film on mad people. We placed the camera, got the lamps ready, disposed the patients in the room. The insane obeyed us with complete abandon, trying very hard not to make mistakes. I was very moved by their behavior and things were going fine. Finally, I could give the order to turn on the lights. In one second, the room was flooded with light. . . . I have never seen again, on any actor's face, such expression of fear. Such total panic. For a very brief moment, the patients remained motionless, as if petrified. It lasted literally a few seconds followed by a scene really hard to describe: the men started having convulsions. Then they screamed, rolled on the floor. In one instant, the room turned into a hellish pit. All the mad people were trying to escape from light as if they had been aggressed by some prehistoric monster. . . . We all stood there, completely stunned. The cameraman didn't even think to stop the camera, to give some orders. Finally, the doctor shouted: "Stop. . . . Cut off the lights." Then, in the room, dark and silent again, we saw piles of corpses, slightly shaking, as if going through the last jumps of agony. I have never forgotten that scene.

Sex Acts Get Adult Theater Closed

Thursday-FEB.9th/1989

By William Murphy
City Hall Bureau Chief

The city closed down a Manhattan movie theater yesterday after two undercover inspectors said they found "omnipresent" unsafe sex between males, sometimes while a young child was in the adult theater.

Police officers and other city employees cleared customers from the Variety Theater at 3 p.m. and padlocked the doors of the building at 110 Third Ave. near 13th Street.

"While the [city] inspectors occasionally observed an usher with a flashlight inside the theater, neither ever observed any theater employee take the slightest action to prevent the high-risk sexual activity that was omnipresent," Health Commissioner Stephen Joseph said in a court affidavit.

"Even more shocking," Joseph continued, "on two occasions a small child approximately eight years old [apparently a theater employee's child] was seen in the theater. There can be no better indication of the reckless indifference displayed by these defendants."

The court order closing the theater was obtained under the State Public Health Council's determination that places such as theaters, bars and bathhouses where anal sex and fellatio occur are a public nuisance because of the possibility that the AIDS virus can be transmitted during such "high-risk" sex.

In legal papers seeking the court order, which the owners can contest at a hearing tomorrow in State Supreme Court in Manhattan, the city said its inspectors observed 57 instances of unsafe sex during 10 inspections.